The *Uttaratantra* in the Land of Snows

The *Uttaratantra* in the Land of Snows

Tibetan Thinkers Debate the Centrality of the Buddha-Nature Treatise

TSERING WANGCHUK

Published by State University of New York Press, Albany

For information, contact State University of New York Press, Albany, NY
www.sunypress.edu

Production, Eileen Nizer
Marketing, Anne M. Valentine

Library of Congress Cataloging-in-Publication Data

Name: Wangchuk, Tsering, 1970– author
Title: The Uttaratantra in the land of snows: Tibetan thinkers debate the
    centrality of the buddha-nature treatise / Tsering Wangchuk: author.
Description: Albany NY : State University of New York Press, [2017]
    Includes bibliographical references and index.
Identifiers: LCCN 2016031424 (print) | LCCN 2017023938 (ebook) |
    ISBN 9781438464671 (e-book) | ISBN 9781438464657 (hc : alk. paper) |
    ISBN 9781438464664 (pb : alk. paper)
Subjects: LCSH: Ratnagotravibh?aga—Criticism, interpretation, etc. |
    Mahayana Buddhism—Tibet Region.
Classification: LCC BQ3027 (ebook) | LCC BQ3027 .W36 2017 (print) |
    DDC 294.3/85—dc23
LC record available at https://lccn.loc.gov/2016031424

10 9 8 7 6 5 4 3 2 1

To my loving family
and in memory of
Awu, Amnyé, and Gen Lozang Gyatso

Contents

Acknowledgments

This book is a product of a long series of conversations with my teachers and colleagues. While words fall short of capturing my immense gratitude for my teachers and colleagues, it is to them that I express my deepest appreciation for any merit that this book might have. To the late Gen Lozang Gyatso, Gen Damchö Gyeltsen, and Gen Gyatso, who taught me Buddhism by example through their ethical standards, contemplative composure, and the knowledge of a Buddhist path and doctrine, I owe my sincerest gratitude. My sincere thanks also go to Gen Kalsang Damdul for his unstaggering support to my project. I also want to thank my classmates at the Institute of Buddhist Dialectics in India for teaching me how to put every Buddhist topic that we studied to a critical inquiry.

I also want to express my gratitude to Professors Ven. Dakpa Sengey, Khenpo Sonam Gyatso, Geshe Yeshe Thabkhey, and Ven. Wangchuk Dorjee Negi at the Central University of Tibetan Studies in Sarnath for their generous time in answering questions regarding many difficult topics found in several Tibetan commentaries on the *Uttaratantra*. My gratitude also goes to Khenpo Choenang of Jonang Monastery in Shimla with whom I had multiple interviews about the buddha-nature concept. Much appreciation goes to the American Institute of Indian Studies for the grant that supported the early stage of my research in India.

In America, I had the privilege to study Buddhism in an academic setting with Professors Jeffrey Hopkins, David Germano, Karen Lang, and Paul Groner of the University of Virginia. I thank all of them for teaching me the tools for studying Buddhist texts. In particular, I would like to extend my heartfelt appreciation to Professors Hopkins and Germano, who not only mentored me during my years as a doctoral student at UVA, but who have continued to offer me guidance and support since I completed my doctoral program. Their scholarship continues to serve as a model for my own work.

The section on Rinchen Yeshé's view of the *Uttaratantra* from chapter 2 has been published as "Can We Speak of Kadam Gzhan Stong?: Tracing the Sources for Other-Emptiness in Early Fourteenth-Century Tibet" in *Journal of Buddhist Philosophy* 2 (2016): 9–22, with the permission from the State University of New York Press. An earlier version of chapter 3 has been published as "Dol po pa shes rab rgyal mtshan on the Mahāyāna doxography—Rethinking the Distinction between Cittamātra and Madhyamaka in Fourteenth-century Tibet" in *Journal of the International Association of Buddhist Studies* 34.1–2 (2012): 321–48, with permission from the International Association of Buddhist Studies. Finally, a previous version of chapter 5 has appeared as "In Defense of His Guru: Dratsepa's Rebuttal to the Challenges Articulated by the Proponents of the Other-Emptiness Doctrine" in *Journal of Indian Philosophy* 39.2 (2011): 147–65, with kind permission from Springer Science+Business Media.

Dr. Gareth Sparham and Professor Klaus-Dieter Mathes read the entire manuscript and offered me invaluable comments and suggestions that gave a new shape to my book. I offer my sincerest gratitude to them for their time and guidance. I am also indebted to SUNY's external reviewers for offering me constructive feedback on the book. My sincerest gratitude also goes to Christopher Ahn, Jessica Kirschner, Eileen Nizer, and Anne Valentine at SUNY for their guidance and editing help. Finally, I want to thank my colleagues at the University of San Francisco for their kind support.

Introduction

General Remarks

Toward the end of a three-year course on Candrakīrti's (ca. 570–640) *Madhyamakāvatāra* at the Institute of Buddhist Dialectics in Dharamsala, which primarily offers a monastic curriculum based on commentaries and works drawn from the Geluk (*dge lugs*) School of Tibetan Buddhism, my whole class humbly requested that our instructor[1] teach us the *Ratnagotravibhāga Mahāyānottaratantraśāstra*, commonly known as the *Uttaratantra* in the Tibetan tradition,[2] a seminal Indian treatise on the concept of buddha-nature (*sangs rgyas kyi rigs*; *buddhagotra*) or tathāgata-essence (*de bzhin gshegs pa'i snying po*; *tathāgatagarbha*).[3] His response, to our disappointment, was that since he had not received the expository transmission (*bshad rgyun*) of the *Uttaratantra* from any of his masters, he could not teach it to us. This rather traditional reply from our elderly guru was quite difficult even for the then young student-monks, who grew up in India and Nepal in the later part of the twentieth-century, to fully comprehend. His response had nothing to do with his lack of knowledge, insofar as many contemporary Tibetan scholars, including the teacher, fervently believe that the *Uttaratantra* is easier to intellectually understand than Madhyamaka classics, such as the *Madhyamakāvatāra* and Nāgārjuna's (ca. 200) *Madhyamakakārikā*. Ironically, our teacher had also constantly reminded us that the meaning of the emptiness of inherent existence taught in the *Madhyamakāvatāra*, a treatise that Geluk scholar-monks hold dear to their hearts, and the meaning of tathāgata-essence explicated in the *Uttaratantra* was the same. He said this even though it is well known that the Geluk School prefers the *Madhyamakāvatāra*'s exposition of ultimate truth over the *Uttaratantra*'s exposition.

1

Several years later, in 2001, far from India, I had begun my graduate program at the University of Virginia in Charlottesville. One of the first seminars I took was on the Madhyamaka system, taught by Professor Jeffrey Hopkins and a visiting Tibetan scholar,[4] an extremely learned young monk from the Amdo region of cultural Tibet. The latter was affiliated with the Jonang (*jo nang*) School of Tibetan Buddhism, which holds a view of emptiness drastically different from that of the Geluk's perspective, articulated by the above-mentioned teacher in Dharamsala, India. The main text that we used in this class was Dölpopa's (*dol po pa shes rab rgyal mtshan*, 1292–1361) *Mountain Doctrine* (*ri chos nges don rgya mtsho*), a seminal work on the Mahāyāna path from the perspective of the Jonang School, which quotes passages from the *Uttaratantra* liberally. It was in this context that the visiting scholar frequently mentioned in class that the emptiness taught in the *Madhyamakāvatāra* was not complete (*nyi tshe ba*), whereas the tathāgata-essence explicated in the *Uttaratantra* was the ultimate emptiness.

These two contemporary views of the *Uttaratantra* vis-à-vis the *Madhyamakāvatāra* demonstrate the complex relationship that the two Indian treatises share in terms of their articulations of ultimate truth for many Tibetan scholars. However, the crucial role that the *Uttaratantra* played in the history of Tibetan Buddhism is yet to receive the scholarly attention it deserves, without which we would only have an impartial knowledge about the historical significance of the *Madhyamakāvatāra* in Tibet. Whereas a considerable number of Western philologists, historians, and philosophers have written about Candrakīrti's *Madhyamakāvatāra* and its place in the intellectual history of Tibetan Buddhism, no Western trained scholar to date has dealt systematically with the place of the *Uttaratantra* in that history, despite its importance within Tibetan Buddhism in general, and Buddhist scholasticism in particular. The two contemporary Tibetan scholars' positions on the relative merits of the *Uttaratantra* vis-à-vis the *Madhyamakāvatāra* and the dearth of modern scholarship on the *Uttaratantra* in Tibet increased my interest in the treatise and led me to a study of the Tibetan commentaries on the Indian commentarial work. Over the course of my study, I set about unraveling the complex processes of the making of the *Uttaratantra* in Tibet, looking for answers to the many historical and doctrinal questions it raises.

My book, then, surveys the literary landscape and analyzes the dynamic intellectual arguments recorded in the Tibetan commentaries on the *Uttaratantra,* as well as the many other Tibetan sources that deal closely with the treatise that emerged between the eleventh and fifteenth centuries. This era saw the *Uttaratantra* translated into Tibetan several times by many scholars and more than a dozen foundational, yet fundamentally distinct, Tibetan commentaries written that ultimately gave rise to several divergent approaches to the *Uttaratantra.* At the core of issues central to understanding these multiple voices that generated the disparate views of this text among Tibetan thinkers are these:

- Is the tathāgata-essence teaching found in the *Uttaratantra* definitive (*nges don; nītārtha*), or is it provisional (*drang don; neyārtha*)? While Tibetan thinkers generally characterize definitive teachings as those that explicitly teach ultimate truth, which is the ultimate purport of the Buddha's teachings, and provisional teachings as those teachings that do not explain ultimate truth clearly and that require further interpretation in order to ascertain the ultimate purport of the Buddha's intent, they disagree on which of the Buddha's teachings are definitive or provisional.

- Does the treatise belong to the middle wheel (*'khor lo bar pa*) or the last wheel (*'khor lo tha ma*) of the Buddha's teachings? Tibetan scholars trace the source for the two wheels of teachings to the *Saṃdhinirmocanasūtra,* an early Mahāyāna text attributed to the Buddha. The sutra speaks of the three sets of the Buddha's teachings: the first wheel, the middle wheel, and the last wheel. Generally speaking, the first is asserted as a set of teachings for Hearers (*nyan thos;* śrāvaka), Buddhist followers of early non-Mahāyāna tradition, whereas the latter two are for the followers of Mahāyāna. The middle-wheel teachings, then, refer to the *Prajñāpāramitāsūtras,* which explain all phenomena without any distinction as empty of its own entity or empty of inherent existence. The last-wheel teachings include the *Saṃdhinirmocanasūtra,* which clarifies how phenomena are empty of their own entity and utilizes terms such as "all-basis-consciousness" (*kun gzhi rnam par shes pa; ālayavijñāna*), "eight consciousnesses," and cognition-only (*rnam par rig pa tsam; vijñaptimātra*),[5] and tathāgata-essence sutras such as *Mahāparinirvāṇasūtra*, *Tathāgatagarbhasūtra*, and so forth.

- Does it teach ultimate truth according to the Cittamātra or Madhyamaka system? Broadly speaking, Cittamātra and Madhyamaka are two schools of thought within the Mahāyāna tradition. The former bases its philosophy on the *Saṃdhinirmocanasūtra* and other Yogācāra works; and it explains our phenomenal world by referring to three natures (*ngo bo nyid gsum; trisvabhāva*)—other-powered or dependent-nature, imputational nature, and throroughly established nature—and other related concepts.[6] On the other hand, Madhyamaka draws its philosophy from the *Prajñāpāramitāsūtras* and others; and it asserts emptiness of inherent existence in all phenomena.[7]

- Does it explicate other-emptiness (*gzhan stong*) or self-emptiness (*rang stong*)? Generally speaking, the former refers to the idea that ultimate truth is empty of defilements that are naturally other than ultimate truth, whereas self-emptiness implies that everything including ultimate truth is empty of its own inherent nature.

The multiplicity of perspectives on the *Uttaratantra* in Tibet is a result of several vicissitudes that we see in the history of Tibetan Buddhism from the eleventh through the fifteenth centuries. Amongst these are the rise and decline of Sangpu (*gsang phu ne'u thog*) monastery as a scholastic institution; the rise and decline of the Sakya (*sa skya*) School as a center for monastic education; the production of new Tibetan translations of Indian treatises; and the ascendancy of the *Madhyamakāvatāra* to popularity and authority. Political, social, and institutional changes are of great importance for ascertaining the full, comprehensive depiction of the textual dynamism of the making of the *Uttaratantra* in Tibet. Nevertheless, while recognizing the importance of extratextual elements such as political and institutional shifts, this book focuses on the intra- and intertextual network of relationships of the Tibetan commentaries on the *Uttaratantra*. Therefore, in the chapters that follow, I lead readers on the journey I undertook to hear the divergent voices addressing these questions on the nature of the *Uttaratantra*; voices that have contributed much to the intellectual history of Tibetan Buddhism. Listening to these opposing voices on the issue of the veracity of the *Uttaratantra* will help us better understand the importance of the treatise and the processes and interplay of exchanges that formed the text. I hope that this text will complement the already existing scholarship on the history of Madhyamaka in Tibet.

Textual Historical Background

The exact date the *Uttaratantra* was written is not known.[8] However, the Tibetan tradition attributes the text in verses to Maitreya,[9] who taught it to Asaṅga (ca. fourth or fifth century) in Maitreya's Pure Land of Tuṣita. According to tradition, Asaṅga, an influential Buddhist interpreter, later wrote a prose commentary on the verses after his return from Tuṣita.[10]

The treatise is divided into five chapters consisting of seven different topics. The first chapter discusses Buddha, Dharma, Saṅgha, and buddha-element (*sangs rgyas kyi khams; buddhadhātu*).

Here is a brief description of each of the first four topics. Buddha generally refers to someone who has fulfilled the personal goal of the complete realization of dharma-body (*chos sku; dharmakāya*) and the goal of the realization of form-body (*gzugs sku; rūpakāya*) for other sentient beings. Dharma in this context is of two natures: the cessation of defilements and the bodhisattva path leading to the cessation. Saṅgha is a community of bodhisattvas who see phenomena as they ultimately exist and who also see distinctive appearances of phenomena. In other words, it is a bodhisattva community that realizes the ultimate reality of all phenomena and that recognizes the multifarious aspect of conventional reality respectively. Buddha-element, the main object of realization, generally refers to the ultimate pure nature of mind that is temporarily obscured by defilements. Much of the first chapter is devoted to the discussion of the buddha-element from ten aspects[11] and how it exists in all sentient beings because of the three reasons[12] using nine metaphors.[13] This chapter, then, becomes the most important chapter of all, as it delineates buddha-element or tathāgata-essence, the most fundamental topic of the *Uttaratantra*, which is also the main focus of my book.

The next three chapters of the *Uttaratantra* explore the nature of enlightenment, enlightened qualities, and enlightened activities, respectively. These three are the resultant state of enlightenment achieved through the four causal factors delineated in the first chapter. The nature of enlightenment is the ultimate reality of mind that is free from all defilements at the resultant state, and it is described with eight aspects.[14] Enlightened qualities refer to the sixty-four awakened qualities[15] such as the ten enlightened powers, thirty-two virtuous marks, and so forth that accompany the achievement of enlightenment or buddhahood. Finally, the enlightened activities of the buddhas are innately natural and uninterruptly for the well-being of others. Thus the treatise consisting of seven topics explicates how individuals can achieve enlightenment within a Mahāyāna system through a realization of the three objects of Mahāyāna refuge and tathāgata-essence. Hence, the treatise is an early map of the path and fruit of the Mahāyāna tradition. The last (fifth) chapter of the *Uttaratantra* explicates the great benefits of having faith in tathāgata-essence, enlightenment, and so forth.

The treatise captivated the hearts and minds of many Tibetan thinkers immediately from the time it was first introduced into Tibet from India in the late eleventh century. To this day, both the root text in verses and the prose commentary continue to exert a strong influence on Tibetan masters and monastics: Tibetan monks of the Nyingma (*rnying ma*), Kagyü (*bka' brgyud*), Sakya, and Jonang schools of Tibetan Buddhism continue to study and transmit its lineage of exposition down to the present day.[16] While the transmission and systematic study of the *Uttaratantra* and its commentary are less common in the contemporary Geluk School, Geluk monastics are familiar with the general theme of the treatise. They know many verses from the root text by heart, which they may cite either in a debate courtyard, in their discourses on the three objects of Mahāyāna refuge, or when debating over the concept of tathāgata-essence.

It was through these Tibetan tradition(s) of the *Uttaratantra* that modern scholars came to know about the *Uttaratantra* in the first half of the twentieth century: first, through Eugene Obermiller's *Sublime Science of the Great Vehicle to Salvation*,[17] a groundbreaking English translation of the treatise from Tibetan, and later through the Sanskrit manuscripts found in Tibet by Rāhula Sāṅkṛtyāyana and later edited by Edward Johnston.[18] Subsequently, in 1966, Japanese scholar Jikido Takasaki compared the Sanskrit manuscripts with both Tibetan and Chinese translations and produced an English translation of what he took to be the core text in his *A Study on the Ratnagotravibhāga*.[19] These early pioneering works provided an impetus to David Ruegg,[20] Susan Hookham,[21] and Klaus-Dieter Mathes[22] to write important works pertaining to the tathāgata-essence concept mentioned in the *Uttaratantra* based primarily on early Tibetan sources. It is through these processes that Buddhist studies scholars, as well as a general international Buddhist readership, have come to know the *Uttaratantra*.

Although the treatise originated in India and was translated into Chinese in the sixth century by Ratnamati, even before Tibet knew anything about Buddhism, it did not initially gain the popularity that it came to have in Tibet in either India or China. The treatise is not cited in any early Indian Buddhist works, with an exception of a few Indian texts from the sixth/seventh century on the tathāgata-essence that are extant only in Chinese translation.[23] However, after several centuries the *Uttaratantra* does gain, or perhaps regain, its significant place in the history of Buddhist literature in India. In the eleventh century in northern India the Indian scholars Ratnākaraśānti (tenth–eleventh centuries),[24] Jñānaśrīmitra (ca. 980–1050),[25] and Maitrīpa (986–1063)[26] began to cite the *Uttaratantra* in their works.[27] Sajjana (eleventh century) and Vairocanarakṣita (eleventh/twelfth centuries) even wrote full-fledged commentaries on the *Uttaratantra* during this period.[28]

Concurrently, Tibet was reemerging from its so-called "dark period," following the reign of Lang Darma (*glang dar ma*, reigned ca. 838–42),[29] a time during which institutional Buddhism declined following the disintegration of the Tibetan Empire.[30] By the eleventh century, Tibet had resumed importing and translating Buddhist texts, building monasteries and temples, and ordaining monks to such an extent that it quickly regained, and even surpassed, the early Buddhist religiocultural activities of the eighth and ninth centuries—a period traditionally known as the early dissemination of Buddhism (*bstan pa snga dar*) in Tibet. It was in such an intellectual milieu that the *Uttaratantra* and its commentary were translated from Sanskrit into Tibetan. Within less than a hundred years, Atiśa (ca. 982–1054) and Naktso (*nag 'tsho lo tsa ba*, 1011–1064),[31] Ngok (*rngog blo ldan shes rab*, 1059–1109) and Sajjana,[32] and Patsap (*spa tshab nyi ma grags*, ca. 1055–1141) produced at least three of the first Tibetan translations,[33] to be followed over the course of the next couple of centuries by three more Tibetan translations.[34] Unfortunately, there is only one complete, extant Tibetan translation available today, the one made by Ngok and Sajjana.

Thus we see that in eleventh-century northern India, Indian scholars and masters gave new life to the then dormant *Uttaratantra* by citing it, writing commentaries about it, and transmitting it to Indian and Tibetan disciples. At the same time, Tibetan scholars working with Indian paṇḍitas introduced the treatise to Tibet through multiple translations executed by some of the most exceptional Buddhist luminaries of the time. Those translations succeeded in introducing the *Uttaratantra* to Tibet and led to an early stage of its dissemination and flourishing. Supplementing the translations, a Tibetan commentarial and oral transmission also developed in the eleventh and twelfth centuries that ensured for the *Uttaratantra* a central role in the intellectual and contemplative developments in the many centuries to follow.

In the earliest period of its transmission from India, according to Tibetan thinkers such as Gö Lotsawa (*'gos lo tsa ba gzhon nu dpal,* 1392–1481) and Kongtrül (*kong sprul blo gros mtha' yas,* 1813–1899), there seem to have emerged two forms of transmitting the teaching of the treatise in Tibet.[35] One exposition is based mainly on what they call the "meditative tradition" (*sgom lugs*), and the other derives from what they call the "dialectic tradition" (*mtshan nyid kyi lugs*).[36] These two early approaches are also referred to as "exposition through the medium of direct perception" (*mngon sum gyi lam gyis bshad pa*) and "exposition through the medium of logical inferences" (*rjes dpag gi lam gyis bshad pa*)[37] respectively, or the "meditative tradition" and the "learning/contemplative tradition" (*thos bsam gyi lugs*).[38] Commentaries written by Ngok and Chapa (*phywa pa chos kyi seng ge,* 1109–1169) are deemed the model for the first form of exposition, whereas those by Tsen Khawoché (*btsan kha bo che,* b. 1021) and Zu Gawé Dorjé (*gzu dga' ba'i rdo rje,* eleventh century)[39] became the archetype for the second commentarial tradition. Unfortunately, the texts by the latter two early scholars are not available.[40]

Although both Tsen Khawoché and Ngok received the *Uttaratantra* transmission from the same master, Sajjana, in Kashmir,[41] they developed their own ways of teaching it based on their particular interests, and on their different background knowledge of other Buddhist texts.[42] Ngok, for example, was only a teenager when he traveled to India. On his return to Tibet, he studied and propagated not only the *Uttaratantra,* but also a number of other important Buddhist epistemological and Madhyamaka texts. Moreover, Tsen Khawoché was already in his midfifties when he traveled to Kashmir, had little background in Buddhist scholastic tradition, and is reported to have said to Sajjana, "Now I have grown old! I cannot master many books. I wish to make the Doctrine of the Blessed Maitreya my death prayer."[43] These two streams of exposition would pave the path for the later Tibetan commentators on the treatise. It was through these mediums of transmission that the treatise captured the hearts and minds of Tibetan scholars, turning the Indian work into a veritable "Tibetan *Uttaratantra*" with its own commentaries and pedagogical methods. It is to those writers and their interpretations of the *Uttaratantra* that we now turn.

Part I

Early Period

Kadam Thinkers Rescue the Treatise

1

Rise of the *Uttaratantra* in Tibet

Early Kadam Scholars Revitalize the Newly Discovered Indian Exegesis

Introduction

The eleventh and twelfth centuries saw the revitalization of Buddhist culture in the form of Tibetan translations of Buddhist texts from India, establishment of monasteries and temples in Tibet, and scholastic study of texts such as the *Five Treatises of Maitreya,* as well as Madhyamaka texts by Indian masters such as Nāgārjuna, Candrakīrti, and Bhāviveka. It was in this cultural milieu that the *Uttaratantra* was first translated into Tibetan from Sanskrit by several Tibetan translators, including Ngok.[1] Not only was Ngok one of the translators, but he was also an early commentator on the Indian treatise. He was born into an aristocratic family and traveled to Kashmir, India, in 1076, where he studied for seventeen years, receiving instruction on the *Uttaratantra.* Upon his return to Tibet, he became the second abbot of Sangpu monastery[2] and contributed greatly to the study of the middle way, perfection of wisdom through his commentary on the *Abhisamayālaṃkāra,* and Buddhist epistemological literature.[3] He is believed to have extensively taught and written on the three middle way treatises, notably, the *Madhymakālaṃkāra* by Śāntarakṣita, the *Madhyamakāloka* by Kamalaśīla, and the *Satyadvayavibhaṅga* by Jñānagarbha. These Indian treatises became instrumental for what would later be referred to as the Svātantrika Madhyamaka with which Ngok and Chapa are associated. His contribution to the field of Buddhist epistemology is equally great as he is credited with founding the "new episteomlogy" (*tshad ma gsar ma*) through his translations and commentaries on Indian Buddhist works on epistemology.

Ngok was not the only commentator on the *Uttaratantra* from that time period. Chapa,[4] from the same monastery, also wrote a commentary on the treatise. He also ascended to the abbatial seat of Sangpu monastery and made valuable contributions to the study of Buddhist philosophy and epistemology. Unlike Ngok, Chapa never went to India to study under Indian scholars, nor did he know Sanskrit.[5] Chapa interpreted Indian treatises such as the *Uttaratantra* according to Ngok's system because of his affiliation with Ngok and Sangpu monastery. As Leonard van der Kuijp argued: "Phya-pa [that is, Chapa], following the trends established by the Rngog-lugs [that is, Ngok's system], was quite active in interpreting the Svātantrika-Madhyamaka doctrines."[6]

As a defender of Svātantrika Madhyamaka, Chapa became the earliest Tibetan critic of Candrakīrti's thoughts regarding middle-way philosophy and had to defend his system against the followers of Candrakīrti, notably, Jayānanda (ca. twelfth century), a staunch proponent of what would be later called Prāsaṅgika Madyamaka.[7] Jayānanda is arguably the first scholar who indicated that the *Uttaratantra* is provisional within the Tibetan intellectual landscape.[8]

Therefore, it is not surprising to find that the two Sangpu scholars praise the *Uttaratantra* as the most definitive and authoritative treatise. Ngok claims that the *Uttaratantra* is the only text that is definitive among the *Five Treatises of Maitreya,* while Chapa refers to the *Uttaratantra* as "the secret of the Mahāyāna."

While the two Sangpu scholars were formidable in disseminating the *Uttaratantra* in Tibet in this early period of the treatise, several other prominent masters from the same era also interpreted the treatise as definitve. Tsen Khawoché and Zu Gawé Dorjé, two lineage holders of the contemplative tradition of the *Uttaratantra*, are believed to have written commentaries on the text that interpreted the treatise in a positive manner, but their commentaries are no longer available. Drolungpa Lodrö Jungné (*gro lung pa blo gros 'byung gnas*, b. eleventh century), one of the four disciples of Ngok and a teacher of Chapa, is believed to have written a commentary[9] to the *Uttaratantra* that accorded with Ngok's presentation of the treatise.[10]

In his *Ornament of the Precious Liberation* (*thar pa rin po che'i rgyan*),[11] Gampopa (*sgam po pa bsod nams rin chen*, 1079–1153), the famed disciple of the most celebrated Tibetan meditation master Milarepa (*mi la ras pa*, 1052–1135), repeatedly cites the *Uttaratantra* as a central textual authority, and he does so in ways that appear to accept its doctrinal expositions straight-forwardly as expressive of the ultimate truth. Not surprisingly, buddha-nature is mentioned as the first point, the causal ground, in his *Ornament of the Precious Liberation*. Furthermore, as Kongtrül states, "Lord Gampopa says that 'The treatise for our Mahāmudrā tradition is *Mahayanottaratantraśāstra* [that is, the *Uttaratantra*] composed by Bhagavan Maitreya."[12]

Mabja (*rma bya byang chub brtson 'grus*, d. 1185), a prominent disciple of Chapa who later went on to study with his master's opponent,[13] states in his commentary on the *Madhyamakakārikā* that the *Uttaratantra* and Candrakīrti's *Madhyamakāvatāra* interpret the last-wheel teachings from a Madhyamaka perspective.[14]

In his *Trees of Clear Realization* (*mngon rtogs ljon shing*), Drakpa Gyeltsen (*grags pa rgyal mtshan*, 1147–1216), one of the luminaries of the Sakya tradition, also demonstrates that the *Uttaratantra* is definitive:

> So, if all sentient beings have the buddha-essence then would it not contradict [the notion] of the cut-off buddha-nature mentioned in the *Sūtrālaṃkāra*? It is not contradictory because the [latter remark] is a provisional statement from the Cittamātra system, whereas here [in the Madhyamaka system] cut off buddha-nature is not possible, as the *Uttaratantra* demonstrates.[15]

It is quite evident that the *Uttaratantra* assumed a significant textual authority for many prominent Tibetan masters from this early period. It is to the two earliest extant commentaries—Ngok's *Condensed Meaning of the Uttaratantra* (*theg chen rgyud bla'i don bsdus pa*)[16] and Chapa's *Illumination of the Meaning of the Uttaratantra* (*theg pa chen po rgyud bla ma'i bstan bcos kyi tshig dang don gyi cha rgya cher bsnyad pa phra ba'i don gsal ba*)[17]—that I now turn.

Ngok and Chapa on the Pervasive Nature of the Buddha-Body

Both Ngok and Chapa offer an interesting interpretation of a well-known verse from the *Uttaratantra* that demonstrates that all beings have tathāgata-essence because of three reasons. The verse reads: "All sentient beings always have the buddha-essence because 1) the buddha-body radiates [to all sentient beings], 2) the suchness [of a buddha and sentient beings] is indivisible, and 3) the buddha-nature exists [in all sentient beings]."[18] In their commentaries, the Sangpu scholars argue that tathāgata-essence found in that verse must be understood in terms of the second reason, which is that suchness is indivisible, without any dualistic entity. Tathāgata-essence must not be connected to either the first reason—the notion that the resultant buddha-body pervades all beings—or the third reason which is that causal buddha-nature exists in all beings. Therefore, tathāgata-essence is neither the resultant buddha-body nor the causal buddha-nature, rather it is the ultimate nature of suchness.

On the first reason, Ngok argues:

> With respect to this [the notion that buddha-body per-vades all sentient beings], the tathāgata stands true [in that buddha-body is fully enlightened, but the notion that] sentient beings possess tathāgata-essence [in this context] is [purely] a designation. Since beings have the lot to achieve buddha-body it is said that it pervades [all sentient beings].[19]

Ngok interprets the first reason—the buddha-body pervades all sentient beings—to merely demonstrate that sentient beings have the potential to achieve buddha-body,[20] not so much to show that they have tathāgata-essence from the perspective of the first reason. Kamalaśīla (eighth century), one of Ngok's influences, also holds a similar position in his *Madhyamakāloka*. The Indian master argues, "That all sentient beings have the tathāgata-essence inevitably shows that all are suitable to achieve the supreme complete buddhahood."[21]

Following in the footsteps of both Kamalaśīla and Ngok, Chapa also shows:

> The suchness of the purified state is the complete buddha-body, the resultant dharma-body. [The term] "radiates" means being pervaded [by dharma-body]. It is also perva-sive in the sense that all sentient beings have the capac-ity to achieve it. With respect to this, the tathāgata is the actual [buddha], but as the essence of sentient beings it is imputed. Because [sentient beings] have the good fortune to achieve dharma-body, dharma-body is designated as pervading [sentient beings].[22]

Hence, both Ngok and Chapa argue that sentient beings do not have tathāgata-essence on the basis of the first reason because they do not have the purified enlightened body of a buddha, rather they have the potential to achieve an englightened state.

However, they agree that sentient beings have the tathāgata-essence from the perspective of the second reason, which is that suchness is indivisible or nondual. As Ngok states, "That both a tathāgata and ordinary beings have [tathāgata] essence is actually the case."[23] The first reason is true only for enlightened beings, but only designated for ordinary beings; the second reason applies to both enlightened beings and sentient beings. Chapa also comments on the second reason as follows:

> [The passage] "because there is no distinction with respect to suchness" [shows] the essence of suchness, the nature of the absence of distinction with respect to emptiness. It is both the essence of a tathāgata and the essence of sentient beings in actuality. This is because the suchness that is devoid of natural defilements [but] endowed with adventitious defilements is the buddha's entity and [it] exists in sentient beings.[24]

Chapa uses language similar to Ngok's to explain the second reason for the existence of tathāgata-essence in sentient beings. Therefore, both Kadam commentators assert that only the second reason establishes an actual link between enlightened beings and sentient beings in terms of their ultimate nature.

In regard to the last reason, Ngok states:

> Since the seed of wisdom and compassion, the predisposition for virtue, [which is] the cause for achieving the state of completely pure suchness, is the cause of a tathāgata, it is imputed as tathāgata. [On the other hand,] it is a fact that it is the essence of sentient beings.[25]

Similarly, Chapa argues, "[The passage] that 'because buddha-nature exists [every one has the tathāgata-essence]' shows that since the cause for achieving [pure] suchness, the virtuous predisposition, the seed of wisdom and compassion is the cause of tathāgata, [buddha-nature is merely] designated by tathāgata, but it is indeed the case that it is the essence of sentient beings."[26] Essentially both Ngok and Chapa argue that the third reason cannot establish a link between enlightened beings and sentient beings in terms of their ultimate nature because it is only a characteristic of sentient beings, but not of enlightened beings.[27]

Therefore, the two Kadam masters argue that sentient beings do not have the tathāgata-essence from the perspective of either the first reason of the resultant essence or the third reason of the causal essence. Rather it is the second reason that becomes the central point for establishing the link between enlightenment and sentient beings. It is the middle reason that shows that sentient beings and tathāgatas are the same in their ultimate nature.[28] In other words, the only thing that sentient beings have in common with enlightened beings is the ultimate nature of their minds.

Ngok and Chapa on Definitive or Provisional Nature in the *Uttaratantra*

Given that the two Sangpu scholars say that the tathāgata-essence is the same as suchness or ultimate truth, they assert that the *Uttaratantra* is a treatise explaining the definitive meaning of the Buddha's teachings. Ngok states, "There are two types of scriptural Dharma: teachings of ultimate truth and teachings of conventional truth."[29] According to him, the Buddha's teachings either explicate the ultimate truth of emptiness or the conventional phenomena. He elaborates on this by saying, "The teachings of the ultimate are like honey because they contain the same flavorful taste. The teachings of conventional phenomena are like fruit because they come in a variety that pervades everywhere."[30] Therefore, Ngok clearly argues that the scriptures that explain the ultimate truth of phenomena, the emptiness of inherent existence, are definitive, whereas the teachings that elaborate on the multifaceted aspects of conventional phenomena are provisional.

Chapa also asserts that the *Uttaratantra* is a definitive work. He uses phrases such as "the supreme meaning" (*mchog gi don*) and "the secret of the Mahāyāna" (*theg pa chen po'i gsang ba*) to refer to the *Uttaratantra*.[31] Chapa contrasts the *Uttaratantra* with the other four texts attributed to Maitreya and concludes that the *Uttaratantra* is superior to the other four. However, unlike Ngok,[32] Chapa states that certain phrases of the *Uttaratantra* are not necessarily definitive. He argues, "The exposition of emptiness in the other one [that is, the middle-wheel teachings] accords with the literal meaning, [while] here [in the last-wheel treatises] the explication that the buddha-element exists as cause requires interpretation. They are not contradictory because this [that is, the explication of the buddha-element being cause in the last-wheel teachings] is not literal."[33] While Chapa shows that the *Uttaratantra* is definitive, he demonstrates that certain phrases in the *Uttaratantra* are not necessarily definitive—such as the passage teaching the buddha-element as cause. This is because for Chapa being a cause in this context entails being conditioned and conventional and something that exists only on the causal state of enlightenment, whereas the buddha-element is unconditioned and ultimate and something that exists pervasively as the ultimate nature on both the causal and resultant levels of englightenment.

Ngok and Chapa on the *Uttaratantra* as a Last-Wheel Treatise

About the difference between the two wheels, Ngok states:

> [A]lthough all characteristics are ultimately negated in the *Prajñāpāramitāsūtras*, [it does not mean that these teachings] contradict with the explanation of [the ultimate character] as the cause for producing enlightened qualities [found] here [in the last-wheel teachings]. The reason is that, [in the middle-wheel teachings] the mere ultimate character is explained from the perspective of the two truths, [whereas] here [in the last-wheel teachings it is shown] as a cause for achieving enlightened qualities by contemplating the [ulti-mate] character explicated there [in the *Prajñāpāramitāsūtras*. So the ultimate] character that is mentioned there [in the *Prajñāpāramitāsūtras*] is established as a cause [in the last-wheel teachings].[34]

Ngok argues that the *Prajñāpāramitāsūtras* or the middle-wheel teachings teach merely the ultimate truth whereas the last-wheel teachings explain the ultimate truth as a causal factor for enlightenment also. Chapa makes Ngok's point more clear by focusing on the subjective mind that realizes the ultimate truth:

> Does [the phrase] "the buddha-element exists" [found in the *Uttaratantra*] not contradict [what the *Prajñāpāramitāsūtras* teach]? There is no contradiction because objects are ultimately empty, but the subjective mind [perceiving the emptiness] produces enlightened qualities. Because of that it is described as a cause."[35]

Therefore, for both Ngok and Chapa, the *Uttaratantra* is a definitive work, and it is also a treatise that explains the meaning of the last-wheel sutras such as the *Tathāgatagarbhasūtra* and the *Śrīmālādevīsūtra*.

Buddha-Element as a Conceived Object

Both Ngok and Chapa address the issue of whether the buddha-element is knowable or not by human consciousness. They describe the ultimate truth or the buddha-element as a knowable object. Ngok, while commenting on how gnosis exists in sentient beings, makes the direct correlation between the object of knowledge and dharma-reality and points out that the wisdom and its object are indivisible.[36] When Ngok dileneates the difference between the buddha-element (the fourth point of the *Uttaratantra)* and enlightenment (the fifth point of the *Uttaratantra)* he points out that the former is the object of knowledge.[37] In both cases, not only is the buddha-element considered an object of knowledge, but it is also specifically discussed in the context of objects of knowledge.

Like Ngok, Chapa also claims it is an object of knowledge. In his *Uttaratantra* commentary, Ngok makes reference to how ultimate truth or buddha-element is not a conceived object of speech and conceptual thought. Ngok states, "The ultimate is not an object of speech; conceptual mind is conventional; because of that the ultimate is not an object of conceptuality. The meaning of [it being] not an object of speech is that it is not a conceived object of speech and conceptual thought."[38]

Chapa provides more explanation as to what Ngok means to hold when he asserts buddha-element is not a conceived object of speech and conceptual thought. He states:

Not being mentioned explicitly means that [the buddha-element] does not appear to the conception in connection with the term-universal; it is only the object-universal that appears to conception in connection with the term-universal. Because all of its self-characteristics do not appear to conception in connection with the term-universal.[39]

As Georges Dreyfus shows Chapa and his followers do not assert that external objects such as a red vase, a chair, and so forth are appearing objects of their respective conceptions; rather it is their object-universals that are the appearing objects of their respective conceptions.[40] Chapa claims that because the buddha-element by itself can never fully be spoken of and cannot be fully conceived by conceptual mind, it is not a conceived object of speech and conceptual cognition. Nonetheless, he states that the object-universal of the buddha-element can be spoken of and can be conceived by conceptual mind. It is through the medium of this that the buddha-element is explained using terms and concepts in the *Uttaratantra* and other tathāgata-essence literature.[41] Chapa discusses the object-universal of the buddha-element within the context of the path of preparation and the path below it,[42] where direct realization of emptiness has not dawned, whereas he speaks of the realization of the actual buddha-element within the context of the path of seeing and above, where individuals have begun to see the buddha-element directly.[43]

Ngok and Chapa Differ on Emphasis

Chapa follows Ngok quite closely not only in terms of content, but also in terms of wording as shown above. In addition to that, Chapa makes use of certain technical terms such as "awakened buddha-element" (*sad pa'i khams*), "ripened buddha-element" (*smin pa'i khams*), and so forth[44] that are found in Ngok's commentary as well.

However, their commentaries differ from each other in terms of emphasis in that Chapa elaborates on issues that are not addressed in Ngok's commentary: (1) Chapa makes more use of the term "all-basis-consciousness"; (2) he makes systematic use of the two terms "naturally abiding buddha-nature" (*rang bzhin gnas rigs*)[45] and "developmental buddha-nature" (*rgyas 'gyur rigs*),[46] in conjunction with the all-basis-consciousness; (3) he mentions the cut-off buddha-nature (*rigs chad*); and (4) he discusses the misconception of emptiness in a Cittamātra system that asserts cut-off buddha-nature.

Ngok uses the term "all-basis-consciousness" only once in his *Uttaratantra* commentary in reference to a stanza apparently quoted from the *Mahāyānābhidharmasūtra:* "The [buddha-] element that has no beginning is the basis for all phenomena. Because it exists, all transmigratory beings exist, and nirvāṇa will also be attained."[47] Commenting on the term "buddha-element," Ngok argues, "That which has such various potentialities is also called all-basis-consciousness."[48] Ngok identifies the buddha-element mentioned in this verse with all-basis-consciousness without offering any futher explanation on it.

On the other hand, Chapa's commentary on the same verse gives a more nuanced description. He argues, "There is certainly no beginning for emptiness, the naturally abiding buddha-nature. Although there is a beginning for the virtuous seed, the developmental buddha-nature, there exists no beginning for its basis, the all-basis-consciousness. Hence, [the developmental buddha-nature] is designated as having no beginning."[49] Although Chapa demonstrates that a relationship between the developmental buddha-nature and the all-basis-consciousness exists, he does not equate the two. However, he shows that the naturally abiding buddha-nature is emptiness.

Chapa shows how the two types of buddha-nature can function as the basis for cyclic existence as well as liberation. He states, "It is through cultivating the correct mind-set that perceives the naturally abiding buddha-nature that the qualities of liberation ensue. Similarly, it is through increasing the power of the contemplatively derived buddha-nature [which is the same as the developmental buddha-nature], that liberation ensues."[50] He argues that the two types of buddha-nature are causes of liberation from cyclic existence. However, he also demonstrates that they function as a basis for cyclic existence. Chapa states:

> It is with emptiness, the naturally abiding buddha-nature, as a basis for misperception that the mistaken mind-set is generated. Through [the mistaken mind-set] karma and afflictions [arise] . . . Although afflictions are not generated through the developmental buddha-nature—the virtuous seed concordant with liberation—afflictions are generated through the all-basis-consciousness, the basis [for the

developmental buddha-nature], that is tainted by the seeds
of afflictions.[51]

Hence, Chapa treats all-basis-consciousness as an important concept
to explain how the developmental buddha-nature functions as a basis
for cyclic existence.

Another issue that Chapa addresses at length in his commentary
is the topic of the cut-off buddha-nature which Ngok does not mention in his commentary.[52] Chapa argues that "because the Natureless-
ness proponents (*ngo bo nyid med par smra ba*) claim that [the naturally
abiding buddha-nature] refers to the reality, emptiness, [they] do not
accept the completely cut-off buddha-nature."[53] Chapa argues that
Madhyamaka proponents like him assert that all sentient beings have
the potential to become a buddha in that their emptiness enables
them to transform.

In response to an unnamed person who claims that the cut-
off buddha-nature exists because it is mentioned in the *Nirvāṇasūtra*,
Chapa affirms the passage requires interpretation, and therefore it is
not to be accepted literally. He demonstrates that the texts that teach
the cut-off buddha-nature are provisional because they are taught (1)
with a certain purpose and (2) with a basis in the Buddha's thought,
and (3) because one can refute the meaning of their explicit teachings.[54]

In the context of his discussion of cut-off buddha-nature, Chapa
mentions Cittamātra. He identifies the proponents of a certain emptiness mentioned in *Asaṅga Commentary* as the exponents of Cittamātra.[55]
However, there is no mention of Cittamātra in Ngok's commentary.
While Chapa endorses the concept of all-basis-consciousness as an
important theme for his presentation of the developmental buddha-
nature in his commentary, he rejects the notion of the cut-off buddha-
nature and sources the incorrect view in this Cittamātra system.[56] For
him, the fact that the *Uttaratantra* teaches all sentient beings as having
the buddha-nature shows that the *Uttaratantra* is a Madhyamaka text,
not Cittamātra.[57]

Chapa discusses the misconceptions of emptiness in two ways
that are not addressed in Ngok's commentary. Chapa mentions the
emptiness of a phenomenon that has become nonexistent through
disintegration and the emptiness of the-one-not-existing-in-another.[58]
The first emptiness refers to an emptiness that comes into existence
through a transformation, as in the case of the emptiness of a vase

produced by the destruction of the vase. The second one is an emptiness of what is simply absent, as in the case of a valley which is
devoid of a large body of water. Although both emptinesses are
referred to as emptiness, they are not actual ultimate truth or real
emptiness according to Chapa.

Conclusion

Although scholars such as Tsen Khawoché, Zu Gawé Dorjé, Gampopa, Mabja, and Drakpa Gyeltsen from this early formative period
contributed to the positive evaluation of the *Uttaratantra*, Ngok and
Chapa made the largest contribution to its scholastic interpetation
by composing the two earliest Kadam commentaries on it. The two
Sangpu thinkers interpreted the text as the most definitive treatise
explicating the last-wheel teachings of the Buddha. Their expositions
on the *Uttaratantra* influenced later scholars, as will be discussed in
the following chapters. At the same time, the seeds of later critiques of
the *Uttaratantra* as provisional are already evident in this time period
as seen in Jayānanda's descriptions. It is to the beginning of the debate
over the definitive nature of the *Uttaratantra* that I now turn.

2

Sowing Seeds for Future Debate

Dissenters and Adherents

Introduction

In chapter 1, I analyzed how Ngok and Chapa, the two early Kadam luminaries from Sangpu monastery, framed the *Uttaratantra* as a significant Mahāyāna treatise by writing two of the earliest Tibetan commentaries on the treatise. Because of their command of Indian Mahāyāna scholastic classics, such as Dignāga's (c. 480–540) and Dharmakīrti's (c. 540–600) works on logic and epistemology, and treatises attributed to Nāgārjuna, Maitreya, Asaṅga, and others, Ngok and Chapa were able to present the newly introduced *Uttaratantra* in a Mahāyāna scholastic language without undermining the textual veracity of the *Uttaratantra* and other tathāgata-essence sutras. Concurrently, scholars who were engaged in the promulgation of *Madhyamakāvatāra* during this early period do not seem to have explicitly repudiated the *Uttaratantra* for teaching tathāgata-essence, irrespective of the fact that Candrakīrti's auto-commentary on the *Madhyamakāvatāra* takes the sutras that teach tathāgata-essence as provisional.[1] In his commentary on the *Madhyamakāvatāra*, Jayānanda states that the Buddha's teachings that explain tathāgata-essence as permanent and independent self are provisional, but even he does not demonstrate that the *Uttaratantra* itself is provisional, nor does he make any comments about its place within the Mahāyāna tradition.[2] Thus, the status of the *Uttaratantra* remained largely uncontested in Tibet in this early period of its dissemination.

This attitude to the *Uttaratantra* changed in the following century, when Sapen, whom David Jackson rightly deems "one of the most influential figures in the transmission of Indian Buddhist religion and learning to Tibet,"[3] challenges the definitive nature of the

Uttaratantra in his *Distinguishing the Three Vows* (*sdom gsum rab dbye*). It is in response to a challenge like this that Rikrel (*bcom ldan rig pa'i ral gri*, 1227–1305) writes his own commentary, the earliest extant Tibetan commentary on the *Uttaratantra* that cites both tantric and sutric sources to corroborate the claims made in the treatise. Other scholars such as Gelong Chöshé (*dge slong chos shes*, thirteenth century),[4] Kyoton Monlam Tsültrim (*skyo ston smon lam tshul khrims*, 1219–1299),[5] Sangpu Lodrö (*gsang phu blo gros mtshungs med*, thirteenth/fourteenth centuries) and Rinchen Yeshé (*rin chen ye shes*, thirteenth/fourteenth centuries) write commentaries on the *Uttaratantra* in favor of the tathāgata-essence literature. The works written by these scholars, juxtaposed with works on the *Madhyamakāvatāra* that emerge at the same time as central works in the middle-wheel literature, a literature that enjoyed great prestige in this period, set the stage for Dölpopa, as will be discussed in next chapter. They provide the intellectual context for Dölpopa's formulation of a unique, but controversial, presentation of Mahāyāna doctrine that utilizes the *Uttaratantra* as the central treatise. So it is these scholars arguing for, or against, the authority of the *Uttaratantra* as a seminal treatise in the Mahāyāna tradition who plant the seeds for disputes that will come to full fruition in the later fourteenth and early fifteenth centuries, when the real drama concerning the authority of the *Uttaratantra* plays out.

Sapen, the Dissenter

As Kevin Vose argues,[6] Sapen's identification and embrace of Prāsaṅgika-Madhyamaka, distinct from Svātantrika-Madhyamaka, arguably settled the doctrinal disputes between Tibetan Madhyamakas. As a proponent of the Madhyamaka view of the emptiness of inherent existence privileging the *Madhyamakāvatāra*, Sapen strongly argues against the tathāgata-essence concept that is central in the *Uttaratantra*. In his important work,[7] *Distinguishing the Three Vows*, Sapen shows that the *Uttaratantra* requires interpretation.[8]

Distinguishing the Three Vows was written circa 1232,[9] when Sapen was about fifty years old.[10] Although the text is neither about the *Uttaratantra* nor tathāgata-essence, it does raise some of the fundamental issues related to tathāgata-essence. It explores and criticizes several doctrinal positions held by other Tibetan Buddhist thinkers of the day. In all, there are fifteen issues that Sapen examines critically in this work,[11] and the tathāgata-essence is one of them. To illustrate the controversial nature of his work, it is reported that people started "gossip[ing] that Sapen's criticisms were motivated by sectarian animosity,"[12] even before Sapen had completed the text. As a consequence of that, Zangtsa (*zangs tsha bsod nams rgyal mtshan*, 1184–1239), Sapen's younger brother, urged him not to complete the book, as it would prove to "be detrimental."[13] In the end, his brother's intervention did not stop Sapen from completing the work.[14]

In verses 59–63 of Sapen's *Distinguishing the Three Vows*,[15] he argues against the presentation of the existence of a tathāgata-essence or sugata-essence endowed with enlightened qualities in sentient beings. Sapen demonstrates that such a position would be tantamount to holding the view of the Sāṃkhya School, that the "result is present in its cause."[16] In this, Sapen agrees with Ngok, Chapa, and Jayānanda, and furthermore, his position anticipates the positions of such later scholars as Dratsépa (*sgra tshad pa rin chen rnam rgyal*, 1318–1388), Butön (*bu ston rin chen grub*, 1290–1364), Rendawa (*red mda' ba gzhon nu blo gros*, 1349–1412), Tsongkhapa (*tsong kha pa blo bzang grags pa*, 1357–1419), and Gyeltsap (*rgyal tshab dar ma rin chen*, 1364–1432). These Buddhist writers agree that tathāgata-essence endowed with enlightened qualities differs from buddha-nature, because the former does not exist in sentient beings, whereas the latter does.

In verses 138–42 of *Distinguishing the Three Vows*,[17] Sapen further argues that the tathāgata-essence teaching in the *Uttaratantra* and other works of the tathāgata-essence literary corpus are provisional, because it meets the three criteria[18] that are characteristics of the Buddha's provisional teachings. The three criteria are the point of reference (*dgongs gzhi*),[19] purpose (*dgos pa*), and counter to the fact (*dngos la gnod byed*). According to Sapen, the point of reference for the tathāgata-essence teachings is emptiness of inherent existence, in that it is the basis of reality that is the primary intention of the Buddha. The purpose for teaching tathāgata-essence discourses is to eliminate the five faults of being discouraged, showing contempt for inferior beings, grasping at unreal things, denigrating authentic teachings, and seeing oneself as superior.[20] The third criterion for those who assert the tathāgata-essence teachings as provisional is that tathāgata-essence as explained in these sutras does not exist, since there are many definitive sutras that teach that all phenomena do not exist inherently.

It is evident from *Distinguishing the Three Vows* that the tathāgata-essence endowed with enlightened qualities does not exist in sentient beings. But does that mean that Sapen completely rejects the existence of tathāgata-essence in sentient beings? In order to address that question, we must turn to his other texts, which, in my opinion, give a fuller picture of his views on this matter.

In *Distinguishing the Three Vows*, Sapen argues that tathāgata-essence, sugata-essence, buddha-essence, and buddha-element are synonyms, but, interestingly, he never mentions the associated term "buddha-nature" in this context. However, in his *Illuminating the Thoughts of the Buddha* (*thub pa'i dgongs pa rab tu gsal ba*), Sapen explains buddha-nature in this way: "The inherent [buddha-]nature exists in all sentient beings. The developmental [buddha-]nature exists [from the time that] one has developed bodhicitta. [The latter] does not exist in those who have not developed [bodhicitta]."[21] Moreover, he continues, "Cittamātra asserts the completely cut-off buddha-nature. The Madhyamaka does not assert [the completely cut-off buddha-nature]."[22] In this context, where he discusses the concept of buddha-nature and how buddha-nature exists in all sentient beings, Sapen never mentions tathāgata-essence and its synonyms mentioned above, nor does he cite the *Uttaratantra* to justify his claim that all sentient beings have buddha-nature.[23]

Furthermore, in his *Letter to the Noble-Minded* (*skyes bu dam pa rnams la zhu ba'i 'phrin yig*), Sapen states, "Regarding tathāgata-essence, I have seen it taught as an interpretable principle in the *Laṅkāvatāra[sūtra]*, the *Mahāyanottaratantra*, the *Madhyamakāvatāra*, and other sutras and [basic Indian Buddhist] treatises. Please investigate whether what I have said concurs with that which is expounded in all sutras and treatises."[24] So Sapen obviously has a problem accepting tathāgata-essence teachings as definitive, whereas he has no issue asserting that buddha-nature exists in all beings. As I will discuss further in chapter 5, in Dratsépa's critique of Dölpopa, Dratsépa shows that Sapen does not assert that tathāgata-essence and buddha-nature are equivalent. However, Sakya scholars such as Rongtön (*rong ston shes bya kun rig*, 1367–1449) argue that Madhyamaka asserts the two to be equivalent, whereas Cittamātra accepts that they are different.[25]

Sapen's refutation of a tathāgata-essence endowed with enlightened qualities existing in sentient beings became the normative position at Sakya monastery. Several of the influential scholars that I consider in the following chapters received their education at Sakya monastery; however, some of them, such as Dölpopa and Sazang (*sa bzang ma ti paṇ chen*, 1294–1376), would challenge this normative Sakya interpretation. Others, such as Rendawa and Tsongkhapa, would elaborate on Sapen's presentation that undermined the authority of the *Uttaratantra* within the Mahāyāna.

Rikrel, the Third Karmapa, and Sangpu Lodrö Defend the *Uttaratantra*

Rikrel was born in the Lhokha (*lho kha*) region of central Tibet and received much of his monastic training at Nartang (*snar thang*) monastery,[26] which was a leading monastic institution at the time.[27] Rikrel wrote sixteen volumes of texts on a variety of topics,[28] such as Buddhist epistemology, perfection of wisdom, and the middle way. He is also known for his work on the catalogue of canonical sources.[29] Among his many works, we find a short commentary on the *Uttaratantra* entitled *Flowers of Ornaments: An Uttaratantra Commentary* (*rgyud bla ma'i ti ka rgyan gyi me tog*).[30] This commentary, as I mentioned above, is the earliest *Uttaratantra* commentary extant in Tibetan that cites passages from tantric texts such as the *Vajraśekharasūtra*,[31] *Guhyasamāja Tantra*,[32] and *Hevajra Tantra*.[33]

Not only did Rikrel and Sapen overlap each other by about twenty-four years, but Rikrel studied under Sapen and knew Sapen's views and thoughts regarding the *Uttaratantra* and other tathāgata-essence literature from firsthand experience.[34] While he does not mention Sapen by name in his commentary, it is very likely that Rikrel composed the commentary as a criticism of views held by Tibetan thinkers such as Sapen regarding the tathāgata-essence literature and also to buttress the *Uttaratantra*'s claims to being a significant text within the Mahāyāna system.[35]

What, then, is Rikrel's view of the *Uttaratantra*? And how does he explain tathāgata-essence? Citing a passage from the *Laṅkāvatārasūtra*,[36] Rikrel, in contrast to Sapen and other scholars at Sakya monastery, argues that all sentient beings have an inherent buddha endowed with enlightened qualities within. Furthermore, citing a passage from the *Hevajratantra*,[37] he even argues that sentient beings are fully enlightened, yet temporarily hampered by adventitious defilements.

Rikrel not only situates the *Uttaratantra* within sutric Mahāyāna literature, but he also includes it in the last wheel as a work expounding on both sutras and tantric literature. He points out that the phrase "supreme continuum" (*bla ma'i rgyud*), which appears in the

Uttaratantra refers to the "profound sutras and tantras such as the *Tathāgatagarbhasūtra*, and so forth,"[38] which the Buddha demonstrated at a "later time." It was perhaps a strategy on the Kadam cataloguer-cum-doxographer's part to situate the treatise within the upper layer of the Mahāyāna literature in the time period when Sapen and others had undermined the authority of the treatise.

Given Rikrel's interpretation of the *Uttaratantra*, it is no wonder that later Jonang scholars would retrospectively include him in the Jonang lineage of other-emptiness transmission, even though he does not employ terms such as "other-emptiness" and "all-basis-gnosis" (*kun gzhi ye shes*), which would become crucial for Dölpopa's presentation of tathāgata-essence. Although Rikrel anticipates much of Dölpopa and his Jonang School's views, Tibetan historians like Pawo Tsuklak Trengwa (*dpa' bo gtsug lag phreng ba*, 1504–1566) know him for his repudiation of the *Kālacakra Tantra*: "Rikrel (*bcom ral pa*) had to say, 'Since this *Kālacakra Tantra* is similar to the doctrine of the Sage Vyāsa, one cannot tell whether it is a Buddhist text or a Hindu text, whether it is a śāstra or a sūtra. Therefore, leave the volume aside.' "[39]

Rikrel was not the only Tibetan thinker of the time to develop a strategy that accorded much canonical importance to the *Uttaratantra*, in contradistinction to the interpretation of tathāgata-essence forwarded by thinkers such as Sapen. The Third Karmapa (a junior contemporary of Rikrel), an influential figure in the Kagyü tradition of Tibetan Buddhism,[40] also argued that the *Uttaratantra* occupied a significant place in the Mahāyāna. Even though his works are primarily oriented towards tantras such as the *Kālacakra*, *Hevajra*, and so on,[41] he studied the *Five Treatises of Maitreya* and texts attributed to Asaṅga, and many of his works are influenced by the *Uttaratantra*, *Mahāyānasūtrālaṃkāra*, and *Dharmadharmatāvibhāga* that are attributed to Maitreya.[42]

The Third Karmapa wrote the first and most extensive Tibetan commentary on Nāgārjuna's *Dharmadhātustava*.[43] In it, he demonstrates, using positive metaphors, that ultimate truth, or the dharma-reality, is none other than tathāgata-essence endowed with all enlightened qualities.[44] He describes ultimate truth in a manner that distinguishes it from the emptiness that is primarily explained in other Madhyamaka texts like Nāgārjuna's *Madhyamakakārikā* and Candrakīrti's *Madhyamakāvatāra*, where emptiness is presented in more negative language. Furthermore, the Third Karmapa composed a summary of the *Uttaratantra* in accordance with the meditative tradition,[45] which establishes the *Uttaratantra* as a definitive text included in the last wheel of the Buddha's teachings. As Klaus-Dieter Mathes demonstrates, "Rangjung Dorje [that is, the Third Karmapa] explains the seven examples of how the dharmadhātu (equated by him with buddha-nature or even the Buddha) abides in all sentient beings."[46] Mathes further says, "To sum up, Rangjung Dorje fully equates the dharmakāya with the dharmadhātu, which is thus inseparably endowed with buddha qualities. The latter are simply hindered by adventitious stains and unfold fully at the time of purification."[47]

In his important work on the topic of tathāgata-essence called *Presentation of the Essence* (*snying po bstan pa*),[48] the Third Karmapa cites the same verse from the *Hevajra Tantra* that Rikrel quotes in his *Uttaratantra* commentary. The Third Karmapa's position regarding the tathāgata-essence and the *Uttaratantra* thus stands in stark contrast to Sapen's interpretation of the *Uttaratantra* and tathāgata-essence literature. Basing their views on the Third Karmapa's explication of tathāgata-essence and his approach to the *Uttaratantra*, Tāranātha and Mangtö Ludrup Gyatso (*mang thos klu sgrub rgya mtsho*, 1523–1596) even claim that the Third Karmapa and Dölpopa met with each other.[49] So planted in the works of the Third Karmapa are further seeds that ripened into the disputes regarding the *Uttaratantra* that followed in the late fourteenth and early fifteenth centuries.

Unlike the two scholars that I have discussed in this section, Sangpu Lodrö[50] was a senior contemporary of both Butön and Dölpopa.[51] Since he was known for his knowledge of the *Five Treatises of Maitreya*,[52] he wrote an extensive commentary on the *Uttaratantra* during the period when the authority of the *Uttaratantra* was being contested. Sangpu Lodrö's commentary[53] frames the *Uttaratantra* in a positive light, arguing that it is a commentary on definitive sutras included in the last-wheel teachings that are "exceedingly secret among the secrets,"[54] and that it teaches that all beings have a tathāgata-essence endowed with enlightened qualities. Gö Lotsawa is partly right in suggesting that Sangpu Lodrö's commentary is in line with Dölpopa's interpretation of the *Uttaratantra*. However, his interpretation of tathāgata-essence as found in the *Uttaratantra* can be seen as a way for the Sangpu scholar to bring the *Uttaratantra* back into the sutric Mahāyāna literature that creates a bridge between the last two wheels in a time period when the treatise had been interpreted differently by Sapen and his critics, Rikrel and the Third Karmapa. Irrespective of it, Sangpu Lodrö does not shy away from criticizing both Ngok[55] and Chapa[56] wherever he deems it necessary.

So, how does Sangpu Lodrö portray the *Uttaratantra* in a positive light? He claims that tathāgata-essence exists in all sentient beings in a fully enlightened form. He states that[57]

> the dharma-body is dharma-reality indivisible from [bud-dha] qualities. Since there is no objection to the fact that the dharma-body exists pervasively in all sentient beings, in the manner of one entity, it is unacceptable to present it, [i.e., the existence of the dharma-body in sentient beings] as [merely] imputed.[58]

Sangpu Lodrö states that the dharma-body does not exist only in buddhas. Since it is no different from dharma-reality (*chos dbyings*), indivisible from enlightened qualities, it literally exists in all sentient beings. He argues for this position using Ngok's and Chapa's readings of the *Uttaratantra* verse as a foil. In contrast to Sangpu Lodrö's position, Chapa and Ngok say that the dharma-body exists in sentient beings only as a potential to achieve enlightenment, not as a fully enlightened entity. Furthermore, Sangpu Lodrö argues:

> Even though defilements exist, they are adventitious [to the buddha-element, because the buddha-element] is naturally pure. [Enlightened] qualities such as the buddha's powers, and so forth naturally exist [in the buddha-element] from a time without beginning. Therefore, there is no new elimi-nation of previously existing defilements, and there is no new achievement of previously non-existent [enlightened] qualities.[59]

Sangpu Lodrö, without using any tantric sources in the way that Rikrel and the Third Karmapa did, is clearly arguing that the tathāgata-essence that exists in sentient beings is endowed with enlightened qualities from a time without beginning, and hence there are no newly attained enlightened qualities. Similarly, he demonstrates that mental defilements are adventitious to, and not inherent in, tathāgata-essence, so no new elimination of defilements is plausible, insofar as they do not naturally or inherently exist in tathāgata-essence, right from the beginning.

Furthermore, he also argues forcefully that the doctrine espoused in the *Uttaratantra* is definitive in meaning and a "secret among the secrets," and that the *Uttaratantra*, therefore, rightfully assumes the role of a central authority within the later Mahāyāna corpus.[60] Nevertheless, even though the *Uttaratantra* and the sutras on which the *Uttaratantra* is based occupy a position of higher scriptural authority than the middle-wheel teachings of the *Prajñāpāramitāsūtras*, Sangpu Lodrö claims that both the middle-wheel scriptures and the *Uttaratantra* teach emptiness. He argues:

> The sutras for the *Uttaratantra* and the *Uttaratantra* [itself] do not contradict the *Prajñāpāramitāsūtras* because the emptiness of inherent existence of all phenomena taught there [in the *Prajñāpāramitāsūtras*] is the dharma-body explicated here [in the last wheel sutras and the *Uttaratantra*]. Teachings describing afflictive emotions, actions, aggregates, and so forth as [similar to] the clouds, etc., in conventional reality [as found in the *Prajñāpāramitāsūtras*] show that afflicted phenomena are adventitious to the nature of mind, [they] are not the nature of mind. It [the nature of mind] is tathāgata-essence . . ."[61]

Sangpu Lodrö, then, contextualizes the *Uttaratantra* within sutric Buddhist literature as do the two early Sangpu commentators, Ngok and Chapa, but unlike them, Sangpu Lodrö explains the meaning of tathāgata-essence in line with Rikrel and the Third Karmapa, arguing that tathāgata-essence is endowed with enlightened qualities. Furthermore, he also presents the content of the *Uttaratantra* more in line with the content of definitive sutras included in the last-wheel teachings, rather than the middle-wheel teachings of the *Prajñāpāramitāsūtras*. It is through these processes that Sangpu Lodrö is able to continue the sutric-based interpretation of the *Uttaratantra* by following a slightly more conservative approach to the treatise.

To sum up, Sapen was a very important scholarly figure in central Tibet, known for his writings on various Buddhist scholastic topics. His treatment of tathāgata-essence literature and the appraisal of the *Uttaratantra* in his *Distinguishing the Three Vows* provoked opposition among other important Tibetan thinkers of the time. Rikrel, the Third Karmapa, and Sangpu Lodrö, aware of the declining popularity of the Madhyamaka interpretation that accommodated the *Uttaratantra* put forth by the two early Kadam masters Ngok and Chapa, and aware that Sapen favored Candrakīrti's *Madhyamakāvatāra* over the

Uttaratantra, devised delicate strategies to relegitimize the authority of the *Uttaratantra* and tathāgata-essence literature.

Rinchen Yeshé's Proto Other-Emptiness Presentation of the *Uttaratantra* and Butön's Reply[62]

As I have argued above, Sapen challenged the early Kadam interpretation of the *Uttaratantra* found in the works of Ngok and Chapa and questioned the authority of the *Uttaratantra* within Mahāyāna literature through advocating for the ultimate truth or emptiness found in works such as *Madhyamakāvatāra*. Rikrel and the Third Karmapa, on the other hand, went beyond even the early Kadam acceptance of the importance of the sutric-centered *Uttaratantra* and associated the treatise with tantric literature as part of a strategy to give it an even more special place within the Mahāyāna. Faced with these competing interpretations, it is not surprising that late thirteenth- and early fourteenth-century Buddhist thinkers appear to shake their heads in disbelief! As I will demonstrate, Rinchen Yeshé wrote his commentary on the *Uttaratantra* in reaction to such interpretations of the *Uttaratantra* offered by Sapen, Rikrel, and the Third Karmapa.

Rinchen Yeshé is a contemporary of Sangpu Lodrö and a teacher to many influential fourteenth-century scholars, including Dölpopa and Gyelsé Tokmé (*rgyal sras thogs med bzang po*, 1295–1369).[63] We know from Stearns' excellent work that Rinchen Yeshé taught the *Five Treatises of Maitreya* to Dölpopa,[64] the exegetical sources that became foundational for Dölpopa's presentation of other-emptiness. Moreover, several fourteenth- and fifteenth-century thinkers, such as Butön, Dratsépa,[65] Tsünpa Pelrin (*btsun pa dpal gyi rin chen*, fourteenth–fifteenth centuries),[66] Zhönnu Gyeltsen (*gzhon nu rgyal mtshan*, fourteenth–fifteenth centuries),[67] and Jonang Zangpo (*rgyal ba jo nang dpal bzang po*, fourteenth–fifteenth centuries)[68] mention the Kadam master in their works. He also shared these teachings with Gyelsé Tokmé, another prominent Kadam scholar reputed for his expertise in the works attributed to Maitreya. Hence, what we can deduce about Rinchen Yeshé's life from these early Tibetan sources is that he is a scholar with high caliber, known for his knowledge of the last-wheel teachings. He also seems to have a reading knowledge of Sanskrit, rather a rare feat for Tibetan scholars in late thirteenth and early fourteenth centuries Tibet. His scholarly life in brief is that he influenced some of the leading fourteenth-century Tibetan thinkers, such as Butön, Dölpopa, and Gyelsé Tokmé, who played significant roles in shaping the future course of Tibetan Buddhist scholasticism. Rinchen Yeshé most likely passed away either in 1345 or 1346.[69]

For his doctrinal position, I have consulted the Kadam master's commentary on the *Uttaratantra*, which is a part of the recent release of dozens of Kadam volumes of previously unknown philosophical texts that predate Dölpopa, and Butön's *Precious Garland of Rebuttals*,[70] the only two sources available at this point on Rinchen Yeshé's doctrinal position. The title of Rinchen Yeshé's *Uttaratantra* commentary is *Rays of the Definitive Meaning* (*rgyud bla ma'i 'grel ba mdo dang sbyar ba nges don gyi snang ba*).[71] As is clear from Rinchen Yeshé's *Rays of the Definitive Meaning*,[72] he meticulously identifies and cites the sutras quoted in Asaṅga's *Uttaratantra* commentary. To offer a few examples of his careful scholarship: he compares Ngok's translations of certain sutric passages that appear in Asaṅga's *Uttaratantra* commentary with earlier Tibetan translations of the same sūtric passages provided by Yeshé Dé (*ye shes sde*, c. 800).[73] Moreover, on several occasions, he chooses Naktso's (*nag 'tsho tshul khrims rgyal ba*, b. 1011) translations of certain passages from the *Uttaratantra* over Ngok's translation.[74] The sutra passages for which he could not locate the title, he says, "did not find the source" (*khungs ma rnyed*).[75] Rinchen Yeshé's careful text-critical analysis is meant to demonstrate that the *Uttaratantra* explicates the ultimate definitive meaning of the *Tathāgatagarbhasūtra*, *Śrīmālādevīsūtra*, *Laṅkāvatārasūtra*, and others,[76] in a time period when the *Uttaratantra* had been deemed less authoritative than Candrakīrti's *Madhyamakāvatāra*.

Rinchen Yeshé quotes from these last-wheel sutras to show that the tathāgata-essence endowed with the marks and signs of a buddha (*sangs rgyas kyi mtshan dang dpe byad*) naturally exists in all sentient beings. For example, he cites a passage from the *Aṅgulimālāsūtra* to argue that sentient beings have the tathāgata-essence endowed with enlightened qualities.[77] Moreover, he argues, "Because freedom from adventitious defilements is the very nature of the tathāgata-element since the primordial time, there are no afflictive emotions that need to be eliminated [from the element]. Because the perfect dharma-reality that is indivisible from enlightened qualities is the very nature of the tathāgata-element, there are no virtuous qualities that need to be newly acquired."[78] Therefore, for Rinchen Yeshé, buddha-nature is not simply a causal potential to achieve enlightenment; rather it is endowed with an inherent enlightened entity that is naturally free from all delusions, but temporarily covered by adventitious defilements.

Moreover, Rinchen Yeshé argues that the ultimate truth is explicated in the later Mahāyāna sutras (*rgyud phyi ma*) that primarily teach definitive meaning. He states, "Mahāyāna is the essence of all teachings of the Sugata. And within Mahāyāna teachings, there are ultimate definitive sutras that primarily teach definitive meaning."[79] He obviously contrasts the last-wheel teachings that teach ultimate definite meaning from the middle-wheel sutras such as the *Prajñāpāramitāsūtras* that, according to him, do not primarily teach the ultimate definitive meaning. Rather, as Rinchen Yeshé argues: "All phenomena that are taught as empty of true existence in the middle wheel teachings, like illusions and so forth, refer [only] to conditioned conventional phenomena. The sugata-essence (*bde gshegs snying po*) that is explained as true and unchanging in the last wheel teachings refers to the ultimate dharma-reality, an unconditioned phenomenon."[80] Therefore, the middle-wheel teachings explain how conventional phenomena, such as tables, chairs, and the like, are empty of inherent existence like an illusory image. These sutras do not explicate the unconditioned ultimate truth that is primarily taught in the definitive last-wheel sutras. Quite interestingly, Rinchen Yeshé uses the term "not truly existent" (*bden med*) to refer to conventional phenomena whose status of existence is no more real than the dream-object that mistakenly appears to the dreamer as the object itself. On the other hand, he uses the term "true" (*bden pa*) to refer to the unconditioned ultimate tathāgata-essence that exits inherently and ultimately.

Now let us turn to Butön's *Precious Garland of Rebuttals*, which complements Rinchen Yeshé's views on tathāgata-essence and the last two wheel teachings found in the latter's *Uttaratantra* commentary. Butön argues in his *Precious Garland of Rebuttals* that the Rinchen Yeshé claims that the emptiness explained in Madhyamaka and Prajñāpāramitā treatises is a nihilistic emptiness (*chad pa'i stong pa nyid*).[81] On the other hand, Rinchen Yeshé states that since the emptiness delineated in texts such as the *Mahāyānasūtrālaṃkāra*, *Uttaratantra*, and tantric texts is endowed with the supreme of all aspects (*rnam kun mchog ldan gyi stong pa nyid*),[82] it is not a nihilistic emptiness.[83] Butön quite rightly argues that Rinchen Yeshé adheres to the view that emptiness of inherent existence is nothing but nonexistence of illusory-like conditioned phenomena, similar to what Dölpopa says with respect to conventional phenomena.[84] According to Butön, Rinchen Yeshé further demonstrates that the tathāgata-essence that exists in all sentient beings is endowed with enlightened qualities, and it is the ultimate emptiness, the ultimate truth.

Furthermore, Butön shows that Rinchen Yeshé asserts the last-wheel treatises, such as the *Saṃdhinirmocanasūtra* and the *Uttaratantra* to be definitive. Butön argues:

> It is mentioned in another letter [from Rinchen Yeshé] that the middle wheel sutras do not teach that they are superior to the last[-wheel teachings]. [On the other hand,] since the last wheel sutra [that is, *Saṃdhinirmocanasūtra*] teaches that it is superior to the middle[-wheel teachings], the content of the last[-wheel sutra] is better. . . . Because the *Mahāyānasūtrālaṃkāra*, the *Uttaratantra*, and so forth comment on the last wheel sutra, their content is better. [Some] assert them as Cittamātra texts, but their content is beyond the four tenet schools [that is, the Sautrāntika, Vaibhāṣika, Cittamātra, and Madhyamaka].[85]

According to Butön, Rinchen Yeshé's view of the *Prajñāpāramitāsūtras* and *Saṃdhinirmocanasūtra* is that the latter is definitive in that it explicates the emptiness that is not merely an emptiness of inherent existence, rather it teaches ultimate truth that is empty of conventional phenomena and defilements. Rinchen Yeshé, furthermore, is believed to have argued that the *Saṃdhinirmocanasūtra* teaches ultimate truth, a point of view that is not found in mainstream fourteenth-century Indian Mahāyāna schools of Tibetan Buddhism. For Butön, these assertions are extremely problematic as he lists the *Saṃdhinirmocanasūtra*, *Mahāyānasūtrālaṃkāra*, and *Uttaratantra* in the category of Cittamātra in his *Catalogue for the Translated Treatises* in 1335.[86] He, therefore, does not assert these treatises to be authoritative in terms of their explication of ultimate truth. On the contrary, Butön holds the position that the *Prajñāpāramitāsūtras*, Candrakīrti's *Madhyamakāvatāra*, and other Madhyamaka treatises teach ultimate truth or emptiness of inherent existence.

It is instructive at this point to briefly compare Rinchen Yeshé's presentation of tathāgata-essence, and his understanding of the relative significance of the last two wheel teachings with Dölpopa's interpretation of Mahāyāna literature. However, I will discuss Dölpopa's view of tathāgata-essence in detail in the following chapter. The two contemporaries undoubtedly share some significant doctrinal similarities. As I mentioned previously, even Butön is believed to have made this observation. According to Künga Drölchok (*kun dga' grol mchog,* 1507–1566), Butön pointed out that Dölpopa's view was very similar to that of Rinchen Yeshé. Both Rinchen Yeshé and Dölpopa argue that the tathāgata-essence endowed with enlightened qualities naturally and permanently exists in all sentient beings; both scholars proclaim that conventional phenomena are empty of inherent existence like an illusion, but the ultimate truth exists inherently; both also rely heavily on sources included in the last-wheel teachings as scriptural authority for their formulation of doctrine, thereby undermining the authority of middle-wheel teachings. Yet, despite the similarities that they share, Rinchen Yeshé does not employ Dölpopa's trademark ideas, such as other-emptiness as a state more exalted than self-emptiness, all-basis-gnosis, Ultimate Cittamātra (*don dam pa'i sems tsam*) as a school superior to Conventional Cittamātra (*kun rdzob pa'i sems tsam*), and Madhyamaka with Appearances (*snang bcas dbu ma*) as a school less exalted than Madhyanaka without Appearances (*snang med dbu ma*).

Conclusion

Sapen, with his majesterial intellect and knowledge of the five sciences (*rig pa'i gnas lnga*), argues against vesting in the tathāgata-essence literature in general, and the *Uttaratantra* in particular, an authoritative status equal to Candrakīrti's *Madhyamakāvatāra,* another popular Indian treatise in thirteenth-century Tibet. This contributes in no small part to limiting the study of the *Uttaratantra.* In reaction, Rikrel and the Third Karmapa argue that the *Uttaratantra* should be vested with significant scriptural authority within the Mahāyāna, citing sources even from tantric texts. Sangpu Lodrö and Rinchen Yeshé then attempt to restore the earlier prestige and authority of the now contested *Uttaratantra* by interpreting its doctrines based on sutric and Indian commentarial texts, without resorting to citations from tantric literature.

These scholars and their works influenced later fourteenth-century *Uttaratantra* scholars. Still it is very difficult to demonstrate with certainty the exact ways in which their influence works itself out in the works of later Tibetan masters like Dölpopa, Sazang, and Butön, whose work is the topic of the following few chapters. Nonetheless, several crucial features of Dölpopa's presentation of the tathāgata-essence are anticipated in the works analyzed here. For instance, Rikrel's exposition of the *Uttaratantra* cites both sutras and tantras and associates[87] the buddha-element with all-basis-consciousness (although Dölpopa uses all-basis-gnosis); Rinchen Yeshé asserts that conventional phenomena are empty of inherent existence in that they are no more real than a dream-object that mistakenly appears as the object itself to dreamers, but he claims that ultimate truth or tathāgata-essence is truly existent, in that it inherently exists as a fully enlight-ened entity; and the Third Karmapa shows that the buddha-element endowed with the marks and signs of a buddha is the same as the all-basis (*kun gzhi*).

Therefore, many of the concepts that Dölpopa would later incor-porate in his well-known works, with their distinctive presentation of the other-emptiness view, were definitely circulating in the first half of the fourteenth century. It is to the works of Dölpopa, Sazang, Gyelsé Tokmé, Gendün Özer (*dge 'dun 'od zer*, thirteenth/fourteenth centuries), and Longchenpa (*klong chen rab 'byams pa*, 1308–1364) that we now turn.

Part II

The Pinnacle Period

The Other-Emptiness Interpretation Spreads

3

Other-Emptiness Tradition

The *Uttaratantra* in Dölpopa's Works

Introduction

As I argued in the previous chapter, Tibetan thinkers such as Sapen, on the one hand, and Rikrel, the Third Karmapa, and others, on the other, laid out a solid platform for the rise of the *Uttaratantra*. The Tibetan scholar who took advantage of this perfect storm of controversy was Dölpopa, a Tibetan writer and doxographer, who brought the *Uttaratantra* and its doctrine of tathāgata-essence to the center and made it the crux of his doctrinal system. As Gö Lotsawa states in *Blue Annals*, "Though many had reproached the All-knowing Jo-mo naṅ-pa [Dölpopa] for having erroneously admitted the Tathāgatagarbha to represent a material truth, numerous persons in dbus and gtsaṅ who had studied assiduously the *Uttaratantra*, appear to have been instructed by him."[1] While Dölpopa's commentary on the Indian treatise does not conjure up the ideas for which he is known,[2] the fact that *Uttaratantra* is at the center of his doctrinal formulation of other-emptiness can be easily found in his *Mountain Doctrine*, a seminal work that presents his doctrinal view in a lucid and erudite manner. In this original work, he uses the treatise liberally to corroborate his views. Hence, it is clear that the *Uttaratantra* played a significant role for Dölpopa for formulating the view of other-emptiness and other attendant ideas that come to be later viewed as controversial and sometimes blasphemous by some Tibetan scholars as discussed in later chapters. Echoing Wilfred Smith, "no text is a scripture in itself and as such. People—a given community—make a text into scripture, or keep it scripture: by treating it in a certain way."[3] Although the treatise had already gained the status of "scripture" by then, it is during this time that the *Uttaratantra* reached its climax.

Predominance of the Last-Wheel Scriptures

Following in the footsteps of the earliest Tibetan commentators of the *Uttaratantra*, fourteenth-century Tibetan thinkers such as Dölpopa, Sazang, Gyelsé Tokmé, and Longchenpa argue that the *Uttaratantra* is a commentarial work on the definitive meaning of the last-wheel sutras.

What does it mean for Dölpopa to say that a certain text is either definitive or provisional? Based on sutras such as the *Akṣayamatinirdeśasūtra* and the *Samādhirājasūtra*, he generally defines those scriptures that explicitly teach conventional truth as provisional and those that clearly explain the ultimate truth as definitive. For instance, he employs the words "self-empty conventional [truth]" (*kun rdzob rang stong*)[4] when he discusses the provisional meaning of the middle-wheel teachings and the "definitive ultimate [truth]" (*don dam nges pa*)[5] to refer to the definitive meaning of last-wheel scriptures. In other words, Dölpopa explicates the concept of provisional meaning in negative language such as phenomena that is empty of inherent existence or nonexistent employing metaphors such as mirages and dreams that connote the notion that things do not exist in the way that they appear to our minds. On the other hand, he describes definitive meaning cataphatically using language such as "inherently pure," "endowed with buddha-qualities," and "ultimately existent" by invoking examples such as the sun and the gold that signify enduring substantiality for ordinary beings.

While Dölpopa and other Tibetan thinkers agree on the definitions expounded in the *Akṣayamatinirdeśasūtra* and the *Samādhirājasūtra*, they do not agree on what constitutes conventional or ultimate truth. Furthermore, Dölpopa invokes the *Saṃdhinirmocanasūtra* as another fundamental source for delineating the distinction between the definitive teachings and the teachings that require interpretation. He states, "The differences of the three wheels of doctrine with regard to requiring interpretation or being definitive and with regard to clearly teaching within good differentiation or not are set forth in the *Sūtra Unraveling the Thought* [*Saṃdhinirmocanasūtra*]."[6] (As you will see later, his opponents, Tsongkhapa and others, strongly disagree with Dölpopa on asserting the *Saṃdhinirmocanasūtra* as a legitimate source for the distinction between definitive meaning and provisional meaning.) Dölpopa expands on what is entailed in "good differentiation":

> In this fashion, the second wheel out of purposeful intent
> teaches that even what are not self-empty are self-empty,

and so on, and is not possessed of good differentiation, that is to say, is not without internal contradictions, and for such reasons [the *Sūtra Unraveling the Thought*] says that [the second wheel] "is surpassable, affords an occasion [for refutation], requires interpretation, and serves as a basis for controversy." About the third wheel by reason that, opposite from those, it differentiates meanings well just as they are, and so forth, [the *Sūtra Unraveling the Thought*] says that it "is unsurpassable, does not afford an occasion [for refutation], is of definitive meaning, and does not serve as a basis for controversy.[7]

Dölpopa essentially argues that the sutras that explicate all phenomena as self-empty or empty of inherent existence require interpretation and sutras that do not make such an explicit statement, rather that clearly make a distinction between phenomena that lack inherent existence and phenomena that do not lack inherent existence are definitive. Therefore, the first wheel requires interpretation and the last wheel does not because the former teaches that conventional phenomena exist inherently, whereas the latter explicitly explains conventional phenomena as empty of inherent existence and tathāgata-essence as ultimate reality which is equivalent to other-emptiness. While Dölpopa does not hesitate to categorize the first or the last wheel as either a provisional or definitive teaching, he does not have such an easy task with the middle-wheel teachings. He says in his *A Brief Distinction* (*gshags 'byed bsdus pa*):

> Moreover, having primarily explained the object of negation, the conventional self-emptiness that is not beyond dependent arising in the middle wheel, the last wheel primarily teaches the basis for negation, the ultimate other-emptiness that is beyond dependent arising. However, it is not the case that the basis for negation is not explained in the middle wheel.[8]

It is clear for Dölpopa that the middle wheel explicates ultimate other-emptiness.[9] Furthermore, Dölpopa demonstrates that the middle wheel creates a linkage to the profound perfection of wisdom which refers to the ultimate other-emptiness expounded in the last wheel.[10]

Considering the definitions mentioned above, does this then mean that Dölpopa asserts the middle-wheel teachings to be definitive? In his

Sun that Illuminates the Two Truths (*bden gnyis gsal ba'i nyi ma*), Dölpopa states, "The Bhagavan explains the first and the second wheels to be provisional in the *Saṃdhinirmocanasūtra*."[11] Jeffrey Hopkins also argues, "The middle wheel of doctrine requires interpretation both because of its lack of clarity on what does and does not ultimately exist and because it overstates the doctrine of self-emptiness when it extends this to the ultimate by declaring it to be without ultimate existence."[12] Therefore, while Dölpopa claims that the middle wheel teaches the ultimate other-emptiness, he demonstrates that it is a teaching of provisional meaning because it explicitly teaches all phenomena to be empty of inherent existence.[13] In other words, it does not explicitly teach ultimate truth. For instance, Dölpopa states in his *Uttaratantra* commentary, "If the notion that the tathāgata-essence exists is a definitive meaning, what is the intention behind the *Prajñāpāramitāsūtras* and so forth that teach that all phenomena are empty of inherent existence, but appear [to exist inherently], like the clouds, dreams, and illusions?"[14]

For Dölpopa, the last-wheel sutras such as *Saṃdhinirmocanasūtra*, *Laṅkāvatārasūtra*, and *Tathāgatagarbhasūtra* and their Indian commentarial sources such as those by Maitreya, Asaṅga, and Vasubandhu are crucial for determining what constitutes ultimate other-emptiness and definitive meaning. In *The Sun that Illuminates the Two Truths*, Dölpopa rhetorically argues that if the sutras that teach tathāgata-essence are not definitive, how could tantric texts such as the *Kālacakra*, *Cakrasaṃvara*, and so forth be definitive?[15] Therefore, he leaves no doubt that the *Uttaratantra* holds a significant place within the Mahāyāna literature, as it teaches the definitive meaning of ultimate truth. Just as the middle wheel is seen as a linkage text to the "profound perfection of wisdom," the last-wheel teachings including the *Uttaratantra* are connecting treatises between sutra and tantra (*mdo sngags gnyis kyi mtshams sbyor gyi gzhung*) in the Jonang tradition.

Is the *Uttaratantra* a Cittamātra Text or a Madhyamaka Text?[16]

As shown in the two preceding chapters, the *Uttaratantra* is generally accepted as a Madhyamaka treatise for much of its early textual history in Tibet. However, in fourteenth century Tibet as will be seen in chapter 5 and chapter 6, scholars such as Butön, Rendawa, and Tsongkhapa would challenge the authority of the text within the Mahāyāna doctrinal scheme by presenting it within the framework of Cittamātra. Their demotion of the *Uttaratantra* within the Mahāyāna doxographical ranking is strategically implemented primarily in response to the doctrinal presentation formulated by Dölpopa. I will now turn to how he presents the two schools.

Citing numerous strategically selected, authoritative Indian sources, partly to justify his interpretation of other-emptiness[17] and in part to respond to the critiques that his opponents level against his reading of Mahāyāna texts, Dölpopa argues the following: (1) Cittamātra is categorized into Conventional Cittamātra (*kun rdzob pa'i sems tsam*) and Ultimate Cittamātra (*don dam pa'i sems tsam*); (2) Cittamātra must not be conflated with Vijñānavāda; (3) Madhyamaka is grouped into Madyamaka without Appearance (*snang med dbu ma*) and Madhyamaka with Appearance (*snang bcas dbu ma*). His Mahāyāna doxography differs significantly from that of other fourteenth-century Tibetan scholars.

In order to examine Dölpopa's Mahāyāna doctrinal classifications, these questions are addressed: What textual sources does Dölpopa have for his classification of Mahāyāna schools? Why and how does he differentiate his Madhyamaka system from Cittamātra? Why and how does he argue for the distinction between Cittamātra and Vijñānavāda?[18] Who directly influences him? These issues will be discussed, primarily, but not exclusively, based upon Dölpopa's *The Sun That Illuminates the Two Truths, A Letter to Ponjangba;*[19] *The Great Calculation of the Fourth Council*[20] and its commentary;[21] and his *Abhisamayālaṃkāra* commentary.[22]

Although much scholarship has been conducted on different ways of categorizing Mahāyāna texts, Dölpopa's interpretation offers much nuanced articulation that is unique to its own historical and intellectual milieu. The international scholarship, thus far, mainly focuses on the doctrinal classifications of Yogācāra-Madhyamaka and Sautrāntika-Madhyamaka,[23] Prāsaṅgika-Madhyamaka and Svātantrika-Madhyamaka,[24] and Sākāra-Cittamātra and Nirākāra-Cittamātra[25] within the textual history of the Buddhist doctrinal systems.[26] Some traditional Tibetan and international scholars assume that Tibetan thinkers have followed the Madhyamaka, as opposed to Cittamātra[27] ever since the beginning of the introduction of Buddhist scholastic tradition in Tibet in the eighth century, and that the traditional Tibetan scholars have preferred Prāsaṅgika-Madhyamaka over Svātantrika-Madhyamaka since the thirteenth century in Tibet.[28] Clearly, as will be shown later, Dölpopa's Mahāyāna classification does not fit into any of these Mahāyāna taxonomies that are often accepted as normative. I will now turn to Dölpopa's nuanced doctrinal classification, which remained largely marginalized for various reasons, notably sectarian, political, and dogmatic.

Classification of Cittamātra

The term *cittamātra* as such is found in many early Mahāyāna sutras with different meanings, as Christian Lindtner argues, "there are different ways of understanding the canonical term cittamātra in Mahāyāna: that of Madhyamka and that of Yogācāra, and perhaps, that of 'Madhyamaka-Yogācāra.'"[29] Therefore, although *cittamātra* is not exclusively employed by the school of thought with the same name, as a proper noun, it is used synonymously with Yogācāra or Vijñānavāda in the history of Mahāyāna doctrinal classification. Since it is this proper name that Dölpopa and other Tibetan scholars of his time are mainly concerned about for their interpretations of what constitutes Cittamātra, I have utilized this word over other terms for the most part in this chapter.

According to M. D'amato,[30] early Cittamātra can be broadly structured into three major phases. In the "first phase" of Cittamātra are included influential texts such as *Saṃdhinirmocanasūtra* and *Yogācāryabhūmi*; in the "second phase" there exist commentarial works such as *Mahāyānasūtrālaṃkāra* and its commentary; and the "third phase," which D'amato refers to as "classical phase" is comprised of Cittamātra works of Asaṅga and Vasubandhu. Irrespective of whether there existed a school of thought called Cittamātra during these phases,[31] later Buddhist scholars take these works and figures[32] to be the foundational sources for Cittamātra. Hence, Cittamātra that Dölpopa and other Tibetan scholars explicate in their works cannot be discussed or properly understood without making reference to these Indian figures or textual sources mentioned here. Furthermore, the Cittamātra that is a point of contention within the Tibetan scholastic milieu during the time of Dölpopa is the Cittamātra that had been criticized by Indian Madhyamaka scholars such as Bhāviveka, Candrakīrti, and Śāntideva in their works. The refutation of Cittamātra by these Indian masters is later faithfully followed by their Tibetan adherents.

Dölpopa obviously has a big challenge here. How could a school that is deemed secondary to Madhyamaka for a long time, at least since the sixth century, in Indian Mahāyāna literature be defended in fourteenth-century Tibet, where Madhyamaka, as opposed to Cittamātra, had been declared the supreme doctrinal view? In order to answer this, we need to understand what Dölpopa's opponents' positions are with respect to Cittamātra. According to Dölpopa, many of his Tibetan contemporaries mistakenly assert the following: (1) *Saṃdhinirmocanasūtra*, *Mahāyānasūtrālaṃkāra*, and so forth are Vijñānavāda texts; (2) the terms such as the "three natures" (*ngo bo nyid gsum*) and "all-basis-consciousness" are unique to Vijñānavāda; (3) Asaṅga and Vasubandhu are proponents of Vijñānavāda *only*. As one could easily deduce from this, Dölpopa's interpretation of Cittamātra clearly differs from the Cittamātra of the "classical phase" and from the Tibetan scholars' view of Cittamātra in fourteenth-century Tibet.

Dölpopa, who is aware of the history of the tension between Madhyamaka and Cittamātra in Indian sources, cannot just refute the views presented by his Tibetan contemporaries without offering any exegetical sources, as he is fully cognizant of the fact that Asaṅga and Vasubandhu explicate Vijñānavāda view in their works. So what he strategically proposes is that these early Indian scholars elucidate in their texts more than the Cittamātra as understood by his Tibetan contemporaries. Hence, he argues that Cittamātra is categorized into Conventional Cittamātra and Ultimate Cittamātra,[33] without making much reference to the more widely known division of Cittamātra.[34] The Conventional Cittamātra, he argues, is the same as Vijñānavāda, which his Tibetan contemporaries mistakenly view as the *only* Cittamātra. He goes on to argue that the Ultimate Cittamātra is the ultimate intention of Asaṅga and Vasubandhu, which his fellow Tibetan scholars and some early Indian masters such as Haribhadra and Vimuktisena do not fully comprehend. It is this Ultimate Cittamātra, he further demonstrates, that is the Great Madhyamaka of other-emptiness, which is at the center of his Mahāyāna view. Furthermore, he employs terms such as "Non-Ultimate Cittamātra" (*don dam min pa'i sems tsam*) and "Ultimate Cittamātra" (*don dam pa'i sems tsam*),[35] and "Mundane Cittamātra" (*'jig rten pa'i sems tsam*) and "Supramundane Cittamātra" (*'jig rten las 'das pa'i sems tsam*)[36] to refer to the two categories respectively. Hence, for Dölpopa, there is no difference between the Ultimate Cittamātra and the Madhyamka that he faithfully follows, which is none other than the Madhyamaka with

Appearance. (More shall be said about this later in the chapter.) Nor does he see any disparity between the Conventional Cittamātra and the Cittamātra that others mistakenly, according to Dölpopa, attribute to be the final view of Asaṅga and Vasubandhu.

So, what is Conventional Cittamātra, and what exegetical sources, if any, does Dölpopa have to support his claim? As Dölpopa argues, "Because mere consciousness is asserted as ultimately existent, it is Cittamātra [Vijñānavāda]."[37] Furthermore, Dölpopa says, "Those who assert that the ultimate phenomena are truly [existent as well as] consciousness are proponents of Cittamātra [Vijñānavāda]. Those who assert that [the ultimate truth] is gnosis that is beyond truly [existent] and consciousness are proponents of Madhyamaka."[38] Therefore, Dölpopa mainly defines Conventional Cittamātra as a school that professes mere consciousness (*rnam shes tsam*) as ultimately existent, which, for him, means that consciousness (*rnam shes*) that is not the domain of gnosis (*ye shes*) is accepted as ultimate reality. Interestingly, because of this, he argues that "Conventional Cittamātra is the same as the well-known Cittamātra of today, and it is called Vijñānavāda."[39] While he asserts that consciousness as ultimately existent is a defining characteristic of Vijñānavāda, he does not accept that the three natures[40] and eight consciousnesses[41] are distinguishing features of Conventional Cittamātra.[42]

As for exegetical sources for the distinction between Vijñānavāda and the Cittamātra that he asserts as the ultimate school of Buddhism, he argues, "In brief, asserting the ultimate phenomena as entity and consciousness is Cittamātra, and asserting [the ultimate phenomena] as gnosis, which is beyond entity and consciousness, is Madhyamaka, as explained in the Śrīkālacakra. . . . and its commentary, Vimalaprabhā."[43] Neither Kālacakra nor Vimalaprabhā provides any correlation between Vijñānavāda and the concepts of the three natures and all-basis-consciousness, rather both texts explain Vijñānavāda within the purview of asserting everything as consciousness only (*rnam shes tsam*).[44] While the term Cittamātra is not employed in both Kālacakra and Vimalaprabhā, the terms "Vijñānavāda" and "Yogācāra" are used interchangeably in Vimalaprabhā to refer to the school that Dölpopa labels as Conventional Cittamātra in his works. The linguistic preference of Vijñānavāda over Cittamātra to distinguish the former from Madhyamaka in these authoritative texts seems to resonate strongly with the distinction that Dölpopa draws between Vijñānavāda and Cittamātra. As already mentioned in this chapter, the former is the same as Conventional Cittamātra, whereas the latter is divided into Conventional Cittamātra, which Dölpopa does not follow, and Ultimate Cittamātra,which he deems as the final view of Mahāyāna Buddhism.

However, one challenge that Dölpopa faces in reconfiguring Cittamātra is the question of authoritative sources for Conventional Cittamātra or Vijñānavāda. Unlike his Tibetan counterparts, he encounters some issue in identifying any sutras or Indian commentarial works as authoritative sources for Vijñānavāda.[45] He also, for obvious reasons, does not claim Asaṅga as a founding father of Vijñānavāda. However, Dölpopa skillfully argues that the *Saṃdhinirmocanasūtra* and treatises attributed to Maitreya and Asaṅga *temporarily* teach Cittamātra.[46] For him, these scriptures *temporarily* teach Vijñānavāda, in that they employ certain Vijñānavāda nomenclatures on the literal basis as a stepping stone for ultimately understanding Ultimate Cittamātra, which is what the sutras ultimately and thoroughly teach. However, Jangsem Gyelwa Yeshé (*byang sems rgyal ba ye shes*, 1247–1320), the second patriarch of the Jonang tradition, explicitly identifies[47] both Asaṅga and Vasubandhu as proponents of Cittamātra or Vijñānavāda and their treatises as textual sources for Cittamātra, without making any distinctions between Conventional Cittamātra and Ultimate Cittamātra.

In brief, as a controversial fourteenth-century Tibetan interpreter of Mahāyāna treatises, Dölpopa goes against the rather mainstream Tibetan configuration of Cittamātra, which is generally seen as inferior to Madhyamaka in terms of its explication of ultimate truth. Using Indian sources, Dölpopa formulates two categories of Cittamātra, notably Conventional Cittamātra and Ultimate Cittamātra. He, thereby, makes the latter school, which is none other than the Madhyamaka that his lineage follows, at the center of his Jonang tradition. It is to the section on the classification of Madhyamaka that we now turn.

Classification of Madhyamaka

As a Tibetan scholar trained at Sakya in fourteenth-century Tibet, Dölpopa is certainly aware of all the Madhyamaka doxographical categories[48] such as the Yogācāra-Madhyamaka and Sautrāntika-Madhyamaka, which were in use between the eighth and eleventh centuries in Tibet, and Prāsaṅgika-Madhyamaka and Svātantrika-Madhyamaka, which dominated the literature dealing with the Tibetan doctrinal system since the thirteenth century. He is also fully cognizant of the growing influence of the Prāsaṅgika-Madhyamaka within the Buddhist scholastic discourse in fourteenth-century Tibet. However, since his main agenda is to delineate the concept of other-emptiness and to criticize the self-emptiness view as a whole, Dölpopa does not express any interest in expounding on the distinction between the Prāsaṅgika-Madhyamaka and Svātantrika-Madhyamaka in his works.[49]

While fourteenth-century Tibetan scholars generally view Prāsaṅgika-Madhyamaka as the highest school of the Mahāyāna system, Dölpopa instead openly argues that the highest Buddhist school must promulgate what he calls "other-emptiness," not self-emptiness. Therefore, real Madhyamaka, for Dölpopa, refers to the school that is free not only from the extreme of mere consciousness as ultimately existent, but also from the extreme of ultimate truth as empty of inherent existence. Hence, Dölpopa proposes that it is Madhyamaka with Appearance[50] that is the highest school of Buddhism, even surpassing what he calls "Madhyamaka without Appearance" into which Dölpopa includes schools such as Prāsaṅgika-Madhyamaka and Svātantrika-Madhyamaka. Therefore, Dölpopa argues that it is this Madhyamaka classification[51] that is a viable Madhyamaka taxonomy, not the ones that are present during his time.

Here, one might ask if Dölpopa has any exegetical sources for his Madhyamaka classification. He argues that the two types of Madhyamaka are found in the *Laṅkāvatārasūtra*.[52]

> Relying on mind-only,
> One does not imagine external objects.
> Relying on non-appearance,
> One passes beyond mind-only.

> Relying on observing reality,
> One passes beyond non-appearance.
> If yogis dwell in non-appearance,
> They do not perceive the great vehicle.[53]

Immediately following the verses from the sutra, Dölpopa concludes, "The intent of the middle[-wheel] sutras, which is beyond Cittamātra, is grounded in the temporary Madhyamaka without Appearance. The intent of the last[-wheel] sutras, which is beyond the temporary Madhyamaka without Appearance, is grounded in the ultimate Madhyamaka with Appearance."[54] Although the exact terms, "Madhyamaka with Appearance" and "Madhyamaka without Appearance," are not evident in the *Laṅkāvatārasūtra*, Dölpopa argues that the verses cited above explain the three Mahāyāna schools—Vijñānavāda, Madhyamaka without Appearance, and Madhyamaka with Appearance—in an ascending hierarchical order on the rung of Mahāyāna doxography.[55]

Furthermore, Dölpopa points to other sources to substantiate his view. As Vesna Wallace claims, "Although the *Kālacakra* tradition acknowledges the Mādhyamika view of emptiness as its primary theoretical foundation, it has its own unique interpretation of emptiness, not only as a mere negation of inherent existence (*svabhāva*), but also as the absence of material constituents of the individual's body and mind. . . . It is a form that is endowed with all the signs and symbols of the Buddha."[56] While the two Madhyamaka categories are not evident in the Kālacakra, the text nevertheless explains emptiness that is not *merely* empty of inherent existence as delineated in the middle-wheel sutras; rather it explicates emptiness endowed with fully enlightened qualities that are found in tathāgata-essence sutras such as the *Tathāgatagarbhasūtra* and *Śrīmāladevīsūtra*. Therefore, it is based on authoritative works such as the *Kālacakra*, *Vimalaprabhā*, and *Laṅkāvatārasūtra* that Dölpopa's distinction between the two Madhyamaka schools can be understood.

While, according to Dölpopa, the *Laṅkāvatārasūtra* is one of the very few sutras where the two Madhyamaka categories are mentioned, there are many sutras such as the *Saṃdhinirmocanasūtra*, *Tathāgatagarbhasūtra* that are included either in the group of ten definitive sutras (*nges don gyi mdo bcu*)[57] or in the set of ten tathāgata-essence sutras (*snying po'i mdo bcu*)[58] that Dölpopa takes to be authoritative sutric sources for Madhyamaka with Appearance. As mentioned above, Dölpopa generally does not accept the *Prajñāpāramitāsūtras*, the foundational sutric sources for the Madhyamaka School that late fourteenth-century Tibetan scholars such as Rendawa and Tsongkhapa propagate, as definitive.[59] In terms of authoritative commentarial works for Dölpopa's Madhyamaka with Appearance, works traditionally attributed to Maitreya, Asaṅga, and Vasubandhu become influential.[60]

To sum up the section, in reaction against his contemporaries, who relied on texts such as the *Prajñāpāramitāsūtras*, *Madhyamakāvatāra* for their interpretation of Mahāyāna doxography, Dölpopa instead employed the *Saṃdhinirmocanasūtra*, works of Maitreya, Asaṅga, and Vasubandhu to make sense of the vast corpus of Mahāyāna doctrinal texts. Hence, in contrast to the distinction (1) between the Cittamātra and Madhyamaka of Mahāyāna doxography and (2) between the Prāsaṅgika-Madhyamaka and Svātantrika-Madhyamaka of Madhyamaka widespread in the Tibetan Buddhist scholastic culture of Dölpopa's time, Dölpopa argued for a distinction (1) between Vijñānavāda and Cittamātra, (2) between Conventional Cittamātra and Ultimate Cittamātra, and (3) between Madhyamaka with Appearance and Madhyamaka without Appearance. Such a reconfiguration of Mahāyāna doxography allowed Dölpopa to interpret Mahāyāna texts in a rather unconventional way for his time, but an interpretation that has its roots in early Indian sources. Such a reconfiguration of Mahāyāna doxography allowed Dölpopa to delimit the significance of the *Prajñāpāramitāsūtras*, Candrakīrti's works such as the *Prasannapadā* and *Madhyamakāvatāra* for his presentation of other-emptiness.

Conclusion

The timing could not have been better for the formulation of Dölpopa's doctrinal presentation of other-emptiness. In Dölpopa's opinion the Madhyamaka hermeneutical devices that Tibetan scholars in general, and Tibetan intellectuals of the fourteenth century in particular, were employing were nothing more than a sign of degeneration of the perfect Buddhist doctrine of the Age of Perfection (*rdzogs ldan gyi bskal pa*).

Although Dölpopa's own *Uttaratantra* commentary never mentions other-emptiness and all-basis-gnosis, which are in some sense "his terms," his seminal work, *Mountain Doctrine*, employs the *Uttaratantra* as a crucial textual source for the presentation of Jonang's path structure based on the view of other-emptiness. He does this without relying on "normative" Madhyamaka texts, such as the *Madhyamakāvatāra* and *Mūlamadhyamakakārikā*. His successful doctrinal presentation would, however, instigate some of the leading scholars, such as Butön, Dratsépa, Rendawa, Tsongkhapa, and Gyeltsap to direct sharp criticisms against his doctrinal formulation. I will examine their criticisms in the third part of the book, but before that I discuss the spread of the *Uttaratantra* in the fourteenth century, where I examine the works of Sazang, Gendün Özer, Gyelsé Tokmé, and Longchenpa.

4

The *Uttaratantra* in Fourteenth-Century Tibet

Introduction

As we look at the number of Tibetan commentaries on the *Uttaratantra* written throughout the history of Tibetan Buddhism, we discover that most of them were written in the fourteenth century. It was not only Dölpopa who played a major role in elevating the authority of the *Uttaratantra* in the fourteenth century, other influential Tibetan exegetes such as Sazang, Gendün Özer, Gyelsé Tokmé, and Longchenpa also contributed to the dissemination of the treatise. It is primarily the works of these four Tibetan thinkers that I examine in this chapter to provide a glimpse into the century that could be referred to as the era of collective effervescence for the *Uttaratantra*.

While Sazang, Gendün Özer, Gyelsé Tokmé, and Longchenpa all interpret the *Uttaratantra* to be definitive, they come from different Tibetan lineages with separate narratives about their religious genealogies. Sazang studied at Sakya monastery and later became one of the most respected students of Dölpopa; Gendün Özer and Gyelsé Tokmé are Kadam masters; Gyelsé Tokmé is reputed for his knowledge of the *Five Treatises of Maitreya*; and Longchenpa is considered as one of the greatest exponents of the Great Perfection tradition of the Nyingma School.[1] One can only imagine the impact that these Tibetan masters with such religious stature had on their followers.

Sazang Follows in His Master's Footsteps

Despite the importance of the *Uttaratantra* in Dölpopa's formulation of the Mahāyāna path structure revolving around the concept of other-emptiness doctrine, the master did not write an extensive commentary on it. However, as is the case with many master-disciple relationships in Tibetan tradition, Sazang would fill up that gap by writing a lengthy commentarial work on the treatise by invoking Dölpopa's thoughts and ideas. As we find at the end of Sazang's *Uttaratantra* commentary:

> At the requests made repeatedly by [my] intelligent
>   disciples,
> [I], Lodrö Gyeltsen Pel, composed [this commentary],
> That delineates the meaning of the profound supreme
>   vehicle,
> As followed by [my] excellent lama [Dölpopa]."[2]

The colophon further adds that Sazang received the transmission of the *Uttaratantra* from Dölpopa,[3] thereby lending authenticity to his voice for his current and future disciples.

While the author takes pride in presenting the view of Dölpopa, Sazang never uses the term "other-emptiness" in the commentary. Nonetheless, true to his words, he interprets the *Uttaratantra* much in the same way as Dölpopa did in his seminal work, the *Mountain Doctrine*. Sazang demonstrates that the *Uttaratantra* comments on the last-wheel sutras, that last-wheel sutras are definitive teachings, that *Prajñāpāramitāsūtras*, unlike the *Saṃdhinirmocanasūtra*, do not make a clear distinction between what constitutes ultimate truth and what does not, and that the last-wheel sutras are Madhyamaka texts as opposed to Cittamātra texts. He also says the ultimate truth or tathāgata-essence, the primary meaning of the last-wheel teachings and the *Uttaratantra*, exists inherently in all beings. Therefore, Sazang uses his *Uttaratantra* commentary to flesh out the doctrine of his guru, thereby further legitimating the centrality of the *Uttaratantra* for the Jonang School.

Toward the beginning of his extensive commentary Sazang points out that Maitreya's works, such as the *Uttaratantra*, clearly and thoroughly describe the dharma-reality or the ultimate truth, which he describes as "the view of the last wheel teaching only."[4] Following his master, Sazang also argues that the ultimate truth or dharma-reality is the primary content of the definitive teachings, whereas conventional truth remains the core meaning of the provisional teachings.[5]

He further elaborates by claiming that the ultimate truth is not empty of inherent existence, rather it exists inherently.[6]

In light of this, Sazang demonstrates that the *Prajñāparamitāsūtra*'s claim that all phenomena are empty of inherent existence must not be taken at face value. He argues, "Although the extensive *Prajñāparamitāsūtra* teaches that all phenomena are empty of inherent nature, one should not accept it literally."[7] Furthermore, in his commentary to *Abhidharmasamuccaya*, Sazang makes a similar point by invoking the last-wheel teaching as a source: "As the *Saṃdhinirmocanasūtra* states, [the *Prajñāpāramitāsūtras*] are not to be taken literally."[8] Moreover, Sazang shows by appealing to the textual authority of the *Saṃdhinirmocanasūtra*[9] that because the last-wheel teaching is definitive, it removes the extremes of both existence and nonexistence, whereas the middle-wheel *Prajñāpāramitāsūtras* eliminate only one extreme, that of existence.[10]

Just as Dölpopa was careful in his formulation of the provisional nature of the middle-wheel teachings, Sazang too is careful with his language when he addresses the issue of the *Prajñāpāramitāsūtras*. He states:

> One might think that everything that is taught in the middle wheel is false. One should not think in this way also because (1) [the middle wheel] primarily teaches the absence of inherent existence with regards to adventitious defilements; (2) since [these sutras] teach the non-existent [phenomena] as non-existent, they are not false; (3) and since the phrases such as "the nature of mind is luminous . . . ," and so forth also show that the dharma-reality exists, the final meaning [of the middle-wheel teachings] is the same as the last wheel, and they are supremely profound as well. However, because the last wheel primarily teaches dharma-reality it should be understood as superior.[11]

Reading it through the lens of the *Saṃdhinirmocanasūtra*, but without undermining the *Prajñāpāramitāsūtras*, Sazang skillfully demonstrates that the former is the textual source *par excellence* for him, his master, and their school.

All of these beg the question: How does Sazang's *Uttaratantra* commentary explain the ultimate truth or dharma reality that is the defining characteristic of the subject matter of definitive teaching? While the commentary does not employ the word "other-emptiness" to describe the ultimate truth, it explains the ultimate truth or tathāgata-essence in the way that other-emptiness is delineated in Dölpopa's works.[12] Sazang characterizes the ultimate truth as permanent entity, partless, beyond consciousness, dharma-body, and inherently existent. On the other hand, conventional truth is not permanent entity, part-less, beyond consciousness, dharma-body, and inherently existent.

Simply put, ultimate truth or tathāgata-essence is a permanent entity because it is not subject to changes brought about by causes and conditions.[13] It is partless because it pervades everything in that it exists as a substratum for all phenomena.[14] It is beyond consciousness because it cannot be perceived by conceptual thought.[15] It is dharma-body[16] because it is the phenomenon *par excellence*, ultimate realization at its purest. As for the ultimate truth or tathāgata-essence being inherently existent, Sazang argues that it refers to something that is the object of gnosis, not of conceptual thought.[17] For him, terms such as "truly existent," "inherently existent," and "naturally existent" are equivalent. Sazang also demonstrates that both tathāgata-essence and its attendant enlightened qualities exist inherently and permanently in the nature of all living beings.[18]

Finally, although his *Uttaratantra* commentary does not explicitly raise the issue of whether last-wheel texts such as the *Saṃdhinirmocanasūtra* and the *Mahāyānasūtrālaṃkāra* explain the view of Cittamātra or Madhyamaka, his commentary on the *Abhidhar-masamuccaya* addresses the question and follows Dölpopa's position quite closely.[19] In it, he clearly demonstrates that these treatises explain Cittamātra temporarily, but ultimately they teach the ultimate truth of the Madhyamaka.

Sazang was only a few years younger than his master, but it appears he first received teachings from Dölpopa sometime in the 1320s when Dölpopa had begun giving his transmission at Jonang. By the time Sazang wrote his *Uttaratantra* commentary, he had already mastered Dölpopa's doctrinal presentation and recognized a parallel between his master's thought and the view presented in the *Uttaratantra*. Sazang created a synthesis of the two thoughts in his *Uttaratantra* commentary. As many Tibetan writers put it, this is perhaps Sazang's best offering of realization (*sgrub pa'i mchod pa*) to his formidable master known as the All-Knowing One (*kun mkhyen dol po pa*).

Two Fourteenth-Century Kadam Masters' *Uttaratantra* Commentaries

As mentioned earlier, commentaries written by other fourteenth-century Tibetan scholars also contributed to a veritable frenzy generated by the *Uttaratantra*. Kadam scholars Gendün Özer and Gyelsé Tokmé each wrote a commentary to the *Uttaratantra*. I will examine their commentaries in this section together because they come from a similar textual community.

We know very little about Gendün Özer,[20] but it is safe to assume that he is a Kadam master who lived between the thirteenth and fourteenth centuries. In his commentary he mentions that he composed it for his students who had requested that he write something that would differ from the "coarse explanation" (*bshad nyog rtsing po*)[21] of the *Uttaratantra* offered by the "early commentators" (*snga rabs pa*)[22] of the Kadam tradition. While Gendün Özer does not intend to succumb to a "coarse explanation" of the Indian treatise, he follows his early Kadam predecessors' exposition in terms of doctrinal position, even though his literary style is different, with numerous poetic verses of admiration. In this time period it is not surprising that he wrote the commentary primarily in consultation with Ngok's Tibetan translation (*rngog 'gyur*) of the *Uttaratantra*, but the author also used the translations made by Naktso and Patsap wherever necessary.[23]

Gyelsé Tokmé is well known from the biographies that his students wrote.[24] He received his monastic education at Bodong E (*bo dong e dgon pa*) and Sakya monasteries and later served as the abbot at Tara (*rta ra*) monastery.[25] He was a prolific writer who is most famously known for *Thirty Seven Practices of a Bodhisattva*, a short text on mind training. Furthermore, he was revered by his followers as the Second Asaṅga (*thogs med gnyis pa*) or the New Asaṅga (*thogs med gsar ma*) for his knowledge of the *Five Treatises of Maitreya*.

Gyelsé Tokmé finished his *Uttaratantra* commentary, *Illuminating the Definitive Meaning of the Uttaratantra*,[26] soon after he completed his commentary on the *Mahāyānasūtrālaṃkāra* at the age of thirty-eight in 1333.[27] To put his commentary in its historical context, already by 1335 Rikrel, the Third Karmapa, Sangpu Lodrö, and Rinchen Yeshé had made known their views regarding the *Uttaratantra* and tathāgata-essence in central Tibet. Furthermore, Dölpopa and Butön had already completed their *Mountain Doctrine* and *History of Buddhism*, respectively, by then. It is not surprising, therefore, that someone who was compared to the famous Indian master Asaṅga was writing a commentary on the *Uttaratantra* at about the same time. Following in the footsteps of other Kadam interpreters of the *Uttaratantra*, both Gendün Özer and Gyelsé Tokmé explicate the *Uttaratantra* within a sutric framework.

Both Kadam scholars shower the *Uttaratantra* with words of praise to elucidate the significance of the treatise within the Mahāyāna tradition. Gendün Özer calls the *Uttaratantra* "the most excellent treatise"[28] and adulates it poetically as follows:

Oh listen! This [the *Uttaratantra*] could be called the "Kanjur"
    (*bka' 'gyur*) that contains the definitive meanings,
Because this is where all the intentions of definitive
    sutras are condensed.
This [the *Uttaratantra*] could be called the "Tengyur"
    (*bstan 'gyur*) that contains the definitive meanings,
Because this is where all expositions of definitive
    commentaries are gathered.
Therefore, those fortunate ones who aspire for definitive
    teachings should seek this out,
As this most certainly explains the definitive meaning.[29]

Gyelsé Tokmé honors the treatise in the following
    manner:
Adorned with the lotuses of the undefiled words,
Endowed with the essence of stamens of the ultimate
    definitive meaning,
Is this lotus grove of the teaching of the Lord Maitreya.
[I] elaborate on it for those who seek the other-
    benefitting honey.[30]

For the two masters, it is clear that the treatise assumed a significant place amongst Buddhist scriptures.

As for how they contrast the last-wheel teachings with the middle-wheel texts, Gendün Özer speaks of the distinction between the middle-wheel and the last-wheel teachings in much the same way as the two earliest Kadam commentators of the *Uttaratantra*. He says about the nature of the middle-wheel teachings, "Where are [all phenomena] taught [as the clouds, dreams, and illusions]? They are taught in the middle-wheel sutras. What is taught [there]? It is taught that each and every individual phenomenon—forms and so forth—is always empty of itself."[31] In contrast, he explains the last-wheel teachings in this way: "Where is [the buddha-element] taught? It is taught in this last wheel sutra . . . What is taught [in the last wheel sutra]? It is taught that all sentient beings have the buddha-element that exists as an essence."[32]

While Gendün Özer argues that the middle-wheel sutras teach all phenomena as empty of themself (*rang rang gis stong pa*) with the metaphor of clouds and dreams, he, like Ngok and Chapa, does not demonstrate that they are provisional teachings requiring interpretation. Similarly, although he shows that the last wheel teaches that the buddha-element exists as an essence (*sangs rgyas kyi khams grub pa snying por gyur pa*), he does not claim that the buddha-element is inherently existent (*rang gi mtshan nyid kyis grub pa*) or truly existent (*bden par grub pa*). Therefore, it is clear that Gendün Özer prefers the last-wheel teachings over the middle-wheel teachings in that the former is more authoritative than the latter.

Keeping the Kadam spirit alive, Gyelsé Tokmé also propounds a similar view of the distinction between the two wheels of teachings. His response to a question on the purpose of teaching the emptiness of inherent existence in the middle-wheel sutras is as follows:

> What is the intention for teaching [in the middle wheel] that [all phenomena] are empty of true existence like the clouds, and so forth? It shows that afflictions, actions engendered by the afflictions, and the aggregates that are the ripened results of the afflictions and the actions are [empty of true existence] like the clouds, and so forth.[33]

Like Gendün Özer, Gyelsé Tokmé argues that only conventional phenomena such as afflictions, actions, aggregates, and so forth are taught as empty of inherent existence in the middle-wheel teachings. Gyelsé Tokmé emphasizes that the last-wheel teachings teach the most definitive meaning of the Buddha's thought. He states, "This meaning, which is depicted by the nine examples in this way, is the profoundest of the profound, and it is the ultimate definitive meaning."[34] Therefore, neither Gendün Özer nor Gyelsé Tokmé harbors any doubts that the tathāgata-essence teachings are somehow less authoritative than the middle-wheel teachings. On the contrary, as their commentaries show, the tathāgata-essence teachings explicate the quintessential ultimate truth.

If the *Uttaratantra* and other tathāgata-essence scriptures teach the ultimate meaning of the Buddha's thought, does this mean that the two Kadam thinkers interpret the tathāgata-essence in much the same way as Dölpopa or Sazang?

Gendün Özer characterizes the buddha-element by its three attendant qualities: the buddha-body, the nature of suchness, and the buddha-nature.[35] For him, the nature of the buddha-element is completely free from afflictions,[36] and positive qualities forever inhere in it.[37] He sums it up nicely in this verse, though without explicitly claiming that sentient beings have buddha-nature endowed with marks and signs of a buddha:

All sentient beings without exception,
Are inherently endowed with positive qualities since the
beginning.
In order to explain that such is the case,
[I] generate the mind [of enlightenment] without deprecating
it.[38]

Gyelsé Tokmé does not diverge from Gendün Özer. He argues:

Since the faults, such as afflictions, and so forth, exist temporarily, as opposed to inherently [in the buddha-element], the qualities such as [enlightened] power, and so forth exist naturally [within the buddha-element]. The buddha-element, at the stage of complete purification, exists in the same way as it existed previously at the stage of impurity. Because of that, [the buddha-element] is the dharma-reality that by nature never changes.[39]

Furthermore, Gyelsé Tokmé equates the naturally purified dharma-body with the tathāgata-essence by arguing that it is precisely because the latter exists in all beings that one can claim that the former exists in all beings also.[40] However, unlike Dölpopa, he never explicitly says in his commentary that sentient beings have a fully enlightened buddha within. It is probably because of framing it in such a way that his student reports that Gyelsé Tokmé believed the doctrinal systems presented by both Dölpopa and Butön to be accurate with its legitimate roots in India. However, as per his student's claim, Gyelsé Tokmé ultimately preferred Butön's presentation over that of Dölpopa.[41]

To sum up, although Gendün Özer and Gyelsé Tokmé diverge from the interpretation of the *Uttaratantra* offered by fourteenth-century thinkers such as Dölpopa and Sazang and thirteenth-century scholars such as Rikrel and the Third Karmapa, they all agreed on the supremacy of the *Uttaratantra* or the tathāgata-essence teachings over the teachings that speak of phenomena as empty of inherent existence. By writing commentaries in favor of the definitive nature of the *Uttaratantra*, these two scholars contributed to the momentum that made the Indian treatise a central text in the fourteenth century.

Longchenpa's View on the *Uttaratantra*

As is the case with other early Nyingma thinkers, Longchenpa did not write a commentary to the *Uttaratantra*. However, his works such as the *Treasury of Words and Meaning* (*tshig don mdzod*),[42] *Treasury of Abiding Reality* (*gnas lugs mdzod*),[43] and *Commentary to the Treasury of the Precious Dharma Reality* (*chos dbyings rin po che'i mdzod kyi 'grel pa*)[44] show the influence of the tathāgata-essence literature in general. His *Treasury of Tenets*, in particular, is replete with citations from the *Uttaratantra*. As Mathes argues,

> Longchenpa's interpretation of buddha nature in his *Treasure of Tenets* (*Grub mtha' mdzod*) deserves our interest for several reasons. First, most of the stanzas dealing with the fourth vajra point (on buddha nature) in the *Ratnagotravibhāga* are quoted and commented upon in thirty continuous pages in the *Treasure of Tenets*. Second, this work's theory of buddha nature plays a central role in linking the dzogchen teachings with older strands of Indian Buddhism. Third is the *Grub mtha' mdzod*'s positive interpretation of the *Ratnagotravibhāga*, maintaining that emptiness needs to be understood in the sense of buddha nature's luminosity, and that such a positive assessment of the ultimate has definitive meaning.[45]

So, Longchenpa also tangentially contributed to the dissemination of the *Uttaratantra* in the fourteenth century by quoting and commenting on numerous verses and passages from the chapter on the buddha-element.

Commenting on a verse from the *Uttaratantra*,[46] Longchenpa says in his *Treasury of Tenets*:

> [In response to a question], "How is it not contradictory that middle[-wheel] sutras, [on the one hand], teach that all phenomena are impermanent like clouds, untrue like dreams, [produced by] the conglomeration of causes and conditions yet lack inherent existence like illusions, and so forth, and on the other hand, here [last-wheel sutras] teach that [the buddha-element] is permanent because it primordially exists without changing, is true because it naturally abides, and is unconditioned because it is not produced by causes and conditions? . . ." [The response is that] this [tathāgata] essence is also empty because it is empty of faults, a conditioned [nature], and so forth, but is not empty in the sense of not having its qualities.[47]

In his use of the *Uttaratantra*, like many other cataphatic interpreters of the Indian treatise, Longchenpa argues that the tathāgata-essence taught in the last-wheel scriptures is empty only of afflictions, impermanence, and illusory phenomena, but not empty of its own inherent enlightened qualities. For instance, he shows, "Because the buddha-element, the enlightened essence that innately exists in sentient beings, is naturally pure and complete with qualities, it is called the nature of the dharma-body."[48] As to what the enlightened qualities are for the Nyingma master, Mathes claims, "Nowhere in the entire *Grub mtha' mdzod* does Longchenpa distinguish between the thirty-two qualities of the dharmakāya and the qualities of the form kāyas. Both types of qualities exist throughout beginningless time."[49] Furthermore, commenting on a verse from the *Uttaratantra* in his *Treasury of Tenets*, Longchenpa argues that there is no affliction that is inherent in the tathāgata-essence since the tathāgata-essence is already inherently pure from beginningless time.[50]

Unlike apophatic interpreters of the *Uttaratantra*, the Nyingma thinker claims that these last-wheel scriptures that explain tathāgata-essence in such manner are definitive, not teachings requiring interpretation. As he concludes the section on the buddha-nature in his *Treasury of Tenets*, again based largely on citations quoted from the

Uttaratantra, he declares, "The meaning of buddha-nature must be asserted and understood only as definitive, not as provisional. Because this topic on the buddha-element [from the *Uttaratantra*] is the essential and difficult-to-realize aspect of the Mahāyāna, that is why it is explained in detail here."[51] David Germano argues that the *Treasury of Words and Meaning* also includes the middle-wheel teachings in the provisional category and includes the last wheel in the definitive meaning category.[52]

Last, to further elucidate the importance of the tathāgata-essence lessons as taught in the last wheel, in his *Treasury of Tenets*,[53] Longchenpa divides the levels of subtlety—ranging from less subtle to the most subtle teachings—of the three wheels of the Buddha's teachings relative to the lifespan of the Buddha. He says the Buddha taught the first wheel, the least subtle teaching, between the ages of thirty-six and forty two;[54] the middle wheel, subtler than the first one, between the ages of forty-three and seventy-two;[55] and the last wheel, the most subtle of the teachings, between the ages of seventy-three and eighty-two.[56]

To sum up this section, even though we do not see in the Nyingma School a particular scholarly interest in this Indian commentarial source until the fourteenth century, it is hardly a historical accident that Longchenpa, the most eminent exponent of the Great Perfection, incorporated much of the buddha-nature chapter of the *Uttaratantra* into his *Treasury of Tenets*. He systematically presents, within the hierarchy of Buddhist texts and thoughts, the *Uttaratantra* as a canonical source for *dzokchen* teachings at the height of the *Uttaratantra* culmination in Tibet.

Conclusion

By the mid-thirteenth century Sapen had already made his views about the tathāgata-essence teachings clear by invoking the authority of Candrakīrti's *Madhyamakāvatāra*. As an apophatic interpreter and proponent of Candrakīrti's *Madhyamakāvatāra*, the price that Sapen had to pay was an undermining of the authority of the *Uttaratantra*. Little did Sapen know that the spark that he had created would have such a lasting impact on the history of the *Uttaratantra* in Tibet. In one century, from the mid-thirteenth to mid-fourteenth, many Tibetan scholars from various sectarian backgrounds wrote commentaries on the *Uttaratantra* defending its presentation of the ultimate truth. To this extent Sapen and his successors can perhaps be seen as having lost the battle against Tibetan giants such as Rikrel, the Third Karmapa, Dölpopa, Longchenpa, and others whose works we examined in this and the previous chapters.

As Northrop Frye poetically states, "History moves in a cyclical rhythm which never forms a complete or closed circle. A new movement begins, works itself out to exhaustion, and something of the original state then reappears, though in a quite new context presenting new conditions."[57] This next cycle in the history of the *Uttaratantra* brings us to Butön, Dratsépa, Rendawa, Tsonkhapa, and Gyeltsap. It is to this final part of the book that we now turn.

Part III

The Argumentation Period

Self-Emptiness Proponents Criticize Other-Emptiness Approach

5

Challenges to the Purely Definitive Nature of the *Uttaratantra*

Zhalu Thinkers Criticize Dölpopa

Introduction

Two eminent scholars, Butön and his disciple Dratsépa, of the Zhalu tradition give an interpretation of the tathāgata-essence literature in their works, Butön's *Ornament That Illuminates Sugata-Essence* (*bde gshegs snying po gsal ba'i rgyan*) and Dratsépa's *Ornament to the Ornament* (*de bzhin gshegs pa'i snying po mdzes rgyan gyi rgyan mkhas pa'i yid 'phrog*) respectively. The former was completed in 1356 and the latter in 1369.

Dratsépa's text was influenced by a dream that he had three years after the death of his master. In the dream, his guru, residing in the Pure Land of Maitreya, gave a testament to his beloved disciple, "There will be an excellent polemical text written by a young monk at the request of others. I have endorsed it with my own seal. It will be of benefit from now on, so do not lose it! It contains many citations from both scriptures and logical reasons. One should not doubt the text because I have consulted it with Maitreya, my master."[1] Dratsépa's commentary is indeed filled with citations from a number of scriptures such as the *Uttaratantra*, affirming his master's position. Dratsépa's work, as he makes explicit in his title, is thus a commentary to Butön's text.

Both criticize Dölpopa in their works. Butön does not mention Dölpopa or his works by name in his *Ornament*, but Dratsépa does not show any hesitancy in explicitly identifying his and his master's opponent. He cites Dölpopa's magnum opus, the *Mountain Doctrine*, by name, often challenging the latter's views.[2]

It is in response to Dölpopa's *Mountain Doctrine* completed by 1333,[3] then, that these two Zhalu thinkers wrote their *Ornaments*. They primarily address issues concerning tathāgata-essence. I will examine both texts, interlacing them, but my main focus is Dratsépa's because his work builds on his master's.

Butön's *Ornament*

Butön sees the *Uttaratantra* as a central commentary on the sutras that teach tathāgata-essence. He quotes the *Uttaratantra* liberally. At the beginning of his text, he states, "Hence, [the word] '*uttara*' in the *Uttaratantra* refers to 'later' since 'later' and 'supreme' have the same [Sanskrit term]. Or, it means 'supreme' since it is the supreme continuum of the Mahāyāna teachings."[4] This follows his remarks that the scriptures that primarily teach tathāgata-essence are "extremely superior" (*shin tu khyad par 'phags*). Therefore, Butön and his counterparts such as Dölpopa and his disciples put the tathāgata-essence teachings such as the *Uttaratantra* higher on the pedestal of Mahāyāna scriptures. However, they differ much in terms of their interpretations of the scriptures.

A quick glance at how Butön and Dratsépa in particular describe Dölpopa and his teachings[5] gives us a sense of how the Zhalu scholars see themselves as the complete opposite to the Jonang masters in their interpretation of the *Uttaratantra*. Butön begins his text with this verse explaining his purpose in composing the *Ornament*:

> The meaning of the extremely profound sugata-essence,
> [Is] taught by the Sugata in his excellent teachings as provisional.
> The impure, unpleasant [interpretation exists] based on not realizing [such],
> Having eliminated [the wrong interpretation], [I] shall expound on the *Ornament*.[6]

The meaning of the first two lines of the verse will become clearer below.

Butön poetically describes Dölpopa's interpretation of the tathāgata-essence teachings as "unpleasant," driven by the mistaken understanding of the Buddha's intention when teaching tathāgata-essence. For Butön, these teachings must not be taken literally; rather they should be understood as provisional.

Criticizing Dölpopa and his followers, Butön repeatedly demonstrates in his work that the following teachings are provisional by citing liberally from many treatises: the teachings that explain that all sentient beings have the tathāgata-essence;[7] those that explicate that the tathāgata-essence is the self;[8] and those that show that the tathāgata-essence is permanent, stable, and independent.[9] Butön sums up his point nicely toward the end of his text:

> Because the meaning of the tathāgata-essence, the object that can only be realized through faith in the Complete Buddha, is extremely difficult to realize and difficult to analyze, one has to realize it by relying upon the teachings of the Buddha. Even amongst the teachings [of the Buddha], since those that are not extensive do not teach [the tathāgata-essence] they cannot unravel the meaning [of the tathāgata-essence]. Even within the extensive teachings [of the Buddha], it is only the later teachings that clearly teach [the tathāgata-essence]. Although [the tathāgata-essence] is implicitly taught in other extensive teachings [such as the *Prajñāpāramitāsūtras*], it is not taught explicitly. Therefore, the meaning of the tathāgata-essence sutras cited in the *Uttaratantra* and its commentary by Asaṅga and [the meaning of the sutras] such as *Mahābherīhārakaparivartasūtra*, and the like that are not explicitly mentioned in these [two commentarial] texts is explained as having the basis in intention, a purpose, and refutations of the explicit claims for the profound meaning by the Bhagavan Maitreya and Ārya Asaṅga in the same way as the Bhagavan did in his sutras. [These citations] are not from other sutras, nor are they from false scriptures, nor is the meaning self-created, as the Bhagavan himself is valid.[10]

Referring to the *Uttaratantra* verse that shows that sentient beings have tathāgata-essence through three reasons,[11] both Butön and Dratsépa argue that the three reasons do not demonstrate that all sentient beings have tathāgata-essence. Rather, they argue that the reason why it is explicated in the tathāgata-essence teachings that all sentient beings have the tathāgata-essence is that sentient beings have

the capability to achieve the dharma-body, because the suchness of
the mind of a buddha and sentient being is indivisible, and because
sentient beings have the buddha-nature for producing the three buddha-bodies.[12] Therefore, Butön claims that the three reasons are the
intention behind the teaching that the tathāgata-essence exists in all
beings, whereas in reality tathāgata-essence does not exist in sentient
beings. Not only is there an intention for such teachings, but there is a
purpose for teaching tathāgata-essence literature as well. The purpose
is to apply antidotes to the five faults mentioned in the *Uttaratantra*.[13]

Finally, he points out that there is a refutation of the explicit
literal meaning of the tathāgata-essence teachings. The refutation is
that since the tathāgata-essence is none other than dharma-body it
cannot and does not exist in sentient beings.[14]

Dratsépa's Commentary[15]

Dratsépa wrote his text in response to the spread of Dölpopa's presentation, which he thinks is "overwhelmed by the force of a great
demon that holds onto reality,"[16] but to be more precise, he wrote the
text to critique those who had raised criticisms against his teacher's
view presented in Butön's *Ornament*. Dratsépa structures his text into
three main sections: the first section, "refuting the misconception with
respect to the teachings of the Buddha"[17] has approximately thirty
pages; the second section, "delineating the profound intention of the
Buddha's teachings"[18] consists of approximately sixteen pages; and
the last section, "rebuttal to the criticisms by the opponents who harm
the Buddha's teachings with an intention motivated by wrong conceptions"[19] has approximately seventy pages. More than half of the
text is devoted to the section where Dratsépa writes a rebuttal to the
criticisms leveled by opponents against his teacher's views explained
in the *Ornament*.

It is not uncommon for the Tibetan scholars of the fourteenth
century to claim that the tathāgata-essence scriptures, such as the
Laṅkāvatārasūtra and *Nirvāṇasūtra* that teach the tathāgata-essence as
a permanent, stable, and enduring self (*rtag brtan ther zug gi bdag*),
are provisional, since Buddhist scriptures generally do not endorse a
concept of *ātman* or self. Therefore, Dratsépa, following the general
Buddhist doctrinal belief that self does not exist, repeatedly argues
that the scriptural passages that say that tathāgata-essence is a permanent, stable, and enduring self require interpretation.

Furthermore, Dratsépa demonstrates that teachings that show that all sentient beings have tathāgata-essence are also interpretable. As Dratsépa strongly proclaims, "Therefore, all sutras and their commentarial works that teach the existence of tathāgata-essence in all sentient beings since beginningless time are interpretable with an intention, [they] are not definitive."[20] Quoting from sutric texts, tantric texts, and Indian and Tibetan commentarial texts that are equally important for Dölpopa and that are cited in Dölpopa's works liberally, Dratsépa argues that not a single sentient being has tathāgata-essence.

For Dratsépa these tathāgata-essence scriptures are not only provisional; they are definitive insofar as they teach that the tathāgata-essence is none other than dharma-body, which is only realized when an ordinary individual becomes fully enlightened. Dratsépa argues, "The actual sugata-essence is the dharma-body of the complete buddha. This never exists in the big corporeal body of sentient beings."[21] The tathāgata-essence that is the same as the dharma-body is definitive. It exists only in buddhas, the enlightened beings; it does not exist in sentient beings, the unenlightened ones.

Therefore, Dratsépa clearly articulates that tathāgata-essence must not be understood as a potential to achieve enlightenment or as an emptiness of inherent nature that exists in all beings; rather he argues that the tathāgata-essence is the ultimate result of enlightenment that manifests only at the end when one's potential to achieve buddhahood has reached its ultimate point.

Hence, Dratsépa concludes that these tathāgata-essence scriptures are a mixture of provisional and definitive meanings because (1) they teach that all sentient beings have the tathāgata-essence and also that the tathāgata-essence is a permanent, stable, and enduring self, neither of which, for Dratsépa, can be accepted literally for the reasons mentioned above; and (2) they teach that the tathāgata-essence is equivalent to the dharma-body of enlightened beings, which is literally acceptable and is definitive. He also argues against Dölpopa's wholesale portrayal of the tathāgata-essence teachings as *only* definitive and also challenges Dölpopa for his assertion that the permanent, stable, and enduring tathāgata-essence exists in all sentient beings.

Here one may wonder if sentient beings do not have tathāgata-essence, how does Dratsépa argue that all sentient beings have a potential to achieve enlightenment? How does he interpret the *Uttaratantra* verse[22] that Tibetan thinkers use to substantiate their view that all sentient beings have tathāgata-essence in the Madhyamaka School? Dratsépa criticizes the more common interpretation of the verse (which is that all sentient beings have tathāgata-essence; therefore they can achieve enlightenment) and argues that the verse requires interpretation, insofar as sentient beings are not enlightened. In order to support his claim, he cites the works of Indian and Tibetan scholars such as Asaṅga,[23] Kamalaśīla,[24] Candrakīrti,[25] Ngok,[26] and Sapen,[27] although none of these scholars, in this context, explicitly claim that sentient beings do not have tathāgata-essence.

Dratsépa was probably aware that these masters did not explicitly make such a statement, but he seems to have been reading their works through the lens of the tathāgata-essence texts, where tathāgata-essence and dharma-body are explained interchangeably. The interchangeability of dharma-body and tathāgata-essence in some Mahāyāna literature is employed to justify Dratsépa's claim that the main point of the *Uttaratantra* verse mentioned above is provisional because no sentient being has the dharma-body of enlightened beings, which is none other than tathāgata-essence.

For Dratsépa, since tathāgata-essence is equivalent to dharma-body, which exists only in enlightened beings, there is a clear distinction between tathāgata-essence and buddha-nature, as the former exists only in enlightened beings. However, quoting from the *Uttaratantra*, he shows that buddha-nature exists in all sentient beings: "The five metaphors demonstrate that since sentient beings have tathāgata-element and the buddha-nature for generating the three buddha-bodies . . ."[28] Dratsépa thus demonstrates that buddha-nature exists only on the causal level of a preenlightenment state, whereas the tathāgata-essence is achieved only on the resultant level of a postenlightenment. Hence, he concludes that all sentient beings can achieve enlightenment because they have buddha-nature.

While Dratsépa proclaims that the tathāgata-essence scriptures are a mixture of interpretable and definitive meanings and that sentient beings do not have tathāgata-essence, both he and Dölpopa agree that the last-wheel tathāgata-essence teachings are higher than, or superior to, the middle-wheel *Prajñāpāramitāsūtras*. For instance, Dratsépa following Butön says, "The third wheel teachings that primarily teach sugata-essence are the foremost, or superior, amongst Mahāyāna scriptures, in the same way that the later teachings on medicine [are superior]."[29] Therefore, both Butön and Dratsépa demonstrate that the last-wheel tathāgata-essence teachings are ranked higher than the middle-wheel teachings. Nonetheless, Dratsépa and Dölpopa differ greatly in terms of how they explain that the tathāgata-essence teachings are superior to the middle-wheel teachings. As Dratsépa carefully explains:

> The later [discourses such as the tathāgata-essence teachings] teach more than the middle [wheel discourse, the *Prajñāpāramitāsūtras*] because they teach a mixture of interpretable and definitive meanings, which is comprehended only by sharp disciples with great intellect, whereas the middle[-wheel] discourse teaches definitive meaning only. [However], [the last-wheel tathāgata-essence teachings] do not teach a superior definitive meaning [that is not taught in the middle wheel] because a definitive meaning that is greater than [the one taught in the middle-wheel teachings] does not exist.[30]

According to Dratsépa, since the definitive meaning is mixed in with the interpretable meaning in the *Laṅkāvatārasūtra*, *Nirvāṇasūtra*, and others, these teachings require a higher intellect to decipher their definitive meaning from their interpretable meaning. However, the purely definitive middle-wheel scriptures do not require such a higher level of intellect to decipher the meaning of the instructions, since it is clearly articulated without mixing in with the interpretable meaning. Therefore, according to Dratsépa, the tathāgata-essence scriptures are superior in terms of how the definitive meaning is explained, not in terms of the definitive content itself, since the definitive meaning that is taught in both the middle-wheel and the tathāgata-essence teachings is exactly the same.

In contrast, Dölpopa generally argues that the last-wheel tathāgata-essence teachings primarily teach definitive meaning of ultimate truth, whereas the middle-wheel scriptures primarily teach interpretable meaning. Furthermore, he maintains that the last-wheel teachings explain the definitive meaning clearly, whereas the middle-wheel scriptures delineate definitive meaning along with interpretable meaning.[31] Therefore, the reasons that Dölpopa uses to show that the last-wheel tathāgata-essence discourses are supreme and the middle-wheel teachings are not supreme are inverted in Dratsépa's critique of Dölpopa's presentation. Although both Dratsépa and Dölpopa agree that the last-wheel tathāgata-essence teachings teach definitive meaning of ultimate truth and that these scriptures are higher on the pedestal than the middle-wheel teachings, they strongly disagree over the importance of the last-wheel sutra, *Saṃdhinirmocanasūtra*, within the Mahāyāna textual corpus.

In response to a challenger (most likely a proponent of Dölpopa's presentation) who cites the passage from the *Saṃdhinirmocanasūtra* that demonstrates that the middle wheel is provisional and the last-wheel teachings are definitive,[32] Dratsépa states, "This [referring to the *Saṃdhinirmocanasūtra*] is a real basis for dispute. Therefore, it is not suitable to be a treatise for distinguishing interpretable and definitive meanings."[33]

Dratsépa is convinced that the *Saṃdhinirmocanasūtra* does not qualify as a legitimate Mahāyāna scripture that clearly differentiates the distinction between what constitutes a definitive meaning and what constitutes a provisional meaning, since it belongs to the Cittamātra School, which he takes as the lower school of the Indian Mahāyāna tradition. Therefore, Dratsépa claims that the sutra does not belong to the Madhyamaka School, which he asserts is the higher school of Indian Mahāyāna tradition. As Dratsépa argues:

> Since the middle wheel [referring to the *Prajñāpāramitāsūtras*] teaches the correct meaning of the absence of elaborations, it is a Madhyamaka [text]; since the last wheel [referring to the *Saṃdhinirmocanasūtra*] teaches the correct meaning as a non-dualistic mind it is a Cittamātra text. Therefore the middle wheel is definitive and the last wheel is interpretable.[34]

Dratsépa argues that the primary difference between the *Prajñāpāramitāsūtras* and the *Saṃdhinirmocanasūtra* in regards to its respective explanation of ultimate truth is that the former teaches absence of elaborations as ultimate truth, whereas the latter describes nondualistic mind as ultimate truth. Furthermore, as Dratsépa claims, one of the main differences between the last-wheel tathāgata-essence teachings in the *Uttaratantra* and teachings in the *Saṃdhinirmocanasūtra* is that the former delineates ultimate truth alongside interpretable meaning, whereas the latter teaches only provisional meaning.

Unlike those who aver that the *Saṃdhinirmocanasūtra* belongs to the Great Madhyamaka School, which, for Dölpopa, is undoubtedly ranked higher than Vijñānavāda, Dratsépa seeks to demonstrate that the last-wheel *Saṃdhinirmocanasūtra* is a Cittamātra scripture. Therefore, while Dölpopa does not make any distinction between the last-wheel tathāgata-essence teachings and the last-wheel

Saṃdhinirmocanasūtra in terms of content, since both primarily teach definitive meaning of ultimate truth, Dratsépa argues that there is a profound difference between the last-wheel tathāgata-essence teachings and the last-wheel *Saṃdhinirmocanasūtra* in terms of content. For Dratsépa, the tathāgata-essence teachings present the philosophical view of the Madhyamaka School. Dratsépa views Dölpopa as someone who interprets the tathāgata-essence teachings as opposite to those of the Madhyamaka writer Candrakīrti.

> Overwhelmed by the force of a great demon that holds onto reality due to degenerated views,

> Certain unwise people lose their wisdom and denigrate Candrakīrti, the greatest of the greatest, at the cost of self-failure.[35]

However, the *Saṃdhinirmocanasūtra* explicates the teaching of the Cittamātra School, whose voice both Dratsépa and Candrakīrti assert cannot be regarded as authoritative for the explication of ultimate self-emptiness. This distinction between the last-wheel tathāgata-essence teachings and the last-wheel *Saṃdhinirmocanasūtra* would later become crucial for Geluk pioneers, such as Gyeltsap and Khedrup (*mkhas grub dge legs dpal bzang*, 1385–1438),[36] for systematizing the huge corpus of Mahāyāna literature.

The *Saṃdhinirmocanasūtra*, the tathāgata-essence teachings, along with the *Uttaratantra* become the foundational scriptures for Dölpopa's presentation of other-emptiness. Based on these foundational Mahāyāna texts, Dölpopa argues that all sentient beings have an actual buddha endowed with all enlightened qualities within them, albeit temporarily covered by impure defilements. The enlightened entity that exists in all beings is buddha-nature, and it is other-emptiness, since it is empty of other phenomena, such as conventional reality and defilements. Dölpopa uses metaphors such as the sun covered by the clouds, pure gold covered with dust, and others found in Mahāyāna classics, to speak of other-emptiness. Furthermore, Dölpopa argues that buddha-nature and its other equivalent nomenclatures such as tathāgata-essence and buddha-element are the supreme self, which, according to Dölpopa, is not to be confused with the concept of self in Hinduism.[37] Therefore, Dölpopa finds the essence of Mahāyāna system in the last-wheel texts, not in the middle-wheel teachings.

Dratsépa challenges the presentation of other-emptiness on several different points and concludes by arguing that other-emptiness is the lowest form of emptiness, and therefore it is not the ultimate truth. He claims:

> Although I fervently assert that other-emptiness exists conventionally and self-emptiness exists ultimately, I do not claim in the way that you [Dölpopa] do that the ultimate other-emptiness exists and conventional self-emptiness does not exist. Furthermore, since other-emptiness is the lowest of emptiness, it does not qualify for the ultimate emptiness.[38]

For Dratsépa other-emptiness is none other than the emptiness that is one-being-empty-of-the-other (*gcig gis gcig stong pa'i stong nyid*) labeled as the lowest emptiness in the *Laṅkāvatārasūtra*.[39] An example for the lowest emptiness mentioned in the *Laṅkāvatārasūtra* would be a house being empty of snakes, which clearly does not align with Dölpopa's presentation of the ultimate other-emptiness.[40]

While Dratsépa does not assert other-emptiness as ultimate truth, he does not completely reject the concept of other-emptiness; rather he claims that the other-emptiness that Dölpopa propagates is only a conventional phenomenon.

Furthermore, Dratsépa strongly believes that there is not a single reliable source that clearly and literally vindicates Dölpopa's notion of other-emptiness, since he demands such a quote:

> Bring a clear citation that states that one must meditate on other-emptiness, known as the basis for pure gnosis, which is sugata-essence that is permanent, stable, static, and free from the other referring to the phenomena of cyclic existence that is to be abandoned, and which is free from conventional self-emptiness that is inherently endowed with all qualities of abandonment and realization since beginningless.[41]

Here it is not simply the case that if Dölpopa or a follower of the Jonang School were to supply a clear quote, Dratsépa would gladly and easily embrace the other-emptiness viewpoint; rather, for Dratsépa, it is to demonstrate that the self-emptiness viewpoint is taught in reliable treatises as ultimate, and it is not taught as referring to a conventional phenomenon only.[42]

Dratsépa does not assert other-emptiness as the ultimate truth. He argues that self-emptiness is the ultimate truth or ultimate reality. Dratsépa concludes, "Therefore, in our Madhyamaka School, self-emptiness refers to the fact that the phenomena that merely exist on the conventional level and emptiness are indivisible and that it is ultimately free from elaborations. Self-emptiness does not refer to [nonexistent phenomena] such as rabbit's horns, barren women's sons, and others."[43] Furthermore, he claims:

> Therefore, the abandonment of all dualities with respect to existence and non-existence, permanence and impermanence, cyclic existence and liberation, self and other, negative and positive phenomena, empty and non-empty, and others in all phenomena and all phenomena being empty of its own self and being ultimately free from all dualistic elaborations is the view of Madhyamaka. Those that teach [such a view] are Madhyamaka treatises.[44]

Therefore, Dratsépa argues that the emptiness that is the ultimate truth is empty of inherent existence, which does not exist separately from conventional phenomena, but rather it exists indivisibly from conventional phenomena. Furthermore, self-emptiness, for Dratsépa, is also beyond any dualistic appearances of an inherent subject and object, self and other, and others. Hence, Dratsépa strongly challenges the existence of other-emptiness that is defined as a phenomenon that exists in separation from conventional phenomena.

To sum up the section: (1) Dratsépa argues that the last-wheel tathāgata-essence teachings are a mixture of definitive and interpretable meanings and that the middle-wheel teachings explicate only definitive meaning (contrast this with Dölpopa's claim that the middle-wheel sutras primarily teach interpretable meaning, and the last-wheel teachings mainly teach definitive meaning); (2) Dratsépa demonstrates that none of them has tathāgata-essence (contrast this with Dölpopa's assertion that all sentient beings have tathāgata-essence within them); (3) Dratsépa states that the teachings that are a mixture of definitive and interpretable meanings are superior (contrast this with Dölpopa's argument that purely definitive teachings are superior); and (4) Dratsépa argues that other-emptiness is a conventional truth, and self-emptiness is an ultimate truth (in contradistinction to Dölpopa's affirmation that self-emptiness is a conventional truth and other emptiness is an ultimate truth).

Therefore, given Dratsépa's positions vis-à-vis Dölpopa's view-points, we can better contextualize the former's indignation with respect to Dölpopa as evidenced by this quote:

> Here someone [referring to Dölpopa], who is conceited, interprets the Buddha's teachings incorrectly. With his evil mind gratified with the poisonous water of biased mind-set, he discards the nectar of the correct view. In such a bad time even if the truth is spoken, it is difficult to find people who will believe it. Therefore, I spoke a bit about the incorrigible view for the purpose of my own mental transformation.[45]

Conclusion

In a time when the fame and name of Dölpopa and his doctrinal pre-sentation of other-emptiness teachings were spreading in central Tibet, challenging the Buddhist doctrinal presentation set forth by Butön and other fourteenth-century Tibetan masters, Dratsépa's critique of Dölpopa's interpretation can be seen as another attempt to repudiate Dölpopa's presentation and to reaffirm the position of his teacher, Butön. It was not just Dölpopa and his followers who were propagat-ing such an interpretation of Mahāyāna literature in central Tibet in the fourteenth century. Some other influential Tibetan scholars, in the earlier part of the fourteenth century, had also argued for a similar interpretation of Mahāyāna literature that Dölpopa later systematized. For instance, the *Uttaratantra* commentaries written by Tibetan schol-ars, such as Rikrel, Sangpu Lodrö, and Rinchen Yeshé clearly resonate with Dölpopa's interpretation of the Mahāyāna treatise.

While I doubt that Dratsépa's arguments against Dölpopa's pre-sentation made any ardent followers of Dölpopa repudiate their doc-trinal claims, even those who disagree with his positions may admit that his strategy for critiquing Dölpopa's presentation was extremely skillful. Dratsépa, basically citing similar sutras, tantras, and other commentarial works that are equally important to Dölpopa and his followers, twists the language that his opponents use and employs it to his advantage. In the end, although Dratsépa may not have suc-ceeded in convincing any of Dölpopa's followers with his scriptural citations and well-formulated reasoning in his *Ornament to the Ornament*, he certainly succeeded in demonstrating to his readers that he had mastered these Buddhist classics and that his faith in his guru, Butön, was unshakable. After all, in Dratsépa's view, it is only through a perfect understanding of ultimate reality with the help of one's guru that individuals can achieve enlightenment.

6

Challenges to the Supremacy of the *Uttaratantra*

Rendawa and Tsongkhapa on Tathāgata-Essence Literature

Introduction

In the previous chapter I explored the ways in which Butön and Drat-sépa interpreted the *Uttaratantra* and the tathāgata-essence literature in contradistinction to that of Dölpopa. The significance of the treatise for the two Zhalu thinkers and for Kadam as well as Jonang scholars inspired scholars such as Rendawa and his student Tsongkhapa to argue for the superiority of Candrakīrti's texts by undermining the *Uttaratantra*. Both thinkers were trained at Sakya monastery where Sapen's *Distinguishing the Three Vows* was studied. They were staunch exponents of Candrakīrti's *Madhyamakāvatāra*, and each wrote a commentary on it, making it a central corpus for defining the ultimate truth. It is to these two thinkers' views on the *Uttaratantra* that we now turn.

Rendawa on the *Uttaratantra* and the Tathāgata-Essence Literature

In his *Distinguishing the Realizations* (*theg pa gsum gyi 'phags pa'i rtogs pa rnam par 'byed pa*), Rendawa says, "Because it is mentioned in the treatise[s] of Glorious Candrakīrti that these masters [such as Asaṅga, Vasubandhu] did not understand the intention of Nāgārjuna correctly [their position that Hearers and Solitary Realizers do not realize the selflessness of phenomena] is not the intent of the Ārya [Nāgārjuna]."[1] Similarly, Rendawa in this text quotes from Candrakīrti's *Madhyamakāvatāra* specifically intending to stress that Candrakīrti is the interpreter *par excellence* of Nāgārjuna's philosophical thought, not Asaṅga, Vasubandhu, Bhāviveka, or others.[2]

Furthermore, in his *Commentary to the Madhyamakāvatāra*, Rendawa succinctly states, "Because previous writers such as Asaṅga, Vasubandhu, and so forth have abandoned afar the noble system of Nāgārjuna . . ."[3]

While Asaṅga and Vasubandhu are extremely important to Dölpopa for his doctrinal systematization, they are not held as authoritative in Rendawa's doctrinal presentation. Similarly, Nāgārjuna's *Mūlamadhyamakakārikā* and Candrakīrti's *Madhyamakāvatāra* are pivotal to Rendawa for his presentation, but they are not held to be as significant in Dölpopa's system for his exposition of other-emptiness.[4] Because of the influence of Candrakīrti's *Madhyamakāvatāra* on Rendawa's presentation of the tathāgata-essence, his approach to the tathāgata-essence teachings is significantly different from that of Dölpopa. For instance, commenting on the section in Candrakīrti's *Madhyamakāvatāra* that references the tathāgata-essence teachings as being provisional, Rendawa states:

> Here, the summary is as follows: if the tathāgata-essence that is taught by the Bhagavan were to be taken literally, then it would not be different from *ātman* [or self] expounded by Tīrthikas. If [the tathāgata-essence teachings] are taught with an intention [by the Buddha] then the questions such as, "What are the basis of intention and the purpose [for teaching the tathāgata-essence]?" follow. The answer is as follows: This is not taken literally rather it has a thought behind it. Having taken emptiness, characterlessness, etc., as the thought behind it, [the Buddha] taught the [tathāgata-essence] for the sake of gradually leading those, who are accustomed to the view of Tīrthikas, and who are not qualified for [the teachings on] profound [emptiness], to [the view of] selflessness.[5]

Following Candrakīrti and Sapen's *Distinguishing the Three Vows*, Rendawa argues that the tathāgata-essence teachings require interpretation as they cannot be accepted at face value. Since he does not assert that every sentient being has all-basis-consciousness, Rendawa differs from Butön and Dratsépa in identifying the basis of intent. While Butön and Dratsépa assert all-basis-consciousness as a basis of intent for the tathāgata-essence teachings, Rendawa replaces the all-basis-consciousness with emptiness as the basis of intent. Butön and Dratsépa cite the verse from the *Mahāyānābhidharmasūtra* in their texts to show that the basis of intent for the tathāgata-essence teachings is all-basis-consciousness.[6]

Furthermore, immediately after the citation mentioned above, Rendawa states:

> However those whose eyes of intellect have been affected by the drink of poison given by evil teachers hold onto the profound sutras [such as the *Tathāgatagarbhasūtra*] taught by the Bhagavan as provisional to be literal. Under the guise of the sugata-essence, they assert a permanent and pervasive self. Not only do they [that is, those evil teachers] stay on the wrong path, they also make others enter into the wrong path. To those who enter into [the wrong path they] give praise and take delight because of [holding] a similar [view]. To those who correctly explain the meaning of emptiness and selflessness, the essence of the Sugata's teachings, [the evil ones] level criticism involving self-repudiating reasons, and so forth, without thinking properly. [The evil ones] secretly call [those who explain emptiness correctly] nihilist. [These evil ones] have even made the Buddhism of the Land of Snows, [which is like the] flames whose supply of firewood is close to exhaustion, completely despicable with the odor of wrong view.[7]

It is without a doubt that "the evil ones" refer to Dölpopa, Sazang, and the like, who assert that a permanent, partless, ultimately existent tathāgata-essence exists in all sentient beings. Rendawa equates such an assertion with the belief in the permanent, unitary, and independent self. Rendawa further points out the popularity of such a view in Tibet, which he deems as the "wrong view."

These citations further suggest that the problem between Rendawa and the "evil ones" is not only regarding what the real nature of emptiness is; rather it also has to do with who is eligible to expound on the meaning of ultimate truth and what text involves explication of the ultimate truth. All of these citations led Jonang scholars to view Rendawa negatively. As Stearns says, "[Rendawa] was viewed by Jonang tradition as a vicious opponent of the teachings of definitive meaning (*nītārtha, nges don*) which had been spread so successfully by Dölpopa."[8]

In the above citations Rendawa criticizes Dölpopa and others for literally accepting the tathāgata-essence teachings as definitive. In the passage below Rendawa argues against the claim that the *Saṃdhinirmocanasūtra* shows the tathāgata-essence teachings to be definitive. He declares:

> Those who assert the permanent sugata-essence that is other than consciousness as the meaning of the last wheel, and claim that this scripture [the *Saṃdhinirmocanasūtra*] proves the last wheel to be definitive are like a woman with her cut-off nose being boastful about her borrowed jewelry. That system [which asserts the permanent tathāgata-essence beyond consciousness as definitive] is even outside of the system of the great charioteers [of the Cittamātra] who accept the last cycle of teachings as definitive.[9]

Rendawa criticizes Dölpopa and others by pointing out that Asaṅga's presentation of definitive sutras differs from Dölpopa's assertion of the tathāgata-essence teachings as definitive. Moreover, Rendawa demonstrates, "Having become familiarized with, and fully understood, the meaning of the scriptures [of Nāgārjuna and Asaṅga], one could engage in commenting on Mahāyāna scriptures. Otherwise, [one] would undoubtedly fall into a deep abyss like blind people who unknowingly walk on a wretched path."[10] This passage makes the immediately preceding citation more clear by arguing that proponents of Mahāyāna scriptures par excellence must know both Nāgārjuna's and Asaṅga's interpretations. (Readers familiar with Dölpopa's works know that Rendawa and Dölpopa come from different textual, hermeneutical backgrounds.) Otherwise, as Rendawa claims, one would be misled like Dölpopa and his followers who profess that the tathāgata-essence is permanent, ultimately existent, and beyond consciousness. This position, as per Rendawa's interpretation of the Indian classics, does not even represent a correct understanding of the texts by Asaṅga, let alone those by Nāgārjuna.

While Rendawa asserts Asaṅga as an important figure for the interpretation of Mahāyāna scriptures, it is Nāgārjuna and Candrakīrti whom he reveres as the supreme commentators of the Mahāyāna scriptures. He states, "So, which tenet among the four schools [that is, Sautrāntika, Vaibhāṣika, Cittamātra, and Madhyamaka] is the thought of the Sugata? Only Nāgārjuna's system is the unmistaken intention of the Sugata's discourses."[11] Rendawa argues that only Nāgārjuna's Madhyamaka system presents the correct ultimate view, not Asaṅga's Cittamātra School. According to Rendawa, Nāgārjuna's system is correctly expounded by Candrakīrti in works such as the *Madhyamakāvatāra*.

If the tathāgata-essence teachings are not definitive, what is definitive and what requires interpretation for Rendawa? He offers the following definition:

> It is as follows: those who follow Ārya Nāgārjuna [hold that] the sutras that conceal [the meaning of emptiness] and that primarily teach conventional truth are [teachings that require] interpretation. Those sutras that primarily teach ultimate truth are definitive sutras. . . . It is asserted that because the existence of incorrect conceptuality is taught in last wheel teachings they require interpretation but because emptiness is clearly taught in the middle [wheel], it is of definitive meaning.[12]

Therefore, Rendawa follows the *Akṣayamatinirdeśasūtra* and the *Samādhirājasūtra* for his interpretation of definitive and provisional meanings of the Buddha's teachings,[13] not the definitions offered in the *Saṃdhinirmocanasūtra*. Rendawa, then, argues that the *Prajñāpāramitāsūtras* are definitive, as they clearly teach the emptiness of inherent existence of all phenomena, whereas the tathāgata-essence teachings and the *Saṃdhinirmocanasūtra* require interepretation because they conceal the meaning of the ultimate emptiness by primarily teaching conventional truth.

In order to realize the emptiness of inherent existence, it is important, Rendawa demonstrates here, to comprehend the meaning of dependent arising:

> Here, if it is a sutra that does not explicitly show the ultimate truth that is the suchness from the perspective of productionlessness and dependent arising, but it explicitly teaches conventional phenomena, then it can be interepreted

to lead to the meaning of emptiness because it is merely taught as a means to enter into [the realization of] the absence of inherent existence.[14]

Rendawa makes it clear that the emptiness that he endorses as the ultimate emptiness is nothing but the absence of inherent existence, which has to be understood within the context of dependent arising, empty of inherent production. While Dölpopa asserts that the self-emptiness is emptiness, he argues that it is not suchness or ultimate truth, for only other-emptiness or the tathāgata-essence can be the ultimate truth. Furthermore, for Dölpopa suchness or ultimate truth cannot be a dependent arising as only conventional phenomena can be dependent arising.[15]

As for whether the *Uttaratantra* is definitive or provisional, Rendawa does not explicitly identify it either as definitive or provisional in the texts that I have consulted. However, Khedrup, a student and a junior contemporary of Rendawa, mentions in his *Presentation of the General Tantric Systems* (*rgyud sde spyi rnam*), "Lama Jé [that is, Rendawa] asserts that [the *Uttaratantra*] is a commentarial work on last-wheel teachings, explicating the view of the Cittamātra School."[16] Moreover, *Blue Annals* reports:

> The Venerable Red-mda'-pa believed at first the *Uttaratantra* to be a Vijñānamātra work, and even composed a commentary from the standpoint of the followers of the Vijñānamātra school. Later, when he became a hermit, he used to sing: "It is impossible to differentiate between the presence and absence of this our Mind. The Buddha having perceived that it penetrated all living beings, as in the example of a subterranean treasure, or the womb of a pregnant woman, had proclaimed all living beings to be possessed of the Essence of the Sugata."[17]

While Khedrup never gives a hint that Rendawa may have developed a new approach to the nature of the *Uttaratantra* later in his life, Gö Lotsawa points out that Rendawa changed his view of the tathāgata-essence later in his life. Gö Lotsawa's statement regarding Rendawa's change of mind with respect to the tathāgata-essence teachings seems to fit with Stearns' observation that Rendawa later in his life put forth a positive assessment of the Kālacakra.[18] Regardless of what Rendawa later thought with respect to the nature of the *Uttaratantra*, these statements still show that the authority of the *Uttaratantra* was debated in fourteenth- and early fifteenth-century Tibet.

Since Rendawa's *Uttaratantra* commentary itself is not extant, it is almost impossible to know how exactly he interpreted the text according to the Cittamātra School. However, we know that Rendawa demotes the tathāgata-essence teachings and promotes the middle-wheel teachings and bases his presentation of the Mahāyāna path on works by scholars such as Nāgārjuna and Candrakīrti, not on works by Asaṅga and Vasubandhu.

Tsongkhapa on the *Uttaratantra* and the Tathāgata-Essence Literature

Tsongkhapa, who studied under both Rendawa and Dratsépa,[19] also criticizes Dölpopa's interpretation of the *Uttaratantra* but employs a different strategy. Tsongkhapa did not write a specific text explaining the *Uttaratantra*, but his views regarding the *Uttaratantra* are found in his *Golden Rosary of Excellent Exposition*, the *Illuminting the Thoughts of Madhyamaka*, and the *Essence of Excellent Exposition*. Moreover, the works of his disciples such as Gyeltsap, Khedrup, and Chöwang Drakpé Pel (*chos dbang grags pa'i dpal*, 1404–1469)[20] set out Tsongkhapa's views on the *Uttaratantra*.[21]

In his *Presentation of the General Tantric Systems*, Khedrup states, "In our system, Jé Rinpoché (*rje rin po che*) [that is, Tsongkhapa] mentions that [the *Uttaratantra*] primarily comments on the meaning of those sutras that are in conformity with the middle-wheel teachings [such as] the *Tathāgatagarbhasūtra*, *Samādhirājasūtra*, *Jñānālokasūtra*, *Aṅgulimālāsūtra*, *Śrīmālādevīsūtra*, and so forth. The content [of the *Uttaratantra*] is in conformity with Prāsaṅgika-Madhyamaka."[22] Khedrup argues that Tsongkhapa takes sutras such as *Tathāgatagarbhasūtra*, *Śrīmālādevīsūtra*, and so forth to be middle-wheel teachings that primarily explain the ultimate truth from the viewpoint of the Prāsaṅgika-Madhyamaka.

Similarly, Chöwang Drakpé Pel states, "The All-knowing Jétsün (*rje btsun*) [that is, Tsongkhapa] repeatedly made the roar of a lion amongst an assembly of scholars [proclaiming that] the ultimate view of the *Abhisamayālaṃkāra* and the *Uttaratantra* falls within the system of Prāsaṅgika-Madhyamaka."[23] Gyeltsap also makes a similar remark, as I will show in the next chapter. Moreover, Buddhist Studies scholars such as Hopkins,[24] Robert Thurman,[25] and David Ruegg claim that Tsongkhapa asserts the *Uttaratantra* to be a Madhyamaka text.[26]

While these scholars might lead us to believe that Tsongkhapa never held the ultimate view of the *Uttaratantra* being anything other than the Prāsaṅgika-Madhyamaka, his *Golden Rosary of Excellent Exposition* gives us a rather complicated answer. Though the *Uttaratantra* is cited quite substantially in the *Golden Rosary of Excellent Exposition* for his exposition of the three buddha-bodies, it is not asserted as an authoritative text for his formulation of emptiness (or ultimate truth) in his works. For instance, Tsongkhapa says:

> Therefore, the proponents of the Madhyamaka School posit that when one realizes the nature of the mind, that is to say, the emptiness in which nothing at all is inherently established, conventionally [speaking] all illusion-like apprehensions are subdued and all illusion-like antidotes are generated. Because of this, that very nature of the mind is posited as the naturally abiding buddha-nature from the conventional perpspective. The proponents of the Cittamātra School assert that the luminous nature of the mind is inherently established on its own at all times and defilements exist [only temporarily that can be] removed by their antidotes; and however much defilements are removed [from the mind] so much are good qualities generated. Because of this they say that [the luminuous nature of the mind] acts as a basis for these two [defilements and virtuous qualities]. Because of this, the dharma-reality [the luminuous nature of the mind] is the buddha-nature. [I] view the former [that is, the Madhyamaka's position on the buddha-nature] as the presentation explicated in the *Abhisamayālaṃkāra* and the latter [that is, what Tsongkhapa interprets to be Cittamātra School's position on the buddha-nature] as the viewpoint explicated in the *Uttaratantra*. Although [both schools] are the same in asserting that the dharma-reality is the buddha-nature, due to the difference in terms of their position on whether the basis of purificiation is truly existent or not, their rationale for presenting the reality as the buddha-nature is not the same.[27]

The contrast between the views of the Madhyamaka School and the Cittamātra School regarding the buddha-nature and the ways in which Tsongkhapa explains the elimination of defilements suggest that the *Abhisamayālaṃkāra* teaches the philosophical view of the Madhyamaka School, and the *Uttaratantra* presents the philosophical view of the Cittamātra School. Therefore, Tsongkhapa suggests that the buddha-nature explained in the *Uttaratantra* is from the viewpoint of the Cittamātra School, not the Madhyamaka School.

Furthermore, the term "final view" (*lta ba mthar thug*) that is found in the quote from Chöwang Drakpé Pel's text seems to suggest that Tsongkhapa had interpreted the *Uttaratantra* from a non-Prāsaṅgika-Madhyamaka perspective, just as he had commented on the *Abhisamayālaṃkāra* from the Svātantrika Madhyamaka. However, Chöwang Drakpé Pel points out that Tsongkhapa *ultimately* interpreted the two texts within the framework of the Prāsaṅgika-Madhyamaka. Therefore, Tsongkhapa's statement in his *Golden Rosary of Excellent Exposition* and his students' utilization of the words "final view" or "final meaning" to refer to the ultimate content of the *Uttaratantra* demonstrate that Tsongkhapa had at some point in his life asserted the *Uttaratantra* as a Cittamātra commentarial work.

While Rendawa seems to have tied the *Uttaratantra* to the Cittamātra School due to the connection that he saw between the tathāgata-essence and the all-basis-consciousness mentioned in texts such as *Laṅkāvatārasūtra*, *Gaṇḍavyūhasūtra*, and *Mahāyānasaṃgraha*, which Rendawa considers as provisional texts, Tsongkhapa appears to have linked the *Uttaratantra* with the Cittamātra School because the buddha-nature in the *Uttaratantra* is explained as "truly existent" (*bden par yod pa*) or "inherently established on its own at all times" (*gshis la rang gi ngo bos dus thams cad du grub*) as found in the above citation. Tsongkhapa does not show any indication that the buddha-nature explained in the *Uttaratantra* is associated with the all-basis-consciousness.

Furthermore, the way that he explicates the buddha-nature from the Cittamātra School in the *Golden Rosary of Excellent Exposition* suggests that the buddha-nature expounded in the *Uttaratantra* refers to the buddha-nature explicated within the context of the presentation of the buddha-nature from the Cittamātra School that does not accept all-basis-consciousness. For instance, Tsongkhapa first explains the buddha-nature from the Cittamātra School that asserts all-basis-consciousness, quoting from the *Śrīmālādevīsūtra* and *Mahāyānasaṃgraha* to show that the buddha-nature is a virtuous seed that is deposited in all-basis-consciousness.[28] In contrast, he explains the buddha-nature from the Cittamātra School that does not assert all-basis-consciousness, quoting from *Bodhisattvabhūmi*, *Śrāvakabhumi*, *Sāgaramegha*, and *Abhidharmasamuccaya* to show that the buddha-nature refers to a naturally acquired virtuous seed that is deposited in the mental consciousness, as opposed to the all-basis-consciousness.[29] The latter presentation of the buddha-nature is followed by his presentation of the buddha-nature from the Madhyamaka School, and it is to the latter buddha-nature that he is referring for the presentation of the difference between the buddha-nature mentioned in the Cittamātra School and the buddha-nature mentioned in the Madhyamaka School. Therefore, according to Tsongkhapa, the *Uttaratantra* follows the Cittamātra School that does not accept the all-basis-consciousness, sometimes known as the Cittamātra School Following Reasoning (*rigs pa'i rjes 'brangs kyi sems tsam*) in Geluk Tenet Literature, but teaches the buddha-nature as truly existent.

If the buddha-nature is explicated in the *Uttaratantra* from the Cittamātra School's point of view, how do we reconcile this with the statement made by his students mentioned above and the remarks made in his own *Illuminating the Thoughts of the Madhyamaka* (*dbu ma dgongs pa rab gsal*), which clearly show that Tsongkhapa asserts the *Uttaratantra* as a Madhyamaka text? I will briefly point out some of the major undertakings that Tsongkhapa took since the completion of his *Golden Rosary of Excellent Exposition* in 1392. He wrote the *Great Exposition of the Stages of Path* in 1402, the *Essence of Excellent Exposition* in 1408, and *Illuminating the Thoughts of the Madhyamaka* in 1418. Furthermore, he founded the Great Monlam (*smon lam*) Ceremony in 1409 and Gaden (*dga' ldan*) monastery in 1409, and instigated his students to build more monastic institutions.[30] Therefore, it seems to me that Tsongkhapa, the author of the *Golden Rosary of Excellent Exposition*, interpreted the buddha-nature explained in the *Uttaratantra* somewhat in line with how his teacher, Rendawa, interpreted it, albeit with some differences. Because of that, Tsongkhapa could not bridge the gap between the *Uttaratantra* and the *Madhyamakāvatāra*, as Gyeltsap and other Geluk scholars would later be able to do. Tsongkhapa appears to have understood these two texts in divergent categories—the *Madhyamakāvatāra* explicating the view of emptiness from the perspective of the Prāsaṅgika-Madhyamaka, and the *Uttaratantra* explaining the view of emptiness from the Cittamātra School.

In contrast, in his *Illuminating the Thoughts of the Madhyamaka*, Tsongkhapa implemented a different strategy that would link the *Uttaratantra* and *Madhyamakāvatāra* in terms of their exposition of ultimate truth. In his *Illuminating the Thoughts of the Madhyamaka*, Tsongkhapa clearly states, "The great master Asaṅga also did not explain the *Uttaratantra* according to the Cittamātra School, rather he explicated it according to the Madhyamaka School."[31] Therefore, in contradistinction to what he had previously asserted in his *Golden Rosary of Excellent Exposition*, Tsongkhapa here argues that the *Uttaratantra* is not a Cittamātra text; rather it is a Madhyamaka treatise.

Tsongkhapa does not assert the tathāgata-essence and the all-basis-consciousness to be exactly the same, as he states:

> The citation from the *Mahāyānābhidharmasūtra* that is utilized to prove all-basis-consciousness in the *Mahāyānasaṃgraha* is cited in [Asaṅga's] *Uttaratantra* commentary [in this way], "It shows that even though sentient beings have the essence, the tathāgata-element, they do not realize it, as [the stanza the *Mahāyānābhidharmasūtra*] 'The element that exists since beginningless time is the basis for phenomena. Due to this all sentient beings [exist], and nirvāṇa is also achieved.'[32] in order to prove that there is the dharma-reality lineage in sentient beings."[33]

Tsongkhapa might very well be criticizing Rendawa, who asserted the *Uttaratantra* as a Cittamātra text, and Dratsépa and other early Tibetan commentators who interpreted the *Uttaratantra* from the Madhyamaka perspective by connecting buddha-nature with all-basis-consciousness. He concludes that the same *Mahāyānābhidharmasūtra* quote that is cited in the *Uttaratantra* commentary does not speak of all-basis-consciousness; rather it refers to the ultimate truth, or the reality.

Tsongkhapa says:

> The explanation of the stanza "that which does not exist in something . . ."[34] that appears in [Asaṅga's] *Uttaratantra* commentary is explained by Asaṅga according to the Madhyamaka exposition, not in conformity with the *Bodhisattvabhūmi*

and the commentary on the *Madhyāntavibhāga*. However, due
to the fear of writing too much, I did not write about this.[35]

In the earlier citation, Tsongkhapa argues that the *Uttaratantra* is not a
Cittamātra text, rather a Madhyamaka text by deciphering the difference between the all-basis-consciousness and the tathāgata-essence. In
the above passage, he shows that the *Uttaratantra* is not a Cittamātra
text by pointing out the difference between the emptiness mentioned
in the Cittamātra texts, such as Asaṅga's *Bodhisattvabhūmi* and the
commentary on the *Madhyāntavibhāga* and the emptiness explicated
in Asaṅga's *Uttaratantra* commentary. Therefore, in his *Illuminating the
Thoughts of the Madhyamaka*, Tsongkhapa claims that the *Uttaratantra*
is a Madhyamaka text, not a Cittamātra text.

Moreover, Tsongkhapa states in the same text that "[Maitreya]
presents the all-basis-consciousness and delineates the position of
the non-existence of external objects in the *Madhyāntavibhāga*, the
Mahāyānasūtrālaṃkāra, and the *Dharmadharmatāvibhāga*, whereas in the
Abhisamayālaṃkāra and the *Uttaratantra* he does not present the all-
basis-consciousness and explicates the position of not negating external
objects."[36] This is the third element that Tsongkhapa adds to his criticism against those who claim that the *Uttaratantra* is a Cittamātra text.
According to Tsongkhapa, Maitreya also structures his texts in two parts,
in just the same way as the Mahāyāna sutras are organized: (1) those
that teach the all-basis-consciousness and the nonexistence of external
objects and (2) those that teach that external objects exist, and all-basis-
consciousness as the eighth consciousness does not exist. Tsongkhapa
argues that since Maitreya's *Madhyāntavibhāga*, *Mahāyānasūtrālaṃkāra*,
and *Dharmadharmatāvibhāga* teach the all-basis-consciousness and the
nonexistence of external objects, they are Cittamātra texts. On the other
hand, because the *Abhisamayālaṃkāra* and the *Uttaratantra*, the other two
texts attributed to Maitreya, present that external objects exist and that
the all-basis-consciousness does not exist as the eighth consciousness,
they are Madhyamaka texts. However, he does not explain further how
the *Uttaratantra* shows that external objects exist in his *Illuminating the
Thoughts of the Madhyamaka*, although the existence of external objects
per se is expounded in great detail in his work.

As will be explained in the next chapter, Gyeltsap elaborates on
these criticisms forwarded by Tsongkhapa. While Tsongkhapa does
not explicitly tie the *Uttaratantra* with the concept of one-vehicle to
show that it is a Madhyamaka text, he points out that if one does

not understand the teachings of all-basis-consciousness as the eighth consciousness, the teachings that show that external objects do not exist, the teachings that explain the other-powered nature and thoroughly established nature as inherently existent, and the teachings that demonstrate three final vehicles as provisional, one will not be able to make the distinction between the Cittamātra School and the Madhyamaka School.[37]

The main reason why Tsongkhapa does not point out the connection between the Madhyamaka School and the one-vehicle concept for proving that the *Uttaratantra* is not a Cittamātra text surely seems to be related to some of the main unique points of the Prāsaṅgika-Madhyamaka that is at the core of his *Illuminating the Thoughts of the Madhyamaka*. For Tsongkhapa, the unique points of the Prāsaṅgika-Madhyamaka are as follows:

> The main unique characteristics [of the Prāsaṅgika-Madhyamaka] are: [1–2] unique ways of negating the all-basis-consciousness that is different in entity from the six collections [of consciousnesses] and self-awareness; [3] the assertion that the independent syllogism (*rang rgyud kyi rtags*) can not generate the view of suchness in an opponent's mental continuum; [4] just as consciousnesss is asserted, so should external objects be asserted; [5] Hearers and Solitary Realizers realize the emptiness of inherent existence; [6] the establishment of the apprehension of phenomena as inherently existent as an afflictive emotion; [7] disintegration as an effective object; [8] because of the establishment [of the seventh uncommon character], there exists an uncommon way of presenting the three times."[38]

However, Gyeltsap will incorporate the concept of one-vehicle as an important theme to criticize those who claim that the *Uttaratantra* is a Cittamātra text, as I will show in the following chapter.

Conclusion

A number of fourteenth-century scholars such as Gendün Özer, Gyelsé Tokmé, Rinchen Yeshé, Dölpopa, and Sazang wrote *Uttaratantra* commentaries and presented it as definitive treatise laying out the nature of ultimate truth. It is in light of this that Rendawa and Tsongkhapa each wrote a commentary on Candrakīrti's *Madhyamakāvatāra* in order to present their view of ultimate truth to at least undermine the significance of the *Uttaratantra* in the philosophical system of Mahāyāna. Therefore, both thinkers leveled criticism against the positions forwarded by Dölpopa and others. Rendawa even went so far as to argue that the *Uttaratantra* is a Cittamātra text (using Cittamātra in a negative sense). His student Tsongkhapa initially argued that the *Uttaratantra* was a Cittamātra text, but later in his life he changed his position and argued that it explained the emptiness of inherent existence, the ultimate truth of the Prāsaṅgika-Madhyamaka, albeit without lending much recourse to the treatise. Unlike these two scholars, Gyeltsap, their student, writes a lengthy commentary on the *Uttaratantra*, and it is to his commentary that we now turn.

Gyeltsap's Commentary on the *Uttaratantra*

A Critique of Dölpopa's Interpretation
of Tathāgata-Essence Literature

Introduction

Gyeltsap, Tsongkhapa, and Khedrup are the three most prominent lineage holders of what would later be known as the Geluk tradition in the Geluk *imaginaire*. Gyeltsap succeeded Tsongkhapa as the lineage holder of the Geluk tradition following the latter's death. Gyeltsap received instruction from Tsongkhapa and Rendawa on the *Uttaratantra*. However, unlike his two masters, who changed their views regarding the status of the *Uttaratantra*, Gyeltsap never held the view that the *Uttaratantra* was a Cittamātra text. In his commentary, Gyeltsap argues that the *Uttaratantra* is a definitive text written from a Prāsaṅgika-Madhyamaka perspective.

Following in the footsteps of his teachers, Gyeltsap criticizes Dölpopa's interpretation by citing sutras and commentarial works that Dölpopa himself considers important. His strategy for criticizing Dölpopa's view of the *Uttaratantra* differs from those used by Butön, Dratsépa, Rendawa, and Tsongkhapa.

As we have seen, the *Uttaratantra* was first introduced to Tibet in the late eleventh century. It quickly became a very significant text in the corpus of Mahāyāna literature in general, and Madhyamaka literature in particular. Two centuries later, however, Butön would include the *Uttaratantra* not in the Madhyamaka section of the *Tengyur* (*bstan 'gyur*; Tibetan translations of treatises), but in the Cittamātra section. Rendawa and Tsongkhapa would also question the importance of the *Uttaratantra* within their detailed explanations of the Madhyamaka presentation of the ultimate truth. In this they privileged Candrakīrti's

Madhyamakāvatāra which was ascending to a significant position akin to the *Uttaratantra* in the Buddhist scholastic tradition.

In his *Uttaratantra* commentary, Gyeltsap shows the strong influence of Tsongkhapa's *Illuminating the Thoughts of the Madhyamaka*. He criticizes those who propose that the *Uttaratantra* is a Cittamātra text, arguing that it explicates the ultimate truth presented in the Prāsaṅgika-Madhyamaka.

How does he criticize those who claim that the *Uttaratantra* is a Cittamātra text? Gyeltsap does not mention his opponents in this context, so it is difficult to say with certainty who his opponents are. We could rule out Tsongkhapa because Gyeltsap had already read Tsongkhapa's *Illuminating the Thoughts of the Madhyamaka* before he completed his *Uttaratantra* commentary.[1] Moreover, Gyeltsap ends each chapter of his commentary with the phrase, "In dependence upon the instruction of Jétsün Lama (*rje btsun bla ma*)"[2] and ends the commentary with the sentence: "Later I received the full kindness of the exposition of the *Uttaratantra* along with [Asaṅga's] commentary from the glorious Jé Rinpoché Lozang Drakpa (*rje rin po che blo bzang grags pa*), the All-knowing One."[3]

Gyeltsap was aware of Rendawa's categorization of the *Uttaratantra* as a Cittamātra text, just as his contemporary and successor Khedrup knew about it.[4] It is also safe to assume that he knew of Butön's inclusion of the *Uttaratantra* in the Cittamātra section of the *Tengyur* catalogue. As discussed below, although Gyeltsap's rationale for demonstrating that the *Uttaratantra* is not a Cittamātra text is based on his and Tsongkhapa's understanding of Prāsaṅgika-Madhyamaka vis-a-vis Cittamātra, it is plausible that both Rendawa and Butön were his target for some of his criticisms. Gyeltsap argues that the *Uttaratantra* is not a Cittamātra treatise because

1. it teaches one final vehicle,

2. it shows that there are followers of the Hearer Vehicle who realize emptiness,

3. it explains emptiness of inherent existence in detail,

4. it is a commentarial work on the Madhyamaka,

5. it states that external objects exist and it does not use the term all-basis-consciousness.

In regard to the first, he states:

[The *Uttaratantra*] explains the tathāgata-essence from the point of view of a resultant tathāgata; it explains it from the point of view of the [ultimate] nature of a tathāgata; and it explains it from the point of view of the cause of a tathāgata. Although the tathāgata-essence is explained in these three ways, it is not asserted that the mere suchness and the dharma-body of a complete buddha are instances of the tathāgata-essence because the *Uttaratantra* and its commentary [by Asaṅga] explain that the tathāgata-essence exists only in sentient beings and in a causal state. To give an example, because the dharma-body activity of the complete buddha, the result achieved through meditating on the path that thoroughly purifies the buddha-element, spreads and pervades to all sentient beings, [since] having the nature to receive the dharma-body activity is a unique characteristic of only sentient beings, all sentient beings have the tathāgata-essence. Even though the suchness that is naturally devoid of defilements is the nature of both sentient beings and buddhas, it is mainly by taking the nature of buddhas into consideration that suchness that exists with the defilements of sentient beings is referred to as tathāgata-essence. Because the suchness that is free from natural defilements, [but] that exists with the defilements of sentient beings exists in all sentient beings it is taught that all sentient beings have tathāgata-essence. Because the buddha-nature, the causal factor for achieving three buddha-bodies, exists in all sentient beings it is taught that all beings have tathāgata-essence.[5]

Gyeltsap thus shows that ultimately both buddhas and sentient beings share the same suchness of mind which is the ultimate nature of mind that is free from natural defilements. Because of this he argues that all sentient beings have tathāgata-essence, and it is through this that he establishes the connection between tathāgata-essence and the concept of one-vehicle, the notion that ultimately there is only the final goal of buddhahood.

As for the second reason mentioned above, Gyeltsap states, "It is shown in the *Uttaratantra* and its commentary [by Asaṅga] that Superior Beings of the Hearer Vehicle realize the selflessness of phenomena."[6] Commenting on a sutric passage,[7] Gyeltsap also says:

Therefore, even the Superior Beings among Hearers and Solitary Realizers directly realize ultimate truth, but, as explained in the *Mūlamadhyamakakārikā*, they do not comprehend it through myriad forms of reasons that cut off elaborations with respect to the ultimate truth. They are not able to realize the ultimate truth, like Mahāyāna followers of high acumen do, through a step by step advancement of a self-powered wisdom regarding the ultimate truth."[8]

In arguing that the *Uttaratantra* explains Hearer and Solitary Realizers perceive emptiness, Gyeltsap presents the *Uttaratantra* within the Prāsaṅgika-Madhyamaka.

As for the third reason demonstrating that the *Uttaratantra* is not a Cittamātra text namely that it explains emptiness of inherent existence in detail, Gyeltsap says, "It is not to be asserted that Ācārya Asaṅga is described as a proponent of Vijñaptimātratā; otherwise it would completely contradict his detailed explanation of the one final vehicle and the presentation of subtle emptiness in his *Uttaratantra* commentary."[9] Gyeltsap argues that the emptiness explained in the *Uttaratantra* and its commentary by Asaṅga is subtle emptiness, and it does not differ from the emptiness that is delineated in the *Prajñāpāramitāsūtras*. Furthermore, he states: "The emptiness of true existence in all phenomena, the ultimate truth that is free of all elaborations, is clearly explained in the *Prajñāpāramitāsūtras* and the *Tathāgatagarbhasūtra* without any difference. Ācārya Asaṅga correctly explains that the emptiness of true existence is the primary meaning of the *Uttaratantra*."[10]

In arguing that the emptiness expounded in the *Prajñāpāramitāsūtras* and the tathāgata-essence explicated in the *Uttaratantra* are the same, Gyeltsap accords the status to the *Uttaratantra* equal to that of Nāgārjuna's *Mūlamadhyamakakārikā*, Candrakīrti's *Madhyamakāvatāra*, and other Madhyamaka treatises which present the ultimate view of Prāsaṅgika-Madhyamaka.

As for Gyeltsap's fourth reason—how the *Uttaratantra* is a commentarial work from the Madhyamaka perspective—he claims that sutras such as the *Tathāgatagarbhasūtra* and other tathāgata-essence treatises teach the same ultimate truth as the middle-wheel sutras do. The *Uttaratantra* is a commentary on sutras such as the *Tathāgatagagarbhasūtra*. Gyeltsap argues that it teaches the same ultimate truth as the ultimate truth explained in the middle-wheel teaching. Hence it is not a Cittamātra text.

On the fifth reason, which is that the *Uttaratantra* teaches that external objects exist and it does not use the term all-basis-consciousness, Gyeltsap says:

> Some assert that the all-basis-consciousness that is explained in the *Mahāyānasaṃgraha* as a different entity from the six collection [of consciousnesses] is the tathāgata-essence. They claim that it is taught in the *Tathāgatagarbhasūtra* and the *Uttaratantra* along with [Asaṅga's] commentary. Such an assertion is held without any critical analysis, because there is not even a partial mentioning of such an all-basis-consciousness in the *Uttaratantra* and its commentary [by Asaṅga]. The system of the *Uttaratantra* is a system that does not assert all-basis-consciousness, [but it] accepts that external objects exist, as I will explain below."[11]

Gyeltsap says some Tibetan scholars explain the *Uttaratantra* from the Cittamātra perspective because they claim Asaṅga cites the same *Mahāyānābhidharmasūtra* verse in his *Mahāyānasaṃgraha* in reference to all-basis-consciousness and in his *Uttaratantra* commentary to refer to the tathāgata-essence.

For Gyeltsap, if the same *Mahāyānābhidharmasūtra* verse were to refer to both the tathāgata-essence and all-basis-consciousness then the *Uttaratantra* would be a Cittamātra text. Gyeltsap's position is that tathāgata-essence and all-basis-consciousness are not the same.

Middle-Wheel and Last-Wheel Teachings

While there is no disagreement between Gyeltsap and Dölpopa about identifying the *Prajñāpāramitāsūtras* as the middle-wheel and the *Saṃdhinirmocanasūtra* as a last-wheel sutra, there is a difference between the two scholars in terms of whether the sutras, such as the *Tathāgatagarbhasūtra*, *Mahāparinirvāṇasūtra*, *Laṅkāvatārasūtra*, and others primarily teach the same ultimate truth of the middle-wheel sutras or not. As explained earlier, Dölpopa argues that sutras such as the *Tathāgatagarbhasūtra*, *Mahāparinirvāṇasūtra*, *Laṅkāvatārasūtra*, and

Saṃdhinirmocanasūtra teach the same ultimate truth. On the other hand, Gyeltsap says, "It is through understanding that the naturally pure buddha-element that is taught in the last wheel and the emptiness that is explained in middle wheel are the same, one can comprehend that the earlier and the later teachings are not contradictory."[12]

Therefore, Gyeltsap argues that the *Tathāgatagarbhasūtra*, *Śrīmālādevīsūtra*, and so forth explain the same ultimate truth as the middle-wheel *Prajñāpāramitāsūtras*, even though the tathāgata-essence teachings are last-wheel sutras. Thus, these last-wheel sutras do not teach the ultimate truth from the Cittamātra perspective that is taught in the last-wheel *Saṃdhinirmocanasūtra*.

Gyeltsap draws a distinction between last-wheel sutras in general and the last-wheel sutra according to the *Saṃdhinirmocanasūtra*. He criticizes those who assert that there is no difference between the tathāgata-essence sutras and the *Saṃdhinirmocanasūtra*: "The assertion that the *Tathāgatagarbhasūtra* is an example for the third-wheel teaching explained in the *Saṃdhinirmocanasūtra* is a nonsensical remark without any knowledge."[13]

While Gyeltsap does not explain that the *Tathāgatagarbhasūtra* is a last-wheel sutra according to the *Saṃdhinirmocanasūtra*, he accepts the sutra as a last-wheel sutra in general. He says that the last wheel according to the *Saṃdhinirmocanasūtra* explains "the imputed nature as empty of true existence,"[14] "the other-powered nature and the thoroughly established nature as truly existent,"[15] and "three final vehicles."[16] On the other hand, the *Tathāgatagarbhasūtra*, a last-wheel sutra, teaches "all phenomena as empty of true existence"[17] and "one final vehicle."[18] Therefore, Gyeltsap makes a distinction between the last-wheel teaching according to the *Saṃdhinirmocanasūtra* and the last-wheel teachings in general. His presentation is more nuanced than Khedrup's explanation of the two wheels.[19] However, both Gyeltsap and Khedrup agree that these tathāgata-essence teachings are all definitive discourses that share the same meaning with the *Prajñāpāramitāsūtras*, not with the *Saṃdhinirmocanasūtra*.

If the *Tathāgatagarbhasūtra* is a last-wheel sutra, would that mean that the *Uttaratantra* is a commentarial work on the last wheel? For Gyeltsap, there is no contradiction in saying that the *Uttaratantra* comments on both last-wheel sutras and the middle-wheel sutras.[20] Gyeltsap's claim, to a degree, echoes the early *Uttaratantra* commentators, such as Ngok and Chapa, who argue that both the middle wheel and the last wheel are definitive in terms of teaching the ultimate reality.

Definitive Meaning and Provisional Meaning

Gyeltsap speaks of the two sets of definitive and provisional meanings. He states, "Generally, the sutras taught by the Bhagavan explain two ways of distinguishing those that require interpretation and those that are definitive. One is explained in the *Akṣayamatinirdeśasūtra* and *Samādhirājasūtra* and the other one in the profound *Saṃdhinirmocanasūtra*."[21] Gyeltsap asserts that all three sutras offer definitions for both definitive and provisional meanings. He does not maintain that all three sutras provide the same definitions. He states, "Because Nāgārjuna, based on the former sutras [that is, the *Akṣayamatinirdeśasūtra* and *Samādhirājasūtra*], clearly distinguishes between the provisional meaning and the definitive meaning, the latter sutra [that is, the *Saṃdhinirmocanasūtra*] is proven to be provisional by default."[22] Gyeltsap follows the definitions explained in these two sutras, not the ones offered in the *Saṃdhinirmocanasūtra* because the latter is a Cittamātra text.

Gyeltsap presents the two sets of definitions for provisional and definitive meaning as follows:

> The first [two sutras, namely, the *Akṣayamatinirdeśasūtra* and *Samādhirājasūtra*] show that those that teach all phenomena as empty of inherent existence are definitive and those that teach persons, aggregates, and so forth in various words and letters are provisional. The latter sutra [referring to the *Saṃdhinirmocanasūtra*], which explains the imputed nature as empty of inherent existence and the other-powered nature and the thoroughly established nature as inherently existent, describes [sutras that] teach all phenomena as empty of inherent existence and that teach all phenomena as inherently existent are provisional. [On the other hand, the sutras that] clearly make the distinction between [what is] not inherently existent and [what is] inherently existent are definitive meaning.[23]

As a follower of the Prāsaṅgika-Madhyamaka, Gyeltsap defines the definitive and provisional teachings as those that primarily teach emptiness of inherent existence, or ultimate truth, and those that primarily teach conventional truth respectively. On the other hand, he offers a separate set of definitions of the definitive and

interpretable teachings from the Cittamātra perspective based on the
Saṃdhinirmocanasūtra.[24]

Self-Emptiness and Other-Emptiness

Gyeltsap criticizes those who assert that the *Uttaratantra* teaches other-
emptiness, and he gives his own explication of the emptiness of inherent existence.

In regard to the first, Gyeltsap argues, "The assertion that there
exists a complete buddha within sentient beings since beginningless
time is different, only in name, from the followers of Īśvara who
accept a permanent self-arisen all-knowing being."[25] This passage and
many of the citations quoted below show how Gyeltsap characterizes
those who assert the other-emptiness in his *Uttaratantra* commentary.
Gyeltsap furthermore states in his polemical tone:

> Some, asserting the ultimate truth as a permanent-entity,
> say that the ultimate truth that is empty of all convention-
> alities is the profound other-emptiness. These are all just
> foolish words.
>
> Does the other-emptiness mean that the ultimate truth
> is empty of being a conventional truth, or does it refer to the
> ultimate truth that is empty of having conventional truth?
> If it is the latter, it would contradict your assertion that the
> ultimate truth pervades all inanimate and animate things,
> [because these things would not have the ultimate truth].
>
> Therefore, ponder upon how the ultimate truth exist-
> ing pervasively in all phenomena and the ultimate truth
> that is the state of having no conventional truth are not
> contradictory!
>
> If it is the former, it would undermine [your assertion]
> that the disciples of the "profound other-emptiness" are
> those with "the most supreme intelligence" because they
> would still have the doubt regarding the permanent-entity
> ultimate truth being a conventional truth and they would
> have to eliminate the doubt.[26]

Here Gyeltsap argues that other-emptiness presented by Dölpopa is not ultimate truth using a two-pronged reason. His examina-

tion proceeds in the following manner. If other-emptiness or ultimate truth is empty of conventional phenomena, it has to be empty of conventional phenomena in one of the following two ways: (1) Other-emptiness has to be empty of *being* conventional phenomena (in that it *is* not conventional phenomenon); (2) Other-emptiness has to be empty of *having* conventional phenomena (in that other-emptiness does not *pervade* or *encompass* conventional phenomena).

Gyeltsap further challenges the proponents of other-emptiness for asserting that dharma-body endowed with two purities—the natural purity and the purity of adventitious defilements—exists in all beings:

Let us analyze the thesis that the dharma-body endowed with two purities exists in sentient beings. 1) Does it mean that the mind of sentient beings that is naturally pure is devoid of all adventitious defilements? 2) Does the dharma-body endowed with two purities exist in sentient beings as the same entity as the mind? 3) Does it exist as a separate entity from one's mind? 4) Does it exist with no relation [to one's mind]?

According to the first, that very sentient beings would be buddhas is an inescapable consequence.

In the second case, is the dharma-body endowed with the two purities that exists in sentient beings i) obscured or ii) not obscured by the adventitious defilements of sentient beings?

If it is obscured, it would contradict being a dharma-body endowed with two purities.

If it is the second [that is, not obscured], then the [assertion that] the mental continuum of sentient beings is one entity with [the dharma-body] endowed with two purities [yet] the mental continuum of sentient beings is inevitably tainted by defilements would not stand.

In the third case (the dharma-body is an entity separate from one's mind), because the two separate entities simultaneously existing cannot be cause and effect, you would have to assert that sentient beings and buddha are of one composite, but this would not be possible at all.

In the fourth case, the pronouncement that the dharma-body endowed with two purities exists inherently beginninglessly without any relationship to sentient beings would contradict all reason.[27]

Here he argues that it is impossible for sentient beings, whose minds are infused with afflictions, to have the dharma-body that is free from defilements.

At the center of Gyeltsap's argument is the proposition that the emptiness of inherent existence as he understands it is the main subject taught in the *Uttaratantra* and the last-wheel sutras that deal with tathāgata-essence. It is also explicitly explained in the *Prajñāpāramitāsūtra*.

As Gyeltsap shows:

> Some, under the guise of explaining the teachings of the Buddha, widely disseminate the self of the non-Buddhist Schools. They say that the *Prajñāpāramitāsūtra*s explain only conventional self-emptiness and without explaining the final ultimate truth, because the final ultimate truth is explained in the last wheel, and its meaning is correctly interpreted in the *Uttaratantra* and its commentary by Asaṅga. One should know that those who say such do not even have the fortune to look at these commentaries.[28]

In brief, Gyeltsap argues that buddha-nature, or tathāgata-essence, does not refer to a fully enlightened entity covered by adventitious defilements. Rather it is the same as the emptiness of inherent existence that is explicated in texts such as the *Prajñāpāramitāsūtras* and *Madhyamakāvatāra*.

Conclusion

Gyeltsap interprets the *Uttaratantra* drawing the concepts of the Prāsaṅgika-Madhyamaka from Tsongkhapa's texts such as the *Illuminating the Thoughts of the Madhyamaka* and the *Essence of Excellent Exposition*. Therefore, his broader agenda is certainly to demonstrate that Tsongkhapa accepted the *Uttaratantra* as a text belonging to the Prāsaṅgika-Madhyamaka and transmitted that instruction to him. So, Gyeltsap claims that both the *Madhyamakāvatāra* and the *Uttaratantra* explain the same meaning of ultimate truth. Hence, they are both definitive works that explicate the intention of the middle wheel.

Moreover, the *Uttaratantra* is a Madhyamaka treatise because it explicates the meaning of the emptiness of inherent existence that is taught in both the *Prajñāpāramitāsūtras* and the *Tathāgatagarbhasūtra*.[29] Gyeltsap argues that there is no difference between the emptiness propounded in these two sutras. For him, the question as to why the *Uttaratantra* is a definitive work is no longer the issue; it is how the *Uttaratantra* is a definitive teaching. Similarly, the question as to why the tathāgata-essence is emptiness is no longer an issue in his commentary; it is how the tathāgata-essence is emptiness.

Whereas both Rendawa and Tsongkhapa criticized Dölpopa and his doctrinal presentation in their works by focusing on sources such as the *Madhyamakāvatāra*, Gyeltsap challenges Dölpopa's presentation by systematically reformulating the *Uttaratantra* from the perspective of the Prāsaṅgika-Madhyamaka. It is partially because of these criticisms that Geluk monks were prohibited from keeping Dölpopa's *Mountain Doctrine* and the *Fourth Council* as Gö Lotsawa would report in his *Blue Annals*.[30]

Conclusion

General Remarks

As Donald Lopez claims, "to study a text is to study the effects of the text in different periods. This history is to be found, among other places, in commentaries—the texts that the text produced."[1] What I have attempted in this book is to trace the history of the *Uttaratantra* in Tibet by analyzing several commentaries on it, or works concerned with it written between the eleventh and fifteenth centuries.[2] As I turn back to its history in Tibet, the Land of Snows, it is not surprising that the treatise gained popularity right from its inception. The rejuvenation of the Buddhist intellectual culture was at its peak in the eleventh and twelfth centuries; the *Uttaratantra* was introduced as a treatise belonging to one of the five texts attributed to Maitreya, the Future Buddha; it was translated into Tibetan by several famed translators of the time such as Ngok, Patsap, and Naktso; the ultimate truth explained in the text was curiously both positivist and negativist (to a certain degree); the text spoke to both intellectuals such as Ngok and Chapa and contemplative practitioners such as Tsen Khawoché and Zu Gawé Dorjé; and it found a text in the name of *Madhyamakāvatāra* that challenged or sometimes complemented it. Given such a historical background, the text was destined to draw the attention of future Tibetan commentators of the period of full assimilation (tenth to mid-thirteenth centuries) and the classical period (mid-thirteenth to sixteenth centuries).[3]

The commentators in the Land of Snows, in particular, do not work in isolation from a community of interpreters where transmission lineage and guru-disciple relationship are crucial. In other words, they interpret the treatise by looking back to the past and by engaging the present within a broader textual community[4] or interpretive community.[5] As I have shown this is precisely what happens in Tibet with the *Uttaratantra*. The text was commented upon by many commentators in its history, creating several groups of fellow exegetes.

Thus, my major task in this book has been to give room for what different voices have to say about the Buddhist philosophical problems connected with the *Uttaratantra* that early Tibetan commentators addressed. Tracing back developments in the literary landscape, I demonstrated that the Tibetan commentators placed the *Uttaratantra* within fields of scholastic or meditative literature. This is reflected in the traditional terms "dialectical tradition" and "meditative tradition" respectively.

At the advent of the Indian treatise's long history in Tibet, the issue was not a hermeneutical one; that is to say, the issue was not whether the treatise was either definitive or interpretable. Rather early commentators laid an emphasis on how one engaged the treatise, either as a scholastic text as Sangpu scholars such as Ngok and Chapa did, or as a meditative manual as mystics such as Tsen Khawoché and Zu Gawé Dorjé did. It was a given that the text taught the definitive meaning of the Buddha's instructions.

However, as the *Madhyamakāvatāra* gained popularity in the Tibetan Buddhist intellectual world, Tibetans began to express reservations. Sapen became the first major Tibetan thinker who questioned the veracity of certain claims made in the *Uttaratantra*, labeling them as requiring interpretation, in contradistinction to the definitive meaning taught in Candrakīrti's text. Sapen, to echo Stanley Fish, executed "a different set of interpretive strategies"[6] which characterized the text differently.

In response to the rise of Candrakīrti's *Madhyamakāvatāra* and Sapen's new reading of the *Uttaratantra*, new textual communities evolved new interpretative strategies. Their interpretations of the *Uttaratantra* found new patterns in the text, thereby producing several new readings. These readings were not constricted by the sacred words or phrases encrypted in wooden block manuscripts; rather they were *limitedly* fluid and contingent upon a contemplative process that went through a stage of hearing (*thos pa*), pondering (*bsam pa*), and gaining meditative understanding (*sgom pa*) of the text, all within a particular lineage or community. The interpretive methods or strategies that these commentators garnered through the tripartite process of hearing, pondering, and contemplative understanding took precedence over the inscribed text of the *Uttaratantra*. If you look for a modern phrase to describe this process, it would be "interpretive methods." This renders nicely the classical Tibetan literary term "'grel lugs" or its oral form "'grel bshad rgyag stangs."

In the two centuries that followed Sapen's new interpretation of the *Uttaratantra*, Tibetan interpreters made use of four broad interpretative methods to make sense of the text. First, Rikrel, Rinchen Yeshé, Sangpu Lodrö, Gendün Özer, and Gyelsé Tokmé employ "the Kadam interpretive method"[7] in their commentaries, arguing for the definitive nature of the treatise and for its great significance within the Mahāyāna corpus. Rinchen Yeshé, Sangpu Lodrö, and Gyelsé Tokmé are known for their knowledge of Maitreya's texts, including the *Uttaratantra*. It is not surprising, therefore, that in the post-Sapen period, which saw the rise of Candrakīrti's *Madhyamakāvatāra* to prominence, they each wrote exhaustive commentaries framing the *Uttaratantra*, within a sutric context, as included in the last-wheel teachings.

Second, "the Jonang interpretative method" is formulated by Dölpopa and Sazang. They built on the Kadam interpretive methods and went so far as to intrepret the *Uttaratantra* as last-wheel teachings, on a par with the *Saṃdhinirmocanasūtra*. They thus distanced the teaching of the *Uttaratantra* from the middle-wheel teachings of the *Prajñāpāramitāsūtras* and made the treatise a central text for the elucidation of other-emptiness. They contrasted this with Candrakīrti's limited interpretation of ultimate truth as found in his *Madhyamakāvatāra*.

Third is the interpretation of the two staunchest proponents of Candrakīrti's *Madhyamakāvatāra*, Rendawa and his disciple, Tsongkhapa. They were ambivalent about the place of the *Uttaratantra* within the Mahāyāna textual tradition, but they nevertheless employed what I refer to as "the Sakya Cittamātra interpretive method." Given the ascendancy of *Uttaratantra* commentaries written in the fourteenth century arguing for the definitive nature of the tathāgata-essence, and given Dölpopa's articulation of Ultimate Cittamātra as the supreme Buddhist school surpassing Prāsaṅgika-Madhyamaka, the only method that seemed to have been available to Rendawa and Tsongkhapa was to give the *Uttaratantra* a status lower than that accorded to the *Madhyamakāvatāra*. However, this interpretive method did not have much impact on future scholars. And even Tsongkhapa himself, for instance, changed his way of explaining the text later in his life.

Fourth and last, Gyeltsap, who studied under both Rendawa and Tsongkhapa, utilized what I call "the Geluk interpretive method." This method allowed Gyeltsap to interpret the *Uttaratantra* from the

Prāsaṅgika-Madhyamaka perspective following, quite counterintuitively, Tsongkhapa's commentary on the *Madhyamakāvatāra*. As a tradition known for looking back to early Kadam for its inspiration in scholasticism and monasticism, this Geluk interpretive method puts the *Uttaratantra* back into the highest Madhyamaka category. In this it is similar to the earlier Kadam tradition. However, quite the opposite to what earlier Kadam scholars such as Chapa, Rinchen Yeshé, and Sangpu Lodrö had imagined, Gyeltsap did so by creating a marriage between Candrakīrti's thought and the *Uttaratantra*, wherein the *Madhyamakāvatāra* is given preference over the *Uttaratantra* for having a clearer explication of the ultimate truth.

These four interpretive methods, developed on the traditional categories of the dialectical tradition and the contemplative tradition, or the Ngok tradition and the Tsen tradition, underscore the complexity of the history of the *Uttaratantra* and the dynamism that informed early Tibetan scholars who engaged with the treatise.

Completing the Cycle

This book has primarily traced the history of the treatise from the eleventh to the mid-fifteenth centuries. It has dealt in detail with the era during which readers favorable to the *Uttaratantra* argued for its legitimacy against its dissenters such as Sapen, Rendawa, and Tsongkhapa. It has not addressed the history of the *Uttaratantra* from the fifteenth century onward,[8] so I shall provide a brief overview of that history to bring the story to its completion.

Since the mid-fifteenth century, as far as I know, no Tibetan commentator has relegated the *Uttaratantra* to the category of interpretable, nor has any accorded a lowly textual status of any other kind to the *Uttaratantra*.

It is safe to assert that *Uttaratantra* commentators since the fifteenth century have written using either the Jonang interpretive method or the Geluk interpretive method, since these two methods have come to dominate the language used to interpret the *Uttaratantra* since that time. The main concern has been more with the identification of the ultimate truth as explained in the *Uttaratantra* and less with defending the definitive nature of the Indian text itself.

Among those who wrote exegeses on the topic of the buddha-nature are Rongtön, Gö Lotsawa, Gorampa (*go rams pa bsod nams seng ge*, 1429–1489), Shakchok (*shakya mchog ldan*, 1428–1507), Kongtrül, and Mipam (*'ju mi pham rgya mtsho*, 1846–1912). They wrote texts related to the tathāgata-essence issue in response to the Geluk or Jonang presentation of tathāgata-essence in the *Uttaratantra*.[9]

Given that Rongtön received his initial scholastic education at Sangpu and later under Yaktön, a great Sakya master, it is not surprising that his commentary follows that of Ngok on the *Uttaratantra*.[10] Furthermore, as a prominent figure who understood himself as upholding a Sakya orthodoxy, he criticizes the claims regarding tathāgata-essence made by Dölpopa and Tsongkhapa even though both were intellectually groomed within and beholden to the Sakya tradition.[11] In contradistinction to Dölpopa and Tsongkhapa, Rongtön's commentary presents the tathāgata-essence as a unity of luminosity and emptiness. He argues that the *Uttatarantra* is a commentary on the definitive meaning of both the middle-wheel and last-wheel teachings.[12]

Rongtön's student Gorampa is a towering figure in Sakya. His commentaries on the Indian Buddhist classics are considered at Sakya monastic institutes to be authoritative. Gorampa is a great polemicist[13] who criticizes Gyeltsap, Dölpopa, and Shakchok.[14] In his *Supplement to the Three Vows* (*sdom gsum kha skong*), he criticizes Gyeltsap and his followers for conflating tathāgata-essence with the mere emptiness of inherent existence. Such tathāgata-essence, in Gorampa's account, is a misrepresentation of tathāgata-essence because the tathāgata-essence must be understood as a unity of luminosity and emptiness.[15] Not surprisingly, Gorampa also argues that the Geluk's tathāgata-essence as the mere emptiness of inherent existence is not ultimate truth.[16] Gorampa critiques Gyeltsap's interpretation of the ultimate truth as nihilist.[17]

The Sakya master also criticizes Dölpopa's view. He says the latter's view of ultimate truth does not represent the view of Madhyamaka since Dölpopa does not extend his deconstructive logic to tathāgata-essence, retaining for it an independent existence.[18]

Gorampa does not just critique Dölpopa and Gyeltsap. He also states:

> Certain persons of coarse mental faculty, holding the eternalistic view [of the Jo nang pas] secretly in their hearts, take sides with the philosophical views of others for the sake of diplomacy, and claim that the Sa skya and Jo nang

pa schools are not incompatible as regards their philosophical views.[19]

The unidentified scholar criticized here is Shakchok.[20] Gorampa takes Shakchok's view of ultimate truth as resembling Dölpopa's view of other-emptiness, not the Sakya position on ultimate truth. Gorampa also criticizes his rival contemporary Shakchok for his claim that buddha-nature does not exist in all sentient beings.[21] (I will say more about this in the following paragraphs.) It is not coincidental that in the fifteenth century when both Jonang's and Geluk's presentations of the *Uttaratantra* were spreading and finding adherents, laying out an alternative to the traditional Sakya doctrine, that Rongtön and Gorampa, the greatest Sakya luminaries of the fifteenth century,[22] are found strongly criticizing the interpretations of ultimate truth being propogated by the Jonang and Geluk schools.

Shakchok is counted a Sakya scholar, and he wrote a commentary on the *Uttaratantra*. His explanation was not, however, in line with that of Rongtön and Gorampa. He studied under Rongtön and would become one of the "Six Ornaments of the Land of Snows" within the Sakya tradition (along with Rongtön and Gorampa).[23] Despite this honorable stature within the Sakya tradition, however, Shakchok is considered controversial because he wrote a text raising questions regarded as challenging Sapen's authoritative *Distinguishing the Three Vows*.[24] At his core Shakchok is a brialliant scholar and polemicist. He criticized the views of both Tsongkhapa[25] and Dölpopa.[26]

As for his interpretation of the *Uttaratantra*, as Yaroslav Komarovski demonstrates, "throughout his life, both in early and later writings, he [Shakchok] showed tremendous respect for this text [*Uttaratantra*] and viewed it as a treatise of definitive meaning."[27] In particular, Shakchok took the *Uttaratantra* to be a representative of the highest school of his tradition,[28] not the Madhyamaka of Nāgārjuna or Candrakīrti.[29] Despite Shakchok's claim that "the primordial positive qualities are forever present in the primordial mind,"[30] he does not claim that the *Uttaratantra* teaches that all beings have the buddha-essence. Rather he construes the buddha-essence as an ultimate truth that is free from a partial form of adventitious defilements. According to Shakchok,[31] such a buddha-essence cannot exist in ordinary beings insofar as they do not directly realize ultimate truth.

He makes a distinctive presentation of the buddha-essence, asserting that the buddha-essence presented in Ngok's and Gyeltsap's

Uttaratantra commentaries, for example, is "imputed," in the sense that it is not the real buddha-essence because it is a mere emptiness characterized by its nonaffirming negative aspect.[32] On the other hand, Shakchok explains that the buddha-essence as delineated in the writings of Jonang scholars such as Dölpopa and Sazang is interpretable because ordinary beings do not have the buddha-essence that is endowed with the buddha-qualities.[33] He says the buddha-essence taught in the *Uttaratantra*, which is neither the emptiness that is mere emptiness, nor the ultimate truth with complete positive qualities, is the definitive meaning of the last-wheel teachings in his systematization of the Mahāyāna.

Thus three of the Six Ornaments of the Land of Snows within the Sakya tradition (Rongtön, Gorampa, and Shakchok) wrote about the tathāgata-essence. In each case what they had to say can be seen as a response to interpretations of the *Uttaratantra* by Jonang and Geluk scholars.

Even while prominent Sakya thinkers were busy presenting their own views about the *Uttaratantra* in response to writings by Jonang and Geluk thinkers, Gö Lotsawa from the Kagyü School penned an exhaustive *Uttaratantra* commentary in 1473. His commentary is the first extensive commentary from the Kagyü School that explicitly presents a Mahāmudra view of the tathāgata-essence. Gö Lotsawa traces the pedigreee of his view back through prominent Kagyü figures such as Gampopa and Jikten Sumgön.[34]

It is noteworthy that this well-known Kagyü historian-cum-commentator wrote a Mahāmudra-based *Uttaratantra* commentary at the same time as Gorampa and Shakchok were writing their works following in the footsteps of Sapen who had criticized the sutra-based Mahāmudra. Gö Lotsawa's Mahāmudra-based *Uttaratantra* commentary is a defense of earlier Kagyü interpretations of the tathāgata-essence against the two illustrious defenders of Sakya in this time period.

As Mathes argues, "Zhonu Pal explains that the emptiness of middling Madhyamaka is approached by the method of nonaffirming negation and assigned to the middle (or second) dharmacakra, whereas supreme Madhyamaka with its "awareness-emptiness" is said to follow the path of affirming negation and belong to the third dharmacakra."[35]

Thus for Gö Lotsawa the *Uttaratantra* is a commentary that explicates the definitive meaning of the last-wheel *Saṃdhinirmocanasūtra*,[36] not the middle-wheel sutras. For Gö Lotsawa the emptiness taught in the last-wheel teachings is the tathāgata-essence, and is the definitive meaning of the Buddha's teachings. However, unlike Dölpopa and the followers of the other-emptiness doctrine, Gö Lotsawa does not claim that the tathāgata-essence is endowed with inherent enlightened qualities. Mathes argues this "would come too close to the non-Buddhist view of an ātman for him."[37] Still, Gö Lotsawa's commentary falls more in line with other-emptiness and less with self-emptiness. In this he anticipates what we will see in the *Uttaratantra* commentary written by the nineteenth-century Kagyü polymath Kongtrül discussed below.

Although Tibetan masters continued to write commentaries on the *Uttaratantra* between the sixteenth and eighteenth centuries,[38] most of them are by Geluk scholars such as Penchen Sonam Drakpa (*pan chen bsod nams grags pa*, 1478–1554),[39] Coné Drakpa Shedrup (*co ne grags pa bshad sgrub*, 1675–1748),[40] and Kachupa Lozang Tsepel (*bka' bcu pa blo bzang tshe 'phel*, 1760–?).[41] Considering the rise of the Geluk power in this period and the political control of central and western Tibet by the Geluk hegemony by the mid-seventeenth century, it is not surprising that other, alternative voices that challenged the status-quo were restricted (to the point that many Kagyü and Jonang monasteries were converted into Geluk ones).

The nineteenth century witnessed the rise of the so-called "nonsectarian" or "*rimé*" movement.[42] The movement can be characterized, in part at least, as an alliance of the non-Geluk schools of Kagyü, Nyingma, and Sakya against Geluk hegemony in the revitalization of scholastic education and monastic culture. It was spearheaded by visionary thinkers and prolific writers such as Kongtrül and Mipam.

Both Kongtrül and Mipam wrote commentaries on the *Uttaratantra*. Indeed, it is noteworthy how many *Uttaratantra* commentaries[43] were written in this same century from a non-Geluk perspective, given the relative dearth of *Uttaratantra* commentaries in the preceding centuries.

Here I will focus briefly on Kongtrül and Mipam, who made great contributions to the honorable Tibetan tradition of writing commentaries to present their own view in response to, or critique of, others' positions—a time-honored literary tradition followed by Tibetan scholars from various backgrounds for centuries.

Kongtrül, a towering figure of the *rimé* movement, showed his utmost respect for the *Uttaratantra* to the extent that he even argued that it could be considered as a sutra, a highly elevated textual status that is reserved for the teachings attributed to the Buddha, as opposed to the status of a *śāstra*, Buddhist texts authored by unenlightened beings. After defining what constitutes a *"bka'"* (sutra) and a *"bstan bcos"* (*śāstra*), he states, "Which one [of the two] is the *Uttaratantra*, the subject of exposition? On the one hand, it could be considered as a sutra approved by the Buddha or as a sutra empowered by the Buddha."[44] There is no doubt that the *Uttaratantra* renders a significant textual authority for Kongtrül. In his lengthy commentary,[45] Kongtrül claims to interpret the *Uttaratantra* in line with the view of the Third Karmapa[46] and Gö Lotsawa's commentary[47] who followed the meditative or experiential approach to the ultimate truth explained in the *Uttaratantra*, as opposed to the dialectical approach.[48] As is the case with those who follow the meditative approach, Kongtrül regards the last-wheel teachings as superior to the middle-wheel teachings.[49] Furthermore, Kongtrül follows in his predecessors' footsteps by claiming that tathāgata-essence is not emptiness in the sense of being a non-affirming negative; rather it is an affirming negative.[50] Most importantly, the Kagyü polymath sees the ultimate view of Gampopa, Jikten Sumgön, and Dölpopa as essentially the same[51] while acknowledging that several Tibetan scholars had criticized Dölpopa's ultimate view.[52] He also asserts that "the nature of tathāgata-essence is that it is free from all adventitious defilements since the beginning"[53] and that "the nature of tathāgata-essence is the indivisible reality that naturally contains ultimate qualities such as [the enlightened] power and so forth since the beginning."[54] Consequently, he does not shy away from pledging his allegiance to the other-emptiness doctrine in his *Uttaratantra* commentary,[55] unlike the *rimé* figures from Nyingma tradition such as Mipam[56] and Khenpo Zhenpen.[57]

Mipam studied under Jamyang Khyentsé Wangpo (1820–1892), Kongtrül, and several other prominent figures of the time. His importance within Nyingma tradition is such that many of his texts including *Lion's Roar: Exposition of Buddha-Nature* are studied at Nyingma commentarial institutes throughout the Himalayan regions.[58] While Kongtrül refers mainly to figures in the lineage of other-emptiness for his source, Mipam in his *Uttaratantra* commentary[59] utilizes Rongtön and Rendawa along with Dölpopa as his sources notwithstanding that his commentary takes jibes at both the Jonang presentation of tathāgata-essence and the Geluk presentation of tathāgata-essence.[60] It is noteworthy that Mipam utilizes Rongtön and Rendawa and that he does not criticize Sakya tradtion in his *Beacon of Certainty,* most probably because of his Sakya *rimé* teacher Jamyang Khyentsé Wangpo.[61] His *Uttaratantra* commentary, the *Instruction from Mipam,* follows that of Rongtön in particular quite closely, at least in its literary style.

In his *Instruction from Mipam,*[62] Mipam interprets both middle-wheel and last-wheel teachings as definitive, but he deems the latter superior to the former because of the unique presentation of the tathāgata-essence. Following Longchenpa, Mipam asserts that tathāgata-essence is empty of adventitious defilements, yet it is not empty of enlightened qualities.[63] Nevertheless Mipam identifies himself as a proponent of self-emptiness.[64]

It is perhaps no accident that Dzemé Rinpoché (*dze smad rin po che,* 1927–1996), a controversial scholar of Geluk tradition,[65] wrote a commentary on the *Uttaratantra* in the twentieth century called *Interlinear Glosses to the Uttaratantra* (*theg pa chen po rgyud bla ma'i bstan bcos kyi mchan 'grel*).[66] His commentary sticks to the classical meaning of the term *"mchan 'grel"* in that it provides explanatory glosses embedded in the root text of the *Uttaratantra.* Furthermore, it does not single out any other thinkers or commentators of the *Uttaratantra* for criticism, nor does it explicitly offer or defend any sectarian position. Given that the two influential *rimé* figures, Mipam and Khenpo Zhenpen (who died in the year that Dzemé Rinpoché was born), wrote *mchan 'grels* ("interlinear glosses") to the *Uttaratantra,* it is worth noting that an erudite Geluk scholar also wrote a commentary with the word *mchan 'grel* in the title. Whether or not Dzemé Rinpoché consciously had their works in mind, he thereby undertakes the important ritual of writing an *Uttaratantra* or the *Sublime Continuum* commentary keeping alive the continuity of a long and important Tibetan commentarial tradition.

Notes

Introduction

1. Gen Damchö Gyeltsen (*rgan dam chos rgyal mtshan*). I am employing the THL's simplified phonetic transcription of Tibetan in this book. For more on the transliteration, see http://www.thlib.org/reference/transliteration.

2. I will refer to the treatise as the *Uttaratantra* because I discuss the history of the text in Tibet. As Jikido Takasaki says, the title *Ratnagotraśāstra* is employed in the Chinese tradition. See Jikido Takasaki, *A Study on the Ratnagotravibhāga (Uttaratantra): Being a Treatise on the Tathāgatagarbha Theory of Mahāyāna Buddhism* (Roma: Istituto Italiano per Il Medio Ed Estremo Oriente, 1966), 5. E. H. Johnston mentions that one of the Sanskrit manuscripts of the text found in Central Asia in the early twentieth century identifies the text by the title *Ratnagotravibhāga*. See E. H. Johnston, foreword to the *Ratnagotravibhāga Mahāyānottaratantraśāstra*, ed., E. H. Johnston (Patna: Bihar Research Society, 1950), v.

3. These terms are used interchangeably, along with "buddha-element" (*sangs rgyas kyi khams; buddhadhātu*) and "sugata-essence" (*bde gshegs snying po; sugatagarbha*), unless otherwised noted.

4. Khenpo Tsültrim Gyamtso (*mkhan po tshul khrims rgya mtsho*).

5. See John Powers, *Hermeneutics and Tradition in the Saṃdhinirmocana-Sūtra* (Leiden: Brill, 1993), particularly chapters, 3, 4, 5.

6. See Jonathan Gold, *Paving the Great Way: Vasubandhu's Unifying Buddhist Philosophy* (New York: Columbia University Press, 2015), chapter 5 on the three natures of Yogācāra philosophy. For a succinct article on the philosophical position of the Yogācāra or Cittamātra, see Dan Lusthaus, "What Is and Isn't Yogācāra," Yogācāra Buddhism Research Association, http://www.acmuller.net/yogacara/articles/intro.html.

7. See Mark Siderits and Shōryū Katsura, *Nāgārjuna's Middle Way* (Boston: Wisdom, 2013).

8. Modern scholars are in agreement that the text was translated by Ratnamati in Chinese in the early sixth century, the earliest translation of the treatise in a language other than Sanskrit. This suggests that a Sanskrit manuscript was available by the early sixth century.

9. In the Tibetan tradition, the verse part is generally referred to as the *Uttaratantra,* or the root text of the *Uttaratantra* (*rgyud bla rtsa ba*), and the prose part, which is attributed to Asaṅga, is referred to as Asaṅga's commentary to the *Uttaratantra* (*rgyud bla thogs 'grel*). Tibetans are not alone in attributing the verse section to Maitreya. Basing on the *Uttaratantra* in the fragment Saka script, Takasaki states that the verses are credited to Maitreya even in Central Asia and India. See Takasaki, *A Study on the Ratnagotravibhāga,* 7. In the Chinese tradition, Fa-tsang (643–712) credited the authorship of the *Uttaratantra* to Sāramati. For an excellent discussion on the issue of the authorship of what came to be known as 'the root text of the *Uttaratantra* and its commentary" (*rgyud bla rtsa 'grel*) in Tibetan Buddhist literature, see Kazuo Kano, *rNgog Blo-ldan-shes-rab's Summary of the Ratnagotravibhāga: The First Tibetan Commentary on a Crucial Source for the Buddha-nature Doctrine* (PhD Dissertation, Hamburg University, 2006), 17–22. Hereafter, *rNgog Blo-ldan-shes-rab's Summary.*

10. See note 9. Takasaki claims that Asaṅga is not mentioned as the author of the prose section in any early Sanskrit manuscripts. See Takasaki, *A Study on the Ratnagotravibhāga,* 7. For a comparative analysis of commentarial literature, see Paul J. Griffiths, *Religious Reading: The Place of Reading in the Practice of Religion* (New York: Oxford University Press, 1999).

11. The ten are entity, cause, result, function, endowment, entry, temporal divisions, ever-pervasive, unchanging, and indivisibility. For an early English translation of the discussion of the ten aspects found in the *Uttaratantra,* see Eugene Obermiller, *The Sublime Science of the Great Vehicle to Salvation Being: A Manual of Buddhist Monism* (Acta Orientalia, IX, 1931), 287–338. Hereafter, *The Sublime Science of the Great Vehicle to Salvation Being.*

12. For the three reasons, see chapter 1, note 18.

13. The nine metaphors are as follows: 1) a buddha seated in a lotus, 2) honey, 3) kernels, 4) gold, 5) precious jewels, 6) sprouts, 7) a previous image of the Buddha, 8) universal king, and 9) a golden form. They are found in the *Tathāgatagarbhasūtra.* For an English translation of the sutra, see William Grosnick, "The Tathāgatagarbha Sūtra," in Donald S. Lopez, Jr., ed. *Buddhism Practice* (New Jersey: Princeton University Press, 1995). For a philological analysis of the nine metaphors as found in the sutra, see Micheal Zimmerman, *A Buddha Within: The Tathāgatagarbhasūtra, the Earliest Exposition o the Buddha-Nature in India.* Bibleotheca Philologica et Philosophica Buddhica IV (Tokyo: Soka University, 2002), 34–39.

14. The eight are 1) entity, 2) cause, 3) result, 4) function, 5) endowment, 6) entry, 7) permanent, and 8) inconceivable. For English translations of the eight aspects found in the *Uttaratantra,* see Takasaki, *A Study on the Ratnagotravibhāga,* 314–35, and Obermiller, *The Sublime Science of the Great Vehicle to Salvation Being,* 370–88.

15. For English translations of the relevant qualities found in the *Uttaratantra,* see Takasaki, *A Study on the Ratnagotravibhāga,* 338–50, and Obermiller, *The Sublime Science of the Great Vehicle to Salvation Being,* 388–97.

16. While the transmissions of the *Uttaratantra* discourse have a longer history in the Kagyü, Sakya, and Jonang schools, in the Nyingma (*rnying ma*) tradition, the transmission seems to have begun with Mipam's (*'ju mi pham rgya mtsho*, 1846–1912) commentary, one of the earliest Nyingma commentaries on the *Uttaratantra* by a Nyingma master. However, Khenpo Yeshe, a Nyingma Khenpo, who is a doctoral student in the Buddhist Studies Program at UC Berkeley, tells me that if the *Uttaratantra* is studied at Nyingma commentarial institutes, Khenpo Zhenphen's *Uttaratantra* commentary is preferred over Mipam's. For more on their commentaries, see my Conclusion.

17. Obermiller's *The Sublime Science of the Great Vehicle to Salvation Being* provides us with a good introduction and several helpful footnotes, but it was not intended to be a work on the Tibetan assimilation of the *Uttaratantra* and the doctrinal issues related to the text.

18. While it is an eye-opening critical edition of the Sanskrit manuscripts, it does not address the issues raised in the Tibetan commentaries on the *Uttaratantra*.

19. Takasaki's seminal work on the *Uttaratantra* has an excellent introduction. He compares the Sanskrit text with both Chinese and Tibetan translations, but his work does not deal with how the Tibetan scholars engaged with the treatise in Tibet between the twelfth and fifteenth centuries.

20. See David Seyfort Ruegg, "The Meanings of the Term Gotra and the Textual History of the Ratnagotravibhāga," *Bulletin of the School of Oriental and African Studies* 39 (1976). In this work, Ruegg primarily deals with how the term "buddha-nature" is explicated in the Indian Buddhist texts by primarily using a post–fourteenth-century Tibetan Geluk interpretation of buddha-nature.

21. S. K. Hookham, *The Buddha Within: Tathagatagarbha Doctrine according to the Shentong Interpretation of the Ratnagogtravibhaga* (Delhi: Sri Satguru, 1992). Hereafter, *The Buddha Within*. Hookham predominantly discusses the tathāgata-essence within the context of other-emptiness view without discussing the issues related to the *Uttaratantra* and the reception of the treatise that I discuss in my book.

22. Klaus-Dieter Mathes, *A Direct Path to the Buddha Within: Gö Lotsawa's Mahāmudra Interpretation of the Ratnagotravibhāga* (Boston: Wisdom, 2008). Hereafter, *A Direct Path to the Buddha Within*. Mathes deals mostly with a fifteenth-century Tibetan commentary on the *Uttaratantra* and does not entertain some of the significant doctrinal issues regarding the *Uttaratantra* before the fifteenth century in Tibet.

23. For a possible influence of the *Uttaratantra* on some early Indian treatises that exist only in Chinese translations, see Kano, *rNgog Blo-ldan-shes-rab's Summary*, 22–23.

24. For the influence of the *Uttaratantra* in Ratnākaraśānti's works, see ibid., 39–49.

25. For the influence of the *Uttaratantra* in Jñānaśrīmitra's works, see ibid., 32–38.

26. For a whole section devoted to the influence of the *Uttaratantra* in Maitrīpa's works, see ibid., 26–32.

27. The *Uttaratantra*'s influences are found in the works of scholars, such as Prajñākaramati (eleventh century), Atiśa, Sajjana, Yamari (ca. 1000–1060), Vairocanarakṣita, Rāmapāla (eleventh century), Sahajavajra (eleventh century), Abhayākaragupta (d. 1125), Śrīrāja Jagaddalāvāsin, Jayānanda, and so forth. See ibid., 49–82.

28. For information about Sajjana's short commentary on the *Uttaratantra* (*Mahāyānottaratantraśāstropadeśa*) consisting of only thirteen verses, see Kano, *rNgog Blo-ldan-shes-rab's Summary*, 505–18; the last few pages (513–18) have the text itself in Sanskrit. For information about Vairocanarakṣita's commentary (*Mahāyānottaratantraṭippaṇī*) consisting of eight folios, see, ibid., 519–57; pages 534–57 have the text itself in Sanskrit.

29. Regarding some problems with his reign date, see Luciana Petech, "The Disintegration of the Tibetan Kingdom," in *The History of Tibet*, ed. Alex McKay (London and New York: Routledge Curzon, 2003), 286.

30. Helmut Hoffman states, "In its course temples and monasteries were desecrated, translation-work brought to a halt, and the foreign monks banished. Tibetan religious were given the choice between returning to lay life or death, and they were forced to participate in hunting expeditions with bows and arrows. This was obviously a period of wild confusion and disorder and the Chinese sources report catastrophes, earthquakes, epidemics and famine. Buddhism was extirpated throughout Central Tibet." "Early and Medieval Tibet," in *The History of Tibet*, ed. Alex McKay (London and New York: Routledge Curzon, 2003), 57.

31. Atiśa and Naktso translated the text at Yerpa (*yer pa*) upon the request of Ngok Jangchup Jungné (*rngog byang chub 'byung gnas*, b. eleventh century). Although no definitive date has been given to the translation, it must have been translated between 1047 and 1054.

32. Ngok and Sajjana translated the text in Kashmir when the former was studying and translating Buddhist texts in India between 1076 and 1093.

33. Although *Blue Annals* mentions that Patsap Nyima Drak (*spa tshab nyi ma grags*, b. 1055) translated the treatise into Tibetan, nowhere in *Blue Annals* does it offer a date or a place for the translation. George Roerich, trans., *The Blue Annals* (Delhi: Motilal Banarsidaas, 1976), 350. Since many of Patsap's texts are believed to have been translated in Kashmir, it is very likely that Patsap translated the *Uttaratantra* in Kashmir during his twenty-three years (most likely from 1077–1100) in India. If Patsap had already translated the treatise before his return to Tibet from India, then the three early translations—one by Naktso and Atiśa, another by Ngok and Sajjana, and one by Patsap—had been completed between 1047 (the year Atiśa arrived in Tibet) and 1100 (the year Patsap supposedly departed from India).

34. It is believed that Marpa Dopa Chökyi Wangchuk (*mar pa do pa chos kyi dbang phyug*, 1042–1136), Yarlung Lotsawa (*yar lung lo tsa ba grags pa rgyal mtshan*, 1242–1346), and Jonang Lotsawa (*jo nang lo tsa ba blo gros dpal*,

ca. 1299–1353) produced three more translations. See Roerich, *Blue Annals,* 359. Kano suggests that these three translations seem to have already become unavailable to Gö Lotsawa (*'gos lo tsa ba gzhon nu dpal,* 1392–1481). See Kano, *rNgog Blo-ldan-shes-rab's Summary,* 98.

35. For information regarding the Tibetan translations and the two streams of interpretations, see Roerich, *Blue Annals,* 347–50. Also see Leonard W. J. van der Kuijp, *Contributions to the Development of Tibetan Epistemology: From the Eleventh to the Thirteenth century* (Wiesbaden: Franz Steiner, 1983), 41–45, for the two streams of transmission of the *Uttaratantra.* Henceforth, *Contributions to the Development of Tibetan Epistemology.*

36. See Mathes, *A Direct Path to the Buddha Within,* 2–3.

37. Kongtrül also speaks of the two in his *Uttaratantra* commentary: "There developed two methods of teaching [the *Uttaratantra*]: explication of [the *Uttaratantra*] through the medium of logical inferences by relying on Madhyamaka treatises and delineation of the meaning of [the tathāgata] essence through the medium of direct perception." *'chad tshul gyi rim pa gnyis su byung ste/ dbu ma'i gzhung la brten pa rjes su dpag pa'i lam gyis bshad pa dang snying po'i don mngon sum gyi lam gyis bshad pa'o//* See Kongtrül Lodrö Tayé, *theg pa chen po rgyud bla ma'i bstan bcos snying po'i don mngon sum lam gyi bshad srol dang sbyar ba'i rnam par 'grel pa phyir mi ldog pa seng ge'i nga ro* (Varanasi: Kagyu Relief and Protection Committee, 1999) 19. Hereafter, *Lion's Roar of the* Uttaratantra.

38. The dialectical tradition is also referred to as "the learning/contemplative tradition" (*thos bsam gyi lugs*). See Kano, *rNgog Blo-ldan-shes-rab's Summary,* 130.

39. For more on Tsen Khawoché and Zu Gawé Dorjé, see Roerich, *Blue Annals,* 347–48. For a list of Tibetan commentaries, see Kano, *rNgog Blo-ldan-shes-rab's Summary,* 594–600.

40. Gelong Chöshé, a Kadam scholar, had access to the commentaries or notes written down by Tsen Khawoché and Zu Gawai Dorjé. It is clear that they were still extant prior to the fifteenth century. See chapter 2, note 4.

41. Tsen Khawoché apparently received the transmission of the *Uttaratantra* through Zu Gawé Dorjé to whom Sajjana entrusted Tsen Khawoché. Sajjana most likely entrusted Tsen Khawoché to Zu Gawé Dorjé because of the language barrier between himself and Tsen Khawoché. On the other hand, Ngok received the transmission directly from Sajjana.

42. Roerich, *Blue Annals,* 347.

43. Ibid.

Chapter 1

1. For more information on the life story of Ngok, see Ralf Kramer, *The Great Translator: Life and Wroks of rNgog Blo ldan shes rab* (München: Indus Verlag, 2007); David P. Jackson, "An Early Biography of rNgok Lo-tsā-ba bLo

ldan shes rab," in *Tibetan Studies: Proceedings of the 6th Seminar of the International Association for Tibetan Studies*, ed. Per Kvaerne (Oslo: Institute for Comparative Research in Human Culture, 1994), 372–92. Also see van der Kuijp, *Contributions to the Development of Tibetan Epistemology*, 29–48, and Kevin Vose, *Resurrecting Candrakīrti: Disputes in the Tibetan Creation of Prāsaṅgika* (Boston: Wisdom Publications, 2009), 45–49, for Ngok's life story.

2. For a brief history of Sangpu Neuthok (*gsang phu ne'u thog*) monastery, see Leonard W. J. van der Kuijp, "The Monastery of Gsang-phu ne'u-thog and Its Abbatial Succession from ca. 1073 to 1250," *Berliner Indologische Studien* 3 (1987): 103–10. The monastery was established by Ngok Lekpé Sherap (tenth–eleventh centuries). For a brief life story of Ngok Lekpé Sherap (*rngog legs pa'i shes rab*), see Vose, *Resurrecting Candrakīrti*, 46–47. Also, see van der Kuijp, *Contributions to the Development of Tibetan Epistemology*, 31–32.

3. In his *Contributions to the Development of Tibetan Epistemology*, 32–33, van der Kuijp says, "While RNgok Lo-tsā-ba [Ngok] is best known for his work in the so-called pāramitāyāna which includes epistemology, prajñāpāramitā, madhyamaka, and abhidharma, his literary activities that pertain to the vajrayāna should also not be underestimated insofar as he translated some eighteen works that fall within this domain of Buddhism." For the abbatial lineage of the Sangpu monastery, see Shunzu Onoda, "Abbatial Successions of the Colleges of gSang phu sne'u thog Monastery" (*Bulletin of the National Museum of Ethnology* 15, no. 4 (1990): 1057.

4. For more information about Chapa, see van der Kuijp, *Contributions to the Development of Tibetan Epistemology*, 59–84.

5. In his *Contributions to the Development of Tibetan Epistemology*, 61, van der Kuijp states, "It is important to stress that Phya-pa was unilingual and had no knowledge of Sanskrit whatsoever; this point is repreatedly underlined by the Tibetan historians themselves."

6. van der Kuijp, *Contributions to the Development of Tibetan Epistemology*, 69.

7. Vose's *Resurrecting Candrakīrti* examines the arguments that the two thinkers formulate in great detail.

8. In his commentary on the *Madhyamakāvatāra*, Jayānanda states, "Moreover, in order to point out [some] other sutras that require interpretation, . . . For instance, those that teach the tathāgata-essence require interpretation." "yang drang ba'i don gyi mdo sde gzhan bstan par bya ba'i phyir . . . dper na de bzhin gshegs pa'i snying po gsungs pa de ni drang ba'i don yin la." See Jayānanda, *dbu ma la 'jug pa'i 'grel bshad* (snga 'gyur rnying ma'i glegs bam rin po che'i dbu phyogs, n.d.), 1057. Henceforth, *Explanation of the Madhyamakāvatāra*. Jayānanda devotes a substantial number of pages to explaining the difference between definitive meaning and provisional meaning and why the tathāgata-essence teachings are provisional. Yet as Kano points out, "[Jayānanda] obviously accepts the Buddha nature doctrine as an authoritative teaching. Jayānanda states it impossible to accept the meaning

of *mithyātvaniyatagora* (or –*dhātu*, "those who are determined to unable to attain the release") literally, since it contradicts to the notion that all sentient beings have the Buddha nature. In this way, he associated the Buddha nature doctrine with the single-vechicle theory." See Kano, *rNgog Blo-ldan-shes-rab's Summary*, 77.

9. However, the commentary is no longer available. See Kano, *rNgog Blo-ldan-shes-rab's Summary*, 183.

10. For a detailed argument that Drolungpa and Ngok held similar views regarding these issues, see Kano, *rNgog Blo-ldan-shes-rab's Summary*, 183–87.

11. See Gampopa Sonam Rinchen, *thar pa rin po che'i rgyan*, in *The Dalai Lama Tibeto-Indological Series XXVI*, ed. Khenpo Sonam Gyalpo (Sarnath: CIHTS, 1999) (henceforth, *Ornament of the Precious Liberation*), wherein the *Uttaratantra* is quoted several times for legitimation, but it is never mentioned explicitly as a definitive work. See Gampopa Sonam Rinchen, *rje dvags po'i zhal gdams dang rje sgom tshul gyi zhus lan, phag gru'i zhus lan* and *rje sgom tshul gyi zhus lan*, Gampopa's Collected Works, vol. KHA (Kathmandu: Shri Gautam Buddha Vihara, 2000) (henceforth, *Responses to Questions*), wherein no reference to the *Uttaratantra* is made . . . See Gampopa Sonam Rinchen, *rje dvags po lha rje'i gsung zhal gyi bdud rtsi thun mong ma yin pa* (*The Uncommon Nectar*), DZA, 317–85, *phyag rgya chen po gsal byed kyi man ngag* (*Instruction on the Mahāmudra*), ZHA, 387–405, *phyag rgya chen po'i rtsa ba la ngo sprod pa zhes kyang bya, snang ba lam khyer gyi rtog pa cig mchog ces kyang bya, phyag rgya chen po gnyug ma mi gyur ba zhes kyang bya* (*Introduction to the Mahāmudra*) YA, 481–509, and *snying po don gyi gdams pa phyag rgya chen po'i 'bum tig* (*Instruction on the Essence*) A, 441–79, Gampopa's Collected Works, vol. 2 (Darjeeling: Kargyud Sungrab Nyamso Khang, 1982) wherein no references to the *Uttaratantra*, the Three Dharma Wheels, and the definitive and provisional meanings are found.

12. *rje sgam po pa'i zhal nas 'o skol gyi phyag rgya chen po 'di'i gzhung ni bcom ldan 'das byams pas mdzad pa'i theg pa chen po rgyud bla ma'i bstan bcos yin no*// See Kongtrül, *Lion's Roar of the* Uttaratantra, 20.

13. It is stated that Mabja had previously studied with Chapa but left the latter to study the Prāsaṅgika-Madhyamaka with Jayānanda (c. 1100). See Vose, *Resurrecting Candrakīrti*, 55.

14. Mabja Jangchup Tsöndü, *dbu ma rtsa ba shes rab kyi 'grel ba 'thad pa'i rgyan* (Sikkim: dpal rgyal ba kar ma pa'i Collections, 1975), 8. Hereafter, *Commentary* to the *Madhyamakakārikā*.

15. *de ltar sems can thams cad sangs rgyas kyi snying po can yin na mdo sde rgyan las rigs chad pa'i gang zag gsungs pa dang mi 'gal lam zhe na mi 'gal te de ni sems tsam pa'i dbang du byas nas drang ba'i don gyi bshad pa yin gyi/ 'dir ni rigs chad pa mi srid de/ rgyud bla ma las rdzogs sangs. . . . zhes gsungs so*// See Drakpa Gyeltsen, *rgyud kyi mngon par rtogs pa rin po che'i ljon shing*, Collected Works, vol. 3 (Varanasi: CIHTS, 1987), 2. Henceforth, *Precious Tree*

of the Tantric Path. Sonam Tsemo (1142–1182), one of the Five Greatest Sakya Masters, quotes from the *Uttaratantra* a few times in his *General Presentation of the Tantric Systems* (*rgyud sde spyi rnam*), but the text does not explicitly mention whether the *Uttaratantra* is a definitive or a provisional work. He talks about the three wheels of the Buddha's teachings, but leaves no allusion as to whether the *Uttaratantra* explicates on the meaning of the middle wheel or the last wheel. For reference, see Sonam Tsemo, *rgyud sde spyi rnam*, Collected Works of Sakya, vol. GA, (no publication date), 50b–51b. Hereafter, *General Tantric Presentation.* Furthermore, he deals with the issues of definitive and provisional texts, but offers no hint as to whether he views the *Uttaratantra* as a definitive or an interpretable work. For more on this, see ibid., 18–20. Moreover, Sonam Tsemo's commentary on Śāntideva's *Bodhicaryāvatāra* never makes reference to the treatise. See Sonam Tsemo, *spyod 'jug gi 'grel ba*, Collected Works of Sakya, vol. CA, (no publication date). Henceforth, *Commentary to the Bodhicaryāvatāra.* On Śāntideva's philosophical thoughts, see David Seyfort Ruegg, *The Literature of the Madhyamaka School of Philosophy in India*, vol. 7, Fasc. 1 (Wiesbaden: Harrassovitz, 1981), 82–86.

16. Ngok Loden Sherap, *theg chen rgyud bla'i don bsdus pa* (Dharamsala: Library of Tibetan Works and Archives, 1993). Hereafter, *Condensed Meaning of the Uttaratantra.*

17. Chapa Chökyi Gyeltsen, *theg pa chen po rgyud bla ma'i bstan bcos kyi tshig dang don gyi cha rgya cher bsnyad pa phra ba'i don gsal ba* (Collected Works of Kadam Masters. vol. 7, Chengdu, si khron mi rigs dpe skrun khang, 2006). Hereafter, *Illumination of the Meaning of the* Uttaratantra.

18. For the verse in Tibetan, see "*theg pa chen po mdo sde'i rgyan dang rgyud bla rtsa 'grel*" in *gangs can rig brgya'i sgo 'byed lde mig*, vol. 27 (Beijing: mi rigs dpe skrun khang, 1998), 81–82. Henceforth, *The Sūtrālaṃkāra and the Uttaratantra.* It is verse 28 of the chapter 1 of the *Uttaratantra* that appears in Takasaki's English translation (p. 197).

19. Ngok states, *phyogs 'di la ni de bzhin gshegs pa ni dngos po yin la, sems can 'di'i snying po can du ni btags pa yin te de thob pa'i skal ba yod pa la des khyab par btags pa'i phyir ro//* See Nogk, *Condensed Meaning of the Uttaratantra*, 57. See also Mathes, *A Direct Path to the Buddha Within*, 28–29 for Ngok's position.

20. " 'It [that is, buddha-body] radiates' means it is pervasive, in that all sentient beings are able to achieve [it].)" *de 'phro ba ni des khyab pa ste, sems can thams cad kyis thob tu rung ba'i phyir khyab pa yin no//* See ibid., 57.

21. *sems can thams cad ni de bzhin gshegs pa'i snying po can no zhes bya ba 'dis kyang thams cad bla na med pa yang dag par rdzogs pa'i byang chub kyi go 'phang thob par rung ba nyid du yongs su bstan te//* See Kamalaśīla, *Madhyamakāloka*, bstan 'gyur, vol. dbu ma (SA), (Beijing: krung go'i bod kyi shes rig dpe skrun khang, 2000), 1383.

22. *rnam par dag pa'i gnas skabs kyi de bzhin nyid ni rdzogs sangs sku 'bras bu chos kyi sku yin la/ de 'phro ba ni des khyab pa ste, sems can thams cad kyis thob tu rung pa'i phyir khyab pa'ang yin no// 'di la de bzhin gshegs pa ni dngos*

yin la, sems can gyi snying po ni btags pa ste/ thob pa'i skal ba yod pa la des khyab par btags pa'i phyir ro// See Chapa, *Illumination of the Meaning of the Uttaratantra*, 229. As I will show later in chapter 2, Sangpu Lodrö Tsungmé criticizes Chapa for the latter's position on the distinction between tathāgata-essence and sentient beings' essence (*sems can gyi snying po*). See Chapa, *Illumination of the Meaning of the Uttaratantra*, 208–10.

23. *de bzhin gshegs pa dang sems can de'i snying po can gnyis ka dngos su yin te . . .* See Ngok, *Condensed Meaning of the Uttaratantra*, 57.

24. *de bzhin nyid dbyer med phyir zhes pa ni stong pa nyid la tha dad med pa'i rang bzhin de bzhin nyid kyi snying po ste/ de bzhin gshegs pa dang sems can gyi snying po gnyi ga dngos su yin te/ de bzhin nyid rang bzhin gyi dri mas dben pa ni glo bur gyi dri ma dang bcas pa'i tshe sangs rgyas kyi rang bzhin yin pa dang sems can gyi rgyud la nges pa'i phyir ro//* See Chapa, *Illumination of the Meaning of the Uttaratantra*, 229.

25. *de bzhin nyid rnam par dag pa'i gnas skabs thob pa'i rgyu dge ba'i bag chags shes rab dang snying rje'i sa bon ni de bzhin gshegs pa'i rgyu yin pas de bzhin gshegs pa zhes btags pa yin la/ sems can gyi snying po ni dngos po kho na yin no//* See Ngok, *Condensed Meaning of the Uttaratantra*, 58. For Mathes' English translation of the passage, see Mathes, *A Direct Path to the Buddha Within*, 28.

26. *rigs yod phyir na zhes bya ba ni de bzhin nyid thob pa'i rgyu dge ba'i bag chags shes rab dang snying rje'i sa bon de bzhin gshegs pa'i rgyu yin pas de bzhin gshegs pa zhes btags pa yin la/ sems can gyi snying po ni dngos po kho nar yin no//* See Chapa, *Illumination of the Meaning of the Uttaratantra*, 229–30.

27. Dratsépa, as is explained in chapter 5, takes a step further and claims that all sentient beings do not have the tathāgata-essence at all. While he cites Ngok's passages on these for a textual justification, Ngok does not explicitly state that sentient beings do not have tathagāta-essence.

28. "Suchness that is naturally devoid of defilement is the nature of a buddha even when it is [defiled] by adventitious obstruction, and it certainly exists in the mental continuum of sentient beings." *de bzhin nyid dri ma rang bzhin gyis dben pa ni glo bur gyi sgrib pa dang bcas pa'i tshe yang sangs rgyas kyi rang bzhin yin pa dang sems can gyi rgyud la nges par gnas pa'i phyir ro//* See Ngok, *Condensed Meaning of the Uttaratantra*, 57.

29. *bstan pa'i chos la yang gnyis te/ don dam pa'i bden pa bstan pa dang kun rdzob kyi bden pa bstan pa'o//* See Ngok, *Condensed Meaning of the Uttaratantra*, 76.

30. *don dam pa bstan pa ni sbrang rtsi dang 'dra ste/ zhim pa'i ro gcig dang ldan pa'i phyir ro// kun rdzob ston pa ni 'bras bu'i snying po dang 'dra ste/ sna tshogs pa kun tu khyab pas so//* See ibid., 78.

31. Chapa, *Illumination of the Meaning of the Uttaratantra*, 164. Some of these words are employed in Sangpu Lodrö Tsungmé's commentary as well.

32. Althogh Ngok states, "So, having observed the ultimate and the conventional [phenomena] mentioned in this way [in the middle-wheel sutras], superior beings' qualities are engendered. Because of this there is no

contradiction in teaching the ultimate emptiness as cause [here in the last wheel] . . . ," he never states that these phrases in the *Uttaratantra* are definitive. *de ltar bstan pa'i don dam pa dang kun rdzob de nyid la dmigs nas 'phags pa'i chos rab tu 'byung bas na don dam pa stong pa nyid de'ang rgyu nyid du rnam par 'jog pa mi 'gal bar ston pa/* See Ngok, *Condensed Meaning of the Uttaratantra*, 90.

33. *gzhan nas stong par bstan pa ni sgra ji bzhin pa yin la/ 'dir khams sangs rgyas kyi rgyur yod par bstan pa dgongs pa can yin pas mi 'gal te/ 'di sgra ji bzhin ma yin pa'i phyir ro//* See Chapa, *Illumination of the Meaning of the Uttaratantra*, 295.

34. *'phags pa shes rab kyi pha rol tu phyin pa la sogs par don dam par mtshan nyid thams cad bkag pa yin yang/ 'dir sangs rgyas kyi chos skye ba'i rgyur bshad pa dang mi 'gal te/ de ni don dam pa'i mtshan nyid tsam bden pa gnyis kyi sgo nas bstan la/ 'dir ni der bstan pa'i mtshan nyid de la dmigs nas sangs rgyas kyi chos 'grub pa'i rgyu yin no zhes der brjod pa'i mtshan nyid de nyid rgyur gzhag pa yin no//* See Ngok, *Condensed Meaning of the Uttaratantra*, 89.

35. *sngar de ltar rnam par bzhag pa ni shes rab kyi pha rol tu phyin pa la sogs pa'i mdor bzhag pa'o//bla ma'i ces bya ba ni rgyud bla ma'i brjod bya de bzhin gshegs pa'i snying po'i mdo 'o// khams yod nyid ces bstan pa mi 'gal lam zhe na mi 'gal te/ yul stong pa yin yang yul can las sangs rgyas kyi chos ksyes bas de rgyur brjod pa'o//* See Chapa, *Illumination of the Meaning of the Uttaratantra*, 296.

36. *sangs rgyas kyi ye shes sems can gyi rgyud la yod pa de gang zhe na chos kyi dbyings so// de ji ltar ye shes yin zhe na bcom ldan 'das kyis chos thams cad mtshan nyid med par skad cig gcig dang ldan pa'i shes rab kyis mkhyen pas na shes rab de shes bya dang dbyer med do//* See Ngok, *Condensed Meaning of the Uttaratantra*, 56.

37. *shes par bya ba ni rtogs par bya ba yin la/ shes par bya ba thams cad kyang de bzhin nyid du 'du bas rtogs par bya ba ni khams so/ de rtogs par byed pa ni shes bya la sgrib pa mtha' dag zad pa'i ye shes yin pas rtogs pa ni byang chub bo//* See Ngok, *Condensed Meaning of the Uttaratantra*, 57.

38. *don dam pa ni ngag gi yul ma yin pa'i phyir te/ rnam par rtog pa ni kun rdzob yin pas don dam pa rtog pa'i yul ma yin pa'i phyir ro// ngag gis brjod du med pa'i don yang 'dir sgra dang rtog pa'i zhen gzhi ma yin pa la dgongs te/* See Ngok, *Condensed Meaning of the Uttaratantra*, 11–12.

39. *de la dngos su brjod du med pa ni rtog pa la sgra spyi dang 'brel bar mi snang ba yin la/ de ni don spyi kho na rtog pa la sgra spyi dang 'brel bar snang gi don rang gi mtshan nyid thams cad rtog pa la sgra spyi dang 'brel bar snang ba med pas/* See Chapa, *Illumination of the Meaning of the Uttaratantra*, 172. For Chapa's view on the typologies of minds and objects, see chapters 22 and 23 of Georges Dreyfus, *Recognizing Reality: Dharamakīrti's Philosophy and Its Tibetan Interpretations* (Albany: State University of New York Press, 1997).

40. See Dreyfus, *Recognizing Reality*, 382–83.

41. *gal te khams stong pa nyid de dngos dang zhen nas kyang brjod du med pa gong du bstan par gong du bstan na 'dir don de brjod pa zhes 'gal lo zhe na/ mi 'gal te khams stong pa nyid don dam pa de zhen nas kyang brjod du med kyang*

stong pa'i don spyi dngos su brjod du yod pa stong pa yongs gcod zhen nas brjod du yod pas 'dir don de brjod pa zhes bya ba yin no// don dam pa'i khams de thob pa ni mthong lam yan chad du gsal snang gis 'ga' yang mthong pa med pa'i tshul gyis stong pa nyid yul du byas pa yin la/ de dang rjes su mthun pa'i lam ni chos mchog man chad pa'i don spyi rnam pas stong pa nyid la dmigs pa ste stong pa'i don spyi shar ba dang phyi rol na stong pa yongs gcod la zhen pa sgro btags la dmigs pa 'khrul pa yin yang sgro 'dogs des mi stong pa'i sgro 'dogs kyi gnyen po byed pas lam du 'gyur te/ See Chapa, *Illumination of the Meaning of the Uttaratantra,* 174.

42. The paths in order are the path of accumulation, path of preparation, path of seeing, path of meditation, and path of no-more learning.

43. Chapa, *Illumination of the Meaning of the Uttaratantra,* 172–74.

44. The terms are "nonabiding nirvāṇa wheel" (*mi gnas pa'i myang 'das kyi 'khor lo*), "jewel cycle" (*dkon mchog gi 'khor lo*), "proximity cause that is in one continuum' (*nye ba'i rgyu rygud gcig tu gtogs pa*), "distant cause that is in separate continuums" (*ring ba'i rgyu rgyud tha dad du gtogs pa*), and "abiding buddha-element" (*gnas pa'i khams*).

45. Naturally abiding buddha-nature generally refers to emptiness or ultimate truth in the *Uttaratantra.*

46. Developmental buddha-nature generally refers to positive deeds that one accumulates over the path in the *Uttaratantra.*

47. *thog ma med dus can gyi khams/ chos rnams kun gyi gnas yin te// de yod pas na 'gro kun dang/ mya ngan 'das pa'ang thob par 'gyur//* The verse appears in the *Asaṅga Commentary* in *The Sūtrālaṃkāra and the Uttaratantra,* 197. It is important to point out here that the *Asaṅga Commentary* itself does not employ "all-basis-consciousness" when commenting on the same stanza. In his *Mountain Doctrine,* Jeffrey Hopkins mentions that Tsongkhapa identifies that the stanza comes from the *Mahāyānābhidharmasūtra.* For reference, see Jeffrey Hopkins, *Mountain Doctrine: Tibet's Fundamental Treatise on Other-Emptiness and the Buddha-Matirx* (Ithaca: Snow Lion, 2006), 760, note 36. Both Butön and Dratsépa, as will be explained in chapter 5, mention that the verse is cited in Asaṅga's *Mahāyānasaṃgraha* where it is referred to as all-basis-consciousness.

48. In his *Condensed Meaning of the Uttaratantra* (p. 83), Ngok states, *de 'dra ba nus pa sna tshogs pa can de la ni kun gzhi'i rnam par shes pa zhes kyang brjod do//* Here, Ngok is referring to the buddha-element which is explained as having the potential to produce both contaminated and uncontaminated phenomena

49. *rang bzhin du gnas pa'i rigs stong pa nyid la sngon gyi dus gzung du gtan med la/ rgyas pa las gyur pa'i rigs dge ba'i sa bon la sngon gyi mtha' gzung du yod kyang de'i rten kun gzhi la sngon gyi mtha' med pa la nye bar btags pa'o//* See Chapa, *Illumination of the Meaning of the Uttaratantra,* 285.

50. *rang bzhin du gnas pa'i rigs la dmigs pa'i tshul bzhin yid la byed pa goms pa las mya ngan las 'das pa'i chos byung la/ yang bsgrubs pa las byung pa'i rigs kyi nus pa 'phel ba las kyang thar pa 'byung pa'i phyir ro//* See Chapa, *Illumination of the Meaning of the Uttaratantra,* 285.

51. *rang bzhin du gnas pa'i rigs stong pa nyid kyis 'khrul gzhi byas nas tshul bzhin ma yin pa yid la byed pa 'byung la/ de las las dang nyon mongs pa dang. . . . bsgrubs pa las byung pa'i rigs thar pa'i cha mthun gyi dge ba'i sa bon las kun nas nyon mongs mi 'byung yang de'i rten kun gzhi la nyon mongs pa'i sa bon bsgos pa las kun nas nyon mongs pa 'byung bas. . . .* See Chapa, *Illumination of the Meaning of the Uttaratantra,* 285–86.

52. For his discussion of the cut-off buddha-nature, see *Illumination of the Meaning of the Uttaratantra,* 233–46. The early sources that are generally cited for the explication of the cut-off buddha-nature are *Nirvāṇasūtra,* Asaṅga's *Yogācārabhūmi* and Maitreya's *Sutrālaṃkāra,* all of which are asserted by many Tibetan scholars as presenting the view of Cittamātra, as opposed to that of the Madhyamaka, which accepts that all sentient beings have the buddha-nature.

53. *ngo bo nyid med par smra bas ni [rang bzhin du gnas pa'i rigs] chos nyid stong pa nyid la smra bas gtan rigs chad pa mi 'dod pa yin no//* See Chapa, *Illumination of the Meaning of the Uttaratantra,* 284.

54. Chapa, *Illumination of the Meaning of the Uttaratantra,* 247.

55. Ibid., 288.

56. For more information on this, see ibid., 284.

57. In his *Illumination of the Meaning of the Uttaratantra* (p. 284), Chapa contrasts the Cittamātra system that asserts the cut-off buddha-nature with the proponents of the Madhyamaka, who assert that all sentient beings have the buddha-nature.

58. *The Sūtrālaṃkāra and the Uttaratantra* (p. 201) refers to the "emptiness-that-is-nonexistence-upon-having-disintegrated" (*zhig nas med pa'i stong pa*). For more information on these terms, see Chapa, *Illumination of the Meaning of the Uttaratantra,* 288–92. Rendawa speaks of these two emptinesses, albeit using slightly different words, severed emptiness (*chad pa'i stong pa nyid*) and secondary emptiness (*nyi tshe ba'i stong pa nyid*) in his *dbu ma la 'jug pa'i rnam bshad de kho na nyid gsal ba'i sgron ma,* dpal ldan sa skya pa'i gsung rab, vol. 13, (Beijing: mi rigs dpe skrun khang, 2003). Henceforth, *The Lamp That Illuminates Suchness.* For information on how Dölpopa explains the emptiness that is the-one-being-empty-of-the-other (*gcig gis gcig stong pa'i stong nyid*) delineated in the *Laṅkāvatārasūtra,* see Jeffrey Hopkins, *Mountain Doctrine: Tibet's Fundamental Treatise on Other-Emptiness and the Buddha-Matrix* (Ithaca: Snow Lion, 2006), 228.

Chapter 2

1. See Candrakīrti, *Commentary on the Madhyamakāvatāra* (*dbu ma la 'jug pa'i bshad pa*) (Cazadero, CA: ye shes sde'i chos 'khor 'khrul dpar khang, 2003), 3101–305.

2. Jayānanda quotes from the *Uttaratantra* a great deal to substantiate many of his views. He wrote the commentary in reaction against Svātantrika interpretation held by Tibetan scholars, such as Chapa and others. See Jayānanda, *Explanation of the Madhyamakāvatāra*.

3. See David Jackson, *The Entrance Gate for the Wise: Sa-skya Paṇḍita on Indian and Tibetan Traditions of Pramāṇa and Philosophical Debate* (Vienna: Arbeitskreis fur Tibetishe und Buddhistische Studien Universitat Wien, 1987), 1. Hereafter, *The Entrance Gate for the Wise*.

4. I presented a paper, "An Early Contemplative Interpretation of Buddha-Nature from a Kadam's Perspective," that examines Gelong Chöshé's short *Uttaratantra* commentary, *The Words of Inconceivable Instruction on the Uttaratantra Treatise* (*bstan bcos rgyud bla ma'ai gdams ngag bsam mi khyab kyi yi ge*), at the International Associaiton for Tibetan Studies Conference in Ulaanbbatar in 2013. I was not able to find any information about the author, but the author identifies himself in the transmission lineage of Tsen Khawoché and Zu Gawai Dorjé. He even mentions that he consulted *Uttaratantra* commentaries or notes written by these two early figures of the contemplative tradition of the *Uttaratantra*. As far as I know, his commentary is the earliest extant commentary that mentions these texts in this context. He interprets the *Uttaratantra* as a definitive text that teaches that the buddha-element is free from defilements. I am working on the article tentatively called "An Early Contemplative Interpretation of Buddha-Nature from a Kadam's Perspective." For the commentary, see Gelong Chöshé, *The Words of Inconceivable Instruction on the Uttaratantra Treatise* (*bstan bcos rgyud bla ma'ai gdams ngag bsam mi khyab kyi yi ge*), in *The Collected Works of Kadam Masters*, vol. 76 (dpal brtsegs bod yig dpe rnying zhib 'jug khang, 2009). I have not included his work for my analysis in this book.

5. His short commentary on the *Uttaratantra* is also from the contemplative tradition of the *Uttaratantra*. Klaus-Dieter Mathes summarizes the commentary in one of his recent articles. Mathes demonstrates that the *Uttaratantra* commentary equates the "buddha-nature (or natural luminosity) with the *dharmakāya*. For his article, see Klaus-Dieter Mathes, "The gzhan stong model of reality: Some more material on its origin, transmission, and interpretation," in the *Journal of International Association of Buddhist Studies* 34, nos. 1–2 (2012): 187–223. For a recent English translation of the commentary, see Karl Brunnhölzl, *When the Clouds Part: The Uttaratantra and Its Meditative Tradition as a Bridge between Sūtra and Tantra* (Boston: Snow Lion, 2014), 777–88. I have not included this *Uttaratantra* commentary as a subject of my analysis in this book.

6. Vose says, "The famed nephew of Sonam Tsemo and Drakpa Gyeltsen and the fourth Sakya hierarch, Sakya Paṇḍita Kunga Gyaltsen (1182–1251), may have ended this period of contested Madhyamaka exegesis [referring to the Prāsaṅgika Madhyamaka and the Svātantrika Madhyamaka

interpretations] when he adopted the Prāsaṅgika view." See Vose, *Resurrecting Candrakīrti*, 59.

7. Jackson says, "Another early Western scholar to notice the importance of the Sdom gsum rab dbye was E. Gene Smith. In his introduction to Kong-sprul's Shes bya kun khyab (1970), p. 4, [Gene] said [*Distinguishing the Three Vows*] was "written largely to refute the dgongs gcig heresy of 'Bri-gung Skyob-pa 'jin-rten-mgon-po.'"" See Jackson, *The Entrance Gate for the Wise*, 47. Jared Rhoton argues, "In his late forties and fifties, Sapan seems to have shifted his main energies toward deeper doctrinal concerns. *A Clear Differentiation of the Three Codes* (*sDom gsum rab dbye*), one of the major works he wrote in mid-life (perhaps in about 1232), reflects this." See Jared Rhoton (trans.), *A Clear Differentiation of the Three Codes: Essential Distinctions among the Individual Liberation, Great Vehicle, and Tantric Systems* (Albany: State University of New York Press, 2002), 15. Henceforth, *A Clear Differentiation of the Three Codes*.

8. Sapen argues that the sutras and the *Uttaratantra* teach the buddha-essence using analogies such as the precious jewel wrapped in dirty clothes should be understood as provisional teachings. Furthermore, he says that Candrakīrti's *Madhyamakāvatāra* speaks of such texts as provisional as well. See Sakya Paṇḍita Kunga Gyeltsen, *sdom gsum rab dbye*, in *The Collected Works of the Founding Masters of Sa-skya*, vol. 12 (Dehradun: Sakya Center, 1993), 17. Henceforth, *Distinguishing the Three Vows*.

9. Jackson includes the *Five Treatises of Maitreya, Madhyamakāvatāra, Mūlamadhyamakakārikā, Catuhśataka*, and *Distinguishing the Three Vows* in the "eighteen of great renown" (*grags chen bco brgyad*) and shows that, according to Zhuchen Tsültrim Rinchen (*zhu chen tsul khrims rin chen*, 1697–1774), the studies of these treatises were established during the time of Yaktön Sangyé Pel (*gyag ston sangs rgyas dpal*, 1350–1414) and Rendawa Zhönnu Lodrö (*red mda' ba gzhon nu blo gros*, 1349–1412) at places such as Sakya and Ngamring (*rngam ring*). See Jackson, *The Entrance Gate for the Wise*, 158, note 72.

10. See Rhoton, *A Clear Differentiation of the Three Codes*, 4.

11. For the fifteen issues, see ibid., 21–22.

12. See ibid., 9.

13. See ibid.

14. According to the story, Sapen had a dream in which he received signs from the Buddha, Manjuśrī and Nāgārjuna indicating that he must complete the work. See ibid.

15. The Tibetan verses are as follows: *mu stegs grangs can pa rnams ni/ gshis la dge sdig yod ces zer// rgyu la 'bras bu gnas par 'dod// bod kyang la la de rjes 'brang// rdo rje rgyal mtshan bsngo ba las/ 'gro kun dge ba ji snyed yod// byas dang byed 'gyur byed pa zhes/ gsungs pa'i dgongs pa 'chad pa la/ kha cig grags can lugs bzhin du/ yod pa'i dge ba zhes bya ba/ rang byung du ni grub par 'dod// de la bde gshegs snying po zer// grangs can lugs 'di mi 'thad pas/ lung dang rigs pas dgag par bya// bde gshegs snying po zhes bya ba/ chos dbyings 'gyur med nyid la*

gsungs// de skad du yang rgyud bla las/ sems ni rang bzhin 'od gsal ba/ nam mkha' *bzhin du 'gyur med gsung//* See Sapen, *Distinguishing the Three Vows*, 9. For an English translation of these verses, see Rhoton, *A Clear Differentiation of the Three Codes*, 49. For information on how the verses are divided, see Rhoton, *A Clear Differentiation of the Three Codes*, 277.

16. For verse 59, see Rhoton, *A Clear Differentiation of the Three Codes*, 49.

17. See ibid., 58. The verses in Tibetan are as follows: '*on kyang mdo sde 'ga' zhig dang/ theg pa chen po rgyud bla mar/ gos ngan nang na rin chen ltar/ sems can rnams la sangs rgyas kyi/ snying po yod par gsungs pa ni/ dgongs pa yin par shes par bya// de yi dgongs gzhi stong nyid yin/ dgos pa skyon lnga spang phyir gsungs// dngos la gnod byed tshad ma ni/ de 'dra'i sangs rgyas khams yod na/ mu stegs bdag dang mtshungs pa dang// bden pa'i dngos por 'gyur phyir dang// nges pa'i don gyi mdo sde dang/ rnam pa kun tu 'gal phyir ro// 'di don de bzhin gshegs pa yi/ snying po'i le'u'i mdo sder ltos// slob dpon zla ba grags pas kyang/ dbu ma la ni 'jug pa las/ bde gshegs snying po drang don du/ gsungs pa de yang shes par gyis//* See Sapen, *Distinguishing the Three Vows*, 17. Rhoton here translates the word "*sangs rgyas khams*" in verse 140 as "Buddha-realm," which I have translated as "buddha-element" in this book. In my discussion with Ven. Drakpa Singgé (*grags pa seng ge*), Lecturer of the Sakya Tradition at the Central University of Tibetan Studies at Sarnath, Varanasi, he said that Sapen explained the teachings of the tathāgata-essence endowed with enlightened qualities as provisional, but the teachings of the tathāgata-essence per se were explained as definitive.

18. See José Cabezón, *Buddhism and Language: A Study of Indo-Tibetan Scholasticism* (Albany: State University of New York Press, 1994), 65–68. Hereafter, *Buddhism and Language*.

19. See David Ruegg, "Purport, Implicature and Presupposition: Sanskrit abhipraya and Tibetan *dgoñs pa/dgons gži* as hermeneutical concepts," *Journal of Indian Philosophy* 13 (1985): 309–25.

20. See *The Sūtrālaṃkāra and the Uttaratantra*, 93.

21. *rang bzhin gyi rigs sems can thams cad la yod/ rgyas pa'i rigs byang chub tu sems bskyed nas yod/ ma bskyed pa la med//* See Sakya Paṇḍita Kunga Gyaltsen, *thub pa'i dgongs pa rab tu gsal ba*, in *The Collected Works of the Founding Masters of Sa-skya*, vol. 10 (tha) (Dehradun: Sakya Center, 1993), 5. Hereafter, *Illuminating the Thoughts of the Buddha*.

22. *gtan rigs chad pa sems tsam pa 'dod// dbu ma pa mi 'dod//* See ibid., 6.

23. However, it is not to say that Sapen does not cite the *Uttaratantra* at all in his *Illuminating the Thoughts of the Buddha*. As a matter of fact, he cites from the text a few times (for instance, see 8 and 10). Nonetheless, *Illuminating the Thoughts of the Buddha* does not discuss how the *Uttaratantra* may or may not be definitive and how it may or may not fit into the three wheels of the Buddha's teachings. The main opponents mentioned in his text are certain Mahāmudra followers.

24. See Rhoton, *A Clear Differentiation of the Three Codes*, 237–38.

25. Rongtön argues, "The *Sūtrālaṃkāra* teaches that the sugata-essence and the [buddha-]nature are different because it shows that sugata-essence exists in all sentient beings, [whereas] there exist sentient beings who are cut off [from the buddha-]nature. Therefore, the assertion that the sugata-essence and the [buddha-]nature are not the same is a position held in the Cittamātra." *mdo sde rgyan las ni bde gshegs snying po dang rigs tha dad du gsungs te bde gshegs snying po sems can thams cad la yod par bshad cing rigs chad kyi sems can yod par bstan pas bde gshegs snying po dang rigs mi gcig par 'dod pa sems tsam pa'i lugs so//* See Rongtön Mawé Senggé, *theg pa chen po rgyud bla ma'i bstan bcos legs par bshad pa* (New Delhi: Yashodhara, 1998), 95. Henceforth, *Explanation of the Uttaratantra.* The *Sūtrālaṃkāra* verse which Rongtön has in mind is most likely this one: *de bzhin nyid ni thams cad la/ khyad par med kyang dag gyur pa/ de bzhin gshegs nyid de yi phyir/ 'gro kun de yi snying po can//* As far as I can tell, this is the only verse from the text that explicitly states that all sentient beings have sugata-essence or tathāgata-essence. See *The Sūtrālaṃkāra and the Uttaratantra*, 19.

26. For a brief life story of Rikrel, see Roerich, *Blue Annals*, 336–39. Also see van der Kuijp, *Contributions to the Development of Tibetan Epistemology*, 266–67, note 61.

27. As *Blue Annals* states, "Two thirds of the Tripitakadharas of that time are known to have gathered at *snar thang* [Narthang monastery]." See Roerich, *Blue Annals*, 337.

28. Ibid.

29. Kurtis Schaeffer and Leornard van der Kuijp, *An Early Tibetan Survey of Buddhist Literature: The Bstan pa rgyas pa rgyan gyi nyi 'od of Bcom ldan ral gri* (Cambridge: Harvard University Press, 2009). Hereafter, *An Early Tibetan Survey of Buddhist Literature.*

30. See Chomden Rikrel, *rgyud bla ma'i ti ka rgyan gyi me tog*, in *The Collected Works of Kadam Masters*, vol. 62 (Chengdu, si khron mi rigs dpe skrun khang, 2009). Henceforth, *Flowers of Ornament.*

31. See Rikrel, *Flowers of Ornament*, 746.

32. See ibid., 753.

33. See ibid., 761.

34. See Schaeffer and van der Kuijp, *An Early Tibetan Survey of Buddhist Literature*, 4–5.

35. Schaeffer and van der Kuijp inform us that Rikrel raises criticisms of Sapen's views on logic and epistemology. See Schaeffer and van der Kuijp, *An Early Tibetan Survey of Buddhist Literature*, 8.

36. The sutra says, "Tathāgata-essence that is naturally luminous, with the characteristic of being completely pure from the beginning, and endowed with marks and signs [of a buddha], exists within the corporeal body of all sentient beings." *de bzhin gshegs pa'i snying po de rang bzhin gyis 'od gsal ba thog ma nas rnam par dag pa'i mtshan nyid mtshan dang dpe byad dang ldan pa sems can thams cad kyi lus kyi nang na mchis pa'o//* See Rikrel, *Flowers of Ornament*, 756.

37. The passage from the tantra states, "Sentient beings are just buddhas. But they are covered by adventitious defilements. Once eliminated, they are just buddhas." *sems can rnams ni sangs rgyas nyid/ 'on kyang glo bur dri mas bsgribs// de bsal na ni sangs rgyas nyid//* See Rikrel, *Flowers of Ornament*, 761. As I discuss in chapter 4, Sazang would cite the same verse in his *Uttaratantra* commentary to make a similar argument that Rikrel makes here.

38. *bla ma'i rgyud ni de bzhin gshegs pa'i snying po la sogs mdo rgyud zab mo rnams so//* See, Rikrel, *Flowers of Ornament*, 763.

39. *bcom ral pas dus 'khor 'di drang srong rgyas pa'i gzhung dang mthun pas phyi nang gang yin dang bka' bstan bcos gang yin mi shes pas po ti zur du byas la zhog zer dgos byung* . . . See Pawo Tsuklak Trengwa, *chos 'byung mkhas pa'i dga' ston* (Sarnath: Vajra Vidya Institute, 2003), 1485. Henceforth, *A Joyous Feast for Scholars*. Rikrel's catalogue, however, paints a slightly different picture. In it, Rikrel includes the Kālacakra but does not include it in the "Tantra" section. Schaeffer and van der Kuijp argue, "A key difference between Bcom ldan ral gri's list and the catalogs of later scriptural collections is that he includes multiple translations of single works. Because the later chapters are organized in accordance with the chronology of translators, different translations of the same work appear in different chapters. See for instance the four entries for the Kālacakra [23.8, 27.135, 28.15, 28.69]." Schaeffer and van der Kuijp, *An Early Tibetan Survey of Buddhist Literature*, 63.

40. For more on the Third Karmapa's life, see Roerich, *Blue Annals*, 488–93.

41. By looking through the works written by the Third Karmapa listed in Kurtis Schaeffer's master's thesis, one can tell that his works are primarily tantric oriented. See Kurtis Schaeffer, *The Enlightened Heart of Buddhahood: A Study and Translation of the Third Karma pa Rang byung rdo rje's Work on Tathāgatagarbha* (MA Thesis, University of Washington, 1995), 14–17. Henceforth, *The Enlightened Heart of Buddhahood*.

42. For information on how the Third Karmapa's writings are influenced by Maitreya's texts, see Karl Brunnhölzl, *In Praise of Dharmadhātu: Nāgārjuna and the Third Karmapa, Rangjung Dorje* (Ithaca: Snow Lion, 2007), 160–93. Khenchen Thrangu also says, "There have been seventeen Karmapas, and among these the Third Karmapa Rangjung Dorje and the Eighth Karmapa Mikyo Dorje showed the greatest scholarship. Mikyo Dorje demonstrated a greater understanding of the sūtra teachings, whereas Rangjung Dorje had greater understanding of the Tantra teachings." *On Buddha Essence: A Commentary on Rangjung Dorje's Treatise* (Boston: Shambala, 2006), xx. Hereafter, *On Buddha Essence*.

43. See Brunnhölzl, *In Praise of Dharmadhātu*, 193.

44. Brunnhölzl says, "The main part of describing the dharmadhātu in its impure phase of being obscured by adventitious stains consists of the *Dharmadhātustava*'s first six examples of butter in milk, a lamp within a vase, an encrusted gem, gold in its ore, rice in its husk, and the banana tree. The

commentary's detailed explanation of these examples emphasizes that the root of being mistaken is just the stainless dharmadhātu being unaware of itself, while there are not the slightest adventitious stains other that that, let alone any that are really existent. The dharmadhātu itself is the Tathagata heart, which does not just refer to mere emptiness." See ibid., 194.

45. See Kongtrül, *Lion's Roar of the* Uttaratantra, 12. Kongtrül also mentions that Karma Könchok Zhönnu (*kar ma dkon mchog gzhon nu*), a student of the Third Karmapa, wrote a detailed commentary to the *Uttaratantra* based on the Third Karmapa's topical summary, and later Karma Trinlé (*kar ma phrin las*) wrote a commentary in a debate format (*sbyor ngag bkod pa'i 'grel pa mdzad*). Ibid. However, none of these commentaries is available for our analysis.

46. Mathes, *A Direct Path to the Buddha Within*, 52.

47. Ibid., 54.

48. In his *On Buddha Essence*, Thrangu gives a lucid commentary on the Third Karmapa's *Presentation of the Essence*. He also offers his own English translation of the Third Karmapa's text. For the verse from the *Hevajra Tantra* quoted in the Third Karmapa's *Presentation of the Essence*, see Thrangu, *On Buddha Essence*, 8.

49. However, Stearns points out that none of the early biographies makes reference to such a meeting. See Cyrus Stearns, *The Buddha from Dölpo: A Study of the Life and Thought of the Tibetan Master SherabGyaltsen* (Albany: State University of New York Press, 1999), 49–50. Henceforth, *Buddha from Dölpo*.

50. While Brunnhölzl claims that Sangpu Lodrö Tsungmé gave teachings to the Third Karmapa, he does not offer any evidence as to why he believes that the former taught these treatises to the latter. I suppose Brunnhölzl came to this conclusion because the Third Karmapa's teacher, Drakpa Senggé (*grags pa seng ge*, 1283–1349) traveled to Sangpu and received these teachings from Sangpu Lodrö Tsungmé. See Brunnhölzl, *In Praise of Dharmadhātu*, 157–58. In his *The Enlightened Heart of Buddhahood*, Schaeffer does not indicate anywhere that the Third Karmapa had any teacher-disciple relationship with Sangpu Lodrö Tsungmé. Schaeffer examined several biographies of the Third Karmapa that are available in both Tibetan and English. See Schaeffer, *The Enlightened Heart of Buddhahood*, 6.

51. *Blue Annals* suggests that Drakpa Senggé had left for Sangpu by 1309 after spending some time in Tsurpu (*mtshur phu*), where the former received initiations from Kagyü masters in 1308. See Roerich, *Blue Annals*, 523–25. Drakpa Senggé would have been twenty-six or twenty-seven years old when he met Sangpu Lodrö Tsungmé, who taught him the *Five Treatises of Maitreya*, etc. So, when Dölpopa was only sixteen, a year before he started receiving instruction on the perfection of wisdom genre, etc. from Kyitön Jamyang Drakpa Gyeltsen (*skyi ston grags pa rgyal mtshan*), Sangpu Lodrö Tsungmé had already established himself as an expert on the *Five Treatises of*

Maitreya. David Ruegg says that Butön, when he was younger, had discussions about the tathāgata-essence issues with Sangpu Lodrö Tsungmé. See David Ruegg, *Three Studies in the History of Indian and Tibetan Madhyamaka Philosophy, Studies in Indian and Tibetan Madhyamaka Thought,* part 1 (Vienna: Arbeitskreis fur Tibetishe und Buddhistische Studien Universitat Wien, 2000), 79, note 176. Henceforth, *Three Studies.*

52. See Roerich, *Blue Annals,* 524–25, 532. Both Drakpa Senggé and Yakdé Penchen (*gyag sde pan chen,* 1299–1378) studied the *Five Treatises of Maitreya* under Sangpu Lodrö Tsungmé. For the speculation of, and critique against, the notion that Sangpu Lodrö Tsungmé is Longchenpa, see Mathes, *A Direct Path to the Buddha Within,* 109–10.

53. Gö Lotsawa mentions that Sangpu Lodrö Tsungmé had already written his commentary before Dölpopa wrote his rather short commentary on the *Uttaratantra.* Gö Lotsawa Zhönnu Pel, *theg pa chen po rgyud bla ma'i bstan bcos kyi 'grel bshad de kho na nyid rab tu gsal ba'i me long* (Kathmandu: Franz Steiner Verlag Stuttgart, 2003), 574. Henceforth, *The Mirror That Illuminates Suchness.*

54. *gsang ba las ches shin tu gsang ba.* See Sangpu Lodrö Tsungmé, *theg pa chen po rgyud bla ma'i bstan bcos kyi nges don gsal bar byed pa'i rin po che'i sgron me* (Arunachal Pradesh: Tibetan Nyingma Monastery, 1974), 22. Henceforth, *The Precious Lamp That Illuminates Definitive Meaning.*

55. Sangpu Lodrö Tsungmé states, "A proponent says that all first four [*Abhisamayālaṃkāra, Sūtrālaṃkāra, Madhyāntavibhāga,* and *Dharmadharmatāvibhāga*] clarify the meaning of the sutras that require interpretation. Such is not the case because it would [absurdly] follow that the first *alaṃkāra* [*Abhisamayālaṃkāra*] did not explain the meaning of the middle wheel correctly as it would be a text explaining the sutras of provisional meaning." *kha cig na re, dang po bzhi ka yang drang ba'i don gyi gsungs rabs kyi don gsal bar byed pa ste zhes gsungs pa ni ma yin te, rgyan dang pos bka' bar pa'i don phyin ci ma log par ma bshad par 'gyur te, drang ba'i don gyi gsungs rabs 'chad byed yin pa'i phyir.* See Sangpu Lodrö Tsungmé, *The Precious Lamp That Illuminates Definitive Meaning,* 13. The scholar whose name is not mentioned is Ngok, who argues that these four treatises are not definitive in his *Uttaratantra* commentary.

56. See chapter 1, note 22.

57. Sangpu Lodrö Tsungmé states, "Here a master [Chapa] states that 'The buddha-element is referred to as dharma-body from the viewpoint of the accomplishment of the pure result; [the buddha-element] is referred to as the causal buddha-nature from the point of view of the potentiality for accomplishing the dharma-body; and [the buddha-element] is suchness from the perspective of the mere suchness that pervades these two [dharma-body and the causal buddha-nature]. As for the resultant essence or the complete buddha, it is the resultant dharma-body, which is on the level of the purified state. That the resultant dharma-body radiates means that it pervades. Because all sentient beings can achieve the resultant dharma-body, it pervades [all beings]. With respect to this, the tathāgata is actual, but sentient beings'

essence is imputed. Because sentient beings have the privilege to achieve the dharma-body, it is imputed that it pervades [all beings].'" *'dir slob dpon 'ga' zhig na re/ de la khams ni rnam par dag pa'i 'bras bu thob pa'i ldog pa nas chos kyi sku zhes bya la/ de thob tu rung pa'i nus pa'i cha nas rgyu rigs zhes bya zhing/ de gnyis la khyab pa chos can gyis khyad par du ma byas pa'i de bzhin nyid tsam gyi ldog pa nas de bzhin nyid do// de la 'bras bu'i snying po ni rdzogs sangs sku ni rnam par dag pa'i gnas skabs kyi 'bras bu chos sku yin la/ de la 'phro ba ni khyab pa ste sems can thams cad kyis thob tu rung pa'i phyir khyab pa yin no// 'di la de bzhin gshegs pa ni dngos yin la/ sems can gyi snying po ni brtags pa ste thob pa'i skal ba yod pa la des khyab par btags pa'i phyir ro. . . . zhes gsung ngo//* See Sangpu Lodrö Tsungmé, *The Precious Lamp That Illuminates Definitive Meaning,* 208–10. While Sangpu Lodrö Tsungmé does not mention Chapa by name here, the quote is found in Chapa's commentary. See Chapa, *Illumination of the Meaning of the Uttaratantra,* 229.

58. *de ni mi 'thad de chos kyi sku ni yon tan dang dbyer med pa'i chos kyi dbyings yin la de sems can thams cad la bdag gcig tu khyab byed du yod pa'i dngos yin pa la gnod byed med pa'i phyir btags pa bar 'jog pa de mi 'thad pa dang.* See Sangpu Lodrö Tsungmé, *The Precious Lamp That Illuminates Definitive Meaning,* 208–10.

59. *. . . nyes pa yod kyang blo bur ba dang ldan pa yin gyi, rang bzhin gyis dag pa dang/ stobs sogs kyi yon tan rnams rang bzhin gyis gdod ma nyid nas ldan pa'i phyir dri ma sngar gsar du spang pa dang/ yon tan sngar med gsar du bsgrubs pa med//* See Sangpu Lodrö Tsungmé, *The Precious Lamp That Illuminates Definitive Meaning,* 253.

60. Sangpu Lodrö Tsungmé states, "Therefore, because both the first [*Abhisamayālaṃkāra*] and the last [*Uttaratantra*] explain the definitive sutras literally, they are definitive. The other three [*Sūtrālaṃkāra, Dharmadharmatāvibhāga,* and *Madhyāntavibhāga*] are provisional because they comment on the meaning of the sutras with provisional meaning that clearly show the three vehicles." *des na thog ma dang tha ma gnyis ni nges pa'i don can gyi bka'i dgongs pa sgra ji lta ba bzhin du 'grel pas nges don yin la/ gzhan gsum ni theg pa gsum gsal par byed pa'i drang don gyi mdo'i dgongs pa 'grel bas drang don yin no//* See Sangpu Lodrö Tsungmé, *The Precious Lamp That Illuminates Definitive Meaning,* 22–23.

61. [*rgyud bla ma'i mdo dang rgyud bla ma' bstan bcos rnams*] *rgyal ba'i yum dang 'gal bar mi 'gyur te/ de las chos thams cad rang bzhin gyis stong par gsungs pa ni 'dir bstan pa'i chos kyi sku nyid yin la/ kun rdzob tu nyon mongs pa dang las dang phung po rnams sprin la sogs pa bzhin du gsungs pa ni kun nas nyon mongs pa'i chos rnams blo bur ba yin gyi/ sems kyi rang bzhin ma yin par bstan la/ de nyid de bzhin gshegs pa'i snying po yin te/* See Sangpu Lodrö Tsungmé, *The Precious Lamp That Illuminates Definitive Meaning,* 377–78.

62. A part of this section appears in my article "Can We Speak of Kadam Gzhan Stong? Tracing the Sources for Other-Emptiness in Early-Fourteenth-Century" *Journal of Buddhist Philosophy* 2 (2016: 9–22).

63. See Tsünpa Pelrin and Zhönnu Gyeltsen, *rgyal sras dngul chu thogs med kyi rnam thar,* (pdal brtsegs bod yig dpe rnying zhib 'jug khang, n.d.), 43, 180. Henceforth, *Biographies of Gyelsé Tokmé Zangpo.*

64. Stearns states, "Dölpopa did indeed study with the Tanak master Rinchen Yeshé. When still quite young, just before his teaching debut at Sakya in 1313, Dölpopa spent about three months at Tanak, where he studied with Rinchen Yeshé and received an explanation of the *Five Treatises of Maitreya*, two of which are the *Highest Continuum [Uttaratantra]* and *Distinguishing Phenomena and True Nature [Dharmadharmatāvibhāga]*" See *Buddha from Dölpo*, 43.

65. Dratsépa says, "He [Butön] also wrote epistles (*dris lan, spriṅ yig*) to various persons including the *chos kyi rgyal po bSod nams lde, gYag sde paṇ chen*, and the *bla ma Rin chen ye śes*." See David Ruegg, *The Life of Bu-Ston Rin Po Che* (Roma: Istituto Italiano per il Medio Estremo Oriente, 1966), 114. Hereafter, *The Life of Bu-Ston Rin Po Che.*

66. He is a student of Gyelsé Tokmé Zangpo (*rgyal sras thogs med bzang po*, 1295–1369). In the biographies of Gyelsé Tokmé Zangpo written by his students, Tsünpa Pelrin and Zhönnu Gyeltsen, Rinchen Yeshé is called "Lama Rinyéwa" (*bla ma rin ye ba*) several times. See Tsünpa Pelrin and Zhönnu Gyeltsen, *Biographies of Gyelsé Tokmé Zangpo*, 43, 51, 56, 68, 82, 97, 180, 198, 201.

67. See chapter 2, note 63.

68. Jonang Zangpo states that Dölpopa had discussions with hundreds of scholars, including Master Senggé Pel (*seng ge dpal*) and Rinchen Yeshé, after Dölpopa completed his study at Sakya monastery. *de nas dgung lo nyer gcig nas sa skyar byon nas slob gnyer dpag tu med pa mdzad nas mthar phyir par gyur to . . . de nas bla ma seng ge dpal dang rin chen ye shes dang . . . la sogs mkhas pa brgya phrag mang po dang bgro gleng mdzad pas khong tshos snga rgol phyi rgol byas kyang chos rje 'dis lung rigs kyi chos skad rgya mtsho phye bas blo gsal de dag zil gyis mnan nas mkhas pa'i grags pas kyab par gyur to//* See Jonang Zangpo, *chos rje kun mkhyen chen po yab sras bco lnga'i rnam thar nye bar bsdus pa ngo mtsar rab gsal*, in *The Collected Works of kun mkhyen dol po pa*, vol. 1 ('Dzam thang, 'Bar khams rdzong: 'Dzam thang dgon pa, 199–), 562–63. Henceforth, *Biographies of the Great Omniscient One, the Father, and His Fourteen Lineage Sons.*

69. While the biography written by Tsünpa Pelrin explains the life story and activities of Gyelsé Tokmé Zangpo in great detail, it does not clearly explain when exactly Gyelsé Tokmé Zangpo had some of the encounters with his fellow scholars. Zhönnu Gyeltsen's biography gives more information. Zhönnu Gyeltsen reports that Gyelsé Tokmé Zangpo went to Chölung (*chos lung*) to see his teacher, Sonam Drakpa (*bsod nams grags pa*, 1273–1345), and a few months later, Sonam Drakpa passed away. Thereafter, Zhönnu Gyeltsen informs his readers that Gyelsé Tokmé Zangpo went to see Rinchen Yeshé, who also passed away shortly after their meeting. See *Biographies of Gyelsé Tokmé Zangpo*, 197–98. However, I have not been able to find any information regarding his approximate birth date, birthplace, or teachers.

70. Butön Rinchen Drup, *'phrin yig gi lan rin po che'i 'phreng ba*, in *The Collected Works of Bu-Ston*, part 26 (LA) edt. by Prof. Dr. Lokesh Chandra, International Academy of Indian Culture (New Delhi, 1971). Henceforth, *Precious Garland of Rebuttals.*

71. It is a 212 folio-long text, which is written in *dbu med* script with dozens of Tibetan abbreviations. See Rinchen Yeshé, *rgyud bla ma'i 'grel ba mdo dang sbyar ba nges don gyi snang ba*, in *The Collected Works of Kadam Masters*, vol. 20 (Sichuan, *dpal brtsegs bod yig dpe rnying zhib 'jug khang*, 2006). Henceforth, *Rays of the Definitive Meaning*.

72. Rinchen Yeshé says, "For the sutras cited without their sources in [Asaṅga's] commentary, I mentioned the titles for those sutras whose sources could be found. [I] could not find sources for some sutras whose sources are not mentioned in [the commentary]. Furthermore, the main reason why the sources for some sutras were not found was partly because those sutras were not translated into Tibetan and partly, without a doubt, because of the lack of diligence, I did not look for them even if they had been translated." *'grel par mdo drangs nas khungs ma rnyed pa smos pa rnams 'dir mdo'i khungs rnyed pa rnams ni mdo'i mtshan smos te bris so// mdo'i khungs ma smos pa 'ga' zhig khungs ma rnyed cing/ gzhan yang rtsa ba'i don la mdo ma rnyed pa kha cig ni bod du ma 'gyur ba dang kha cig ni 'gyur yang brtson 'grus zhan pas blta ma nus pas ma rnyed par zad do// 'grel par grangs pa rnams dang 'gyur gyi khad yod pa rnams ni 'grel pa dpe yod cing 'gyur bzang ngan brtag pa'i phyir mdo'i 'gyur mdzad pa po rnams kyi ji lta ba bzhin bris so// 'grel pa'i 'gyur dang mi 'dra ba'i mdo rnams dang 'grel pa na mi bzhugs pa'i mdo drangs pa rnams ni gang na bzhugs pa'i mdo de nyid legs par bltas te bris pa yin pas yid ches pa'i gnas su bya'o//* See ibid., 442–43.

73. See ibid., 51, 151.

74. For Naktso's translation, see ibid., 293, 349, 353, 361, 375, 401. For his preference of Naktso's translation over Ngok's translation, see ibid., 293, 375.

75. See ibid., 83, 95, 167.

76. Rinchen Yeshé lists sixteen sutras that he argues are "supremely profound and difficult to be realized" (*mchog tu zab cing rtogs par dka' ba*) and that are foundational for the *Uttaratantra*. See ibid., 25.

77. The passage that is quoted in the commentary is this: "The unconditioned buddha-element endowed with the limitless marks and signs of a buddha exists in all sentient being." *ma byas pa'i sangs rgyas kyi khams mtshan dang dpe byad bzang po mtha' yas pas brgyan pa sems can thams cad la yod do//* See Rinchen Yeshé, *Rays of the Definitive Meaning*, 170. Furthermore, Rinchen Yeshé cites a passage from the *Mahāparinirvāṇasūtra*: "For example, blind people do not see the sun and the moon, but if qualified doctors treat them with medicine [they] will see [the sun and the moon. However,] it is not the case that the sun and the moon that did not exist before came into existence now. So, the nirvāṇa is like [the sun and the moon] in that it exists since the beginning, not recently." *dper na dmus long dag nyi ma dang zla ba mi mthong ste/ sman dpyad mkhas pas sman byas na snang zhing mthong bar 'gyur te/ nyi ma dang zla ba de yang sngon med pa la da lta yod pa ma yin no// mya ngan las 'das pa yang de dang 'dra ste thog ma nas yod pa yin gyi/ da ltar gzod yod pa ma yin no zhes pa dang/* See ibid.

78. *gang gi phyir rang bzhin gyis yongs su dag pa de bzhin gshegs pa'i khams 'di la bsal bar bya ba kun nas nyon mongs pa'i rgyu mtshan ni 'ga' yang med de/ gdod ma nas glo bur ba'i dri ma dang bral ba ni 'di'i rang bzhin yin pa'i phyir ro// 'di la rnam par byang ba'i rgyu mtshan gsar du gzhag par bya ba cung zad yod pa ma yin te/ yon tan rnam par dbe ba med pa'i chos yang dag pa'i chos nyid ni 'di'i rang bzhin yin pa'i phyir ro//* See ibid., 268.

79. *bde bar gshegs pa'i gsung rab thams cad kyi snying por gyur pa theg pa chen po/ de'i nang nas kyang nges don gtso bor ston pa don dam rnam par nges pa'i mdo/* See ibid., 25. For a long list of sutras that primarily teach definitive meaning, see ibid.

80. *des na bka' bar par chos thams cad sgyu ma lta bu la sogs pa bden med du gsungs pa ni kun rdzob 'dus byas kyi chos rnams la dgongs pa yin la, bka' tha mar bde gshegs snying po bden pa 'gyur med du gsungs pa ni don dam chos dbyings 'dus ma byas la dgongs pa yin no//* See ibid., 275.

81. Butön says, "If I were to make a speculation about your letter, this is what [you] seem to have intended. The meaning of Madhyamaka and Prajñāpāramitā is nihilistic emptiness or inanimate emptiness in the way that a few Tibetan scholars explain it. The emptiness [explained] there is not the emptiness endowed with the supreme of all aspects." *khyed kyi yi ge de la bdag gis 'og dpag byas na/ 'di 'dra zhig dgongs par go ste/ dbu ma pa dang phar phyin gyi don de da lta bod kyi mkhas pa re re gnyis gnyis kyis 'chad pa bzhin du chad pa'i stong pa'am bem po'i stong pa nyid yin gyi/ de'i stong pa de rnam kun mchog ldan gyi stong pa yang min//* See Butön, *Precious Garland of Rebuttals*, 205.

82. Butön says, "The treatises such as *Sūtrālaṃkara* are like tantric vehicle because the emptiness explained there is emptiness endowed with all aspects and meditating on it is done through self-awareness." *mdo sde rgyan la sogs pa ni sngags kyi theg pa dang mtshungs te/ stong pa nyid ni rnam kun mchog ldan gyi stong pa nyid yin la/ sgom pa yang rang rig pa'i tshul du sgom pa yin no//* See ibid.

83. See Hopkins, *Mountain Doctrine*, 14.

84. Stearns has this to say about Dölpopa's view on self-emptiness, "Phenomena at the relative level are empty of self-nature (*rang stong*) and are no more real than the fictitious horn of a rabbit or the child of a barren woman." See Stearns, *Buddha from Dölpo*, 2–3.

85. *yi ge logs shig pa de na/ bka' bar pa nas 'di tha ma las khyad par du 'phags par ma bshad la/ bka' tha ma nas 'di bar pa las khyad par du 'phags par bshad pas tha ma brjod bya bzang ngo// des na mdo sde rgyan dang rgyud bla sogs bka' tha ma'i dgongs 'grel yin pas brjod bya bzang ngo// de dag sems tsam du bzhed pa yang mang mod kyi/ grub mtha' bzhi ga las brgal ba'i don yin no zhes bya ba gda.'* See Butön, *Precious Garland of Rebuttals*, 201.

86. See his *bstan 'gyur gyi dkar chag yid bzhin nor bu'i dbang gi rgyal po'i phreng ba (Catalogue for the Translated Treatises), The Collected Works of Bu-Ston*, vol. 26, Lhasa, Zhol Publications, 2000.

87. See, Rikrel, *Flowers of Ornament*, 749–50.

Chapter 3

1. Roerich, *Blue Annals*, 349–50. Some two centuries later Jonang Künga Drölchok would trace Dölpopa's interpretation of the *Uttaratantra* to Tsen Khawoché's transmission of it. On this, see Stearns, *Buddha from Dölpo*, 42–43. In an interview, Khenpo Chönang (*mkhan po chos snang*), a contemporary Jonang scholar, told me that there are two transmissions of the *Uttaratantra*: the transmission for meditators (*bya rgyun*) and the transmission of exposition (*bshad rgyun*). According to him, there is not much difference between the two, except that the latter involves more explication than the former, and both are present within the Jonang School.

2. See Mathes, *A Direct Path to the Buddha Within*, 75–84, for Dolpopa's interpretation of the *Uttaratantra*.

3. Wilfred Smith, *What Is Scripture?: A Comparative Approach* (Minneapolis: Fortress, 2005), 18. Hereafter, *What Is Scipture?*

4. See Dölpopa, *lta ba shan 'byed yid kyi mun sel*, *Collected Works of Dol po pa shes rab rgyal mtshan*, vol. 6 (Dzamthang, bar khams rdzong), 682. Henceforth, *Distinguishing Views*.

5. See Dölpopa, *Distinguishing Views*, 682. Furthermore, he states, "Because if one realizes the gnosis-body of all tathāgatas that is ultimate, permanent, and reality, which is the meaning of *Mañjuśrīnamasaṃgīti*, one realizes the oneness of the ultimate definitive meaning of all vehicles." *mtshan yang dag par brjod pa'i don de bzhin gshegs pa thams cad kyi ye shes kyi sku don dam rtag pa chos kyi dbyings shes na theg pa thams cad kyi mthar thug nges pa'i don gcig tu shes pa de'i phyir//* See Dölpopa, *so so skye bo'i pan di ta la sogs pa'i 'khrul pa lung bstan pa*, Collected Works of Dol po pa shes rab rgyal mtshan, vol. 6, pp. 603–616 (Dzamthang, bar khams rdzong), 611. Henceforth, *Criticism against Ordinary Scholars*.

6. Hopkins, *Mountain Doctrine*, 581.

7. Ibid., 582. Tāranātha says that these three wheels actually do not contradict one another, rather the first wheel of the Dharma primarily teaches conventional truth, the middle wheel briefly explains definitive meaning, and the last wheel explicates only the ultimate definitive. *'khor lo rnam gsum dgongs pa gcig tu bsgrubs/ . . . 'on kyang dang por kun rdzob gtso bor bstan/ bar du nges don phyed tsam/ tha mar ni nges don don dam rdzogs par bstan pa yin//* See Jetsün Tāranātha in his *gzhan stong dbu ma'i rgyan* in rdzogs ldan chos mchog dbu ma gzhan stong gi chos skor, vol. 7 (Shang Kang: Thenma, 2005), 144. Henceforth, *Ornament of the Other-Emptiness Madhyamaka*. Tāranātha also affirms that the first wheel is provisional, the middle wheel is temporarily definitive (*gnas skabs nges don*), and the last wheel is ultimately definitive (*mthar thug nges don*). See Jetsün Tāranātha, *tshul gnyis rnam 'byed nges don 'jug ngogs*, in *rdzogs ldan chos mchog dbu ma gzhan stong gi chos skor, deb bdun pa, shang kang then ma dpe skrun khang*, 2005, 241. Henceforth, *Entry to the Definitive Meaning*.

8. *de yang 'khor lo bar pa yang dgag bya'i chos kun rdzob rang stong dang, rten 'brel las ma 'das pa gtso cher bstan nas dgag pa'i gzhi don dam gzhan stong*

rten 'brel las 'das pa ni 'khor lo tha mar gtso cher bstan te/ 'khor lo bar par yang dgag bya'i gzhi ma bstan pa yang ma yin no// See Dölpopa, *gshags 'byed bsdus pa,* Collected Works of Dölpopa Sherap Gyeltsen, vol. 6, 367–400, (Dzamthang, bar khams rdzong), 390. Henceforth, *A Brief Distinction.* See Hopkins, *Mountain Doctrine,* 196–97 for a similar statement.

9. This is why I think Matthew Kapstein explains the middle-wheel teachings "to be in some sense definitive too," according to Dölpopa. For reference, see Matthew Kapstein, *Reason's Traces: Identity and Interpretation in Indian and Tibetan Buddhist Thought* (Boston: Wisdom, 2001), 301. Hereafter, *Reason's Traces.*

10. Dölpopa says that the middle wheel is "*sher phyin zab mo la mtshams sbyor ba.*" See Dölpopa, *chos dbyings bde ba chen po'i 'ja' sa,* Collected Works of Dölpopa Sherap Gyeltsen, vol. 6, 355–66 (Dzamthang, bar khams rdzong), 357. Henceforth, *Proclamation of the Great Bliss of Dharmadhātu.* In one of the interviews that I had with Khenpo Chönang of the Jonang School in Shimla in 2006, he mentioned that the middle-wheel teachings were "temporary provisional meaning" (*gnas skabs kyi drang don*).

11. *bka' 'khor lo dang po dang gnyis pa drang don du bcom ldan 'das kyis mdo dgongs pa nges 'grel du gsungs la . . .* See Dölpopa Sherap Gyeltsen, *bden gnyis gsal ba'i nyi ma,* in *The Collected Works of Dölpopa Sherap Gyeltsen,* vol. 6, 695–726 (Dzamthang: bar khams rdzong), 723. Henceforth, *The Sun That Illuminates the Two Truths.*

12. Hopkins, *Mountain Doctrine,* 24. Tāranātha argues that there is no evidence to show that the middle wheel is definitive and the last wheel is provisional; rather several sutras such as *Saṃdhinirmocanasūtra, Nirvāṇasūtra,* and *Aṅgulimālasūtra* speak of the former as provisional and the latter as definitive. *bar pa nges don phyi ma drang don du/ ston byed mdo sde gsal po gang na'ang med// bar pa drang don phyi ma nges don du/ dgongs pa nges 'grel mnyang 'das chen po dang/ sor 'phreng sogs kyi mdo las gsal bar bshad//* See Tāranātha, *Ornament of the Other-Emptiness Madhyamaka,* 146–47. Similarly, Tāranātha argues that there is no scriptural reason to show that the middle wheel is definitive and the last wheel provisional. See Tāranātha, *Entry to the Definitive Meaning,* 249.

13. More on the distinction between the middle-wheel teachings and the last-wheel teachings, see Jeffrey Hopkins, *The Essence of Other Emptiness* (New York: Snow Lion, 2001), 120. Hereafter, *The Essence of Other Emptiness.*

14. *de ltar de bzhin gshegs pa'i snying po yod pa nyid nges pa'i don yin na/ rgyal ba'i yum la sogs pa las chos thams cad stong pa nyid de sprin dang rmi lam dang sgyu ma bzhin du snang yang rang bzhin med pa'o zhes gsungs pa'i dgongs pa gang yin zhe na. . . .* See Dölpopa, *theg pa chen po rgyud bla ma'i bstan bcos legs bshad nyi ma'i 'od zer* (Collected Works of Dölpopa Sherap Gyaltsen, vol. 2), 103. Henceforth, *The Sunlight Exposition.*

15. Dölpopa, *The Sun That Illuminates the Two Truths,* 722.

16. Much of this material has appeared in my article "Dol po pa shes rab rgyal mtshan on Mahāyāna doxography: Rethinking the Distinction

between Cittamātra and Madhyamaka in Fourteenth-Century Tibet" *Journal of the International Association of Buddhist Studies* 34, nos.1–2 (2012): 321–48.

17. See Stearns, *Buddha from Dölpo*, 41–83.

18. On the usual interchangeability of these two terms, see Paul Williams (with Anthony Tribe), *Buddhist Thought: A Complete Introduction to the Indian Tradition* (London and New York: Routledge, 2000), 154. Hereafter, *Buddhist Thought*.

19. Dölpopa, *dpon byang ba'i phyag tu phul ba'i chos kyi shan 'byed*, in *The Collected Works of Kun mkhyen dol po pa* ('Dzam thang, 'Bar khams rdzong: 'Dzam thang dgon pa, 199–), vol. 6, 401–602. Henceforth, *A Letter to Pönjangwa*.

20. Dölpopa, *bka' bsdu bzhi pa'i don bstan rtsis chen po*, in *The Collected Works of Kun mkhyen dol po pa* ('Dzam thang, 'Bar khams rdzong: 'Dzam thang dgon pa, 199–), vol. 6, 165–202. Henceforth, *The Great Calculation of the Fourth Council*. For an English translation of the text, see Stearns, *Buddha from Dölpo*, 135–204.

21. See Dölpopa, *bka' bsdu bzhi pa'i don bstan rtsis chen po phyogs med ris med ces bya ba'i 'grel pa*, in *The Collected Works of Kun mkhyen dol po pa* ('Dzam thang, 'Bar khams rdzong: 'Dzam thang dgon pa, 199–), vol. 6, 219–72. Henceforth, *Commentary on the Fourth Council*.

22. See Dölpopa, *shes rab kyi pha rol tu phyin pa man ngag gi bstan bcos mngon par rtogs pa'i rgyan gyi rnam bshad mdo'i don bde blag tu rtogs pa*, in *The Collected Works of Kun mkhyen dol po pa* ('Dzam thang, 'Bar khams rdzong: 'Dzam thang dgon pa, 199–), vol. 5, 243–618. Henceforth, *Abhisamayālaṃkāra Commentary*. Dölpopa mentions in his own *The Sun That Illuminates the Two Truths* that a detailed explanation of the distinction between the two schools is given in his *Abhisamayālaṃkāra Commentary*.

23. Georges Dreyfus and Sara McClintock state: "Although the early Tibetan author Ye shes sde (eighth c.) is usually credited with the first use of the terms "mDo sde spyod pa'i dbu ma" (*Sautrāntika-Madhyamaka) and "rNal 'byor spyod pa'i dbu ma" (*Yogācāra-Madhyamaka), we also find Kamalaśīla in his subcommentary on Śāntarakṣita's MA referring to the "two paths of the Madhyamaka" (MAP, D 128a: *dbu ma'i lam gnyis*) in a context in which it seems clear that one path upholds external objects conventionally, while the other follows the Yogācāra or Cittamātra tradition of rejecting external objects." See Georges Dreyfus and Sara McClintock, *The Svātantrika-Prāsaṅgika Distinction: What Difference Does a Difference Make?* (Boston: Wisdom Publications, 2003), 33–34, n 6. Hereafter, *The Svātantrika-Prāsaṅgika Distinction*. Also, see David Seyfort Ruegg, *The Buddhist Philosophy of the Middle: Essays on Indian and Tibetan Madhyamaka* (Boston: Wisdom, 2010), 162, n. 7. Hereafter, *The Buddhist Philosophy of the Middle*.

24. See Dreyfus and McClintock, *The Svātantrika-Prāsaṅgika Distinction*.

25. For an excellent discussion of the term *cittamātra* in the Mahāyāna system from the beginning until Kamalaśīla, see Christian Lindtner, "Cittamātra in Indian Mahāyāna until Kamalaśīla," *Wiener Zeitschrift für die Kunde südasiens und Archiv für indische Philosophie* 41 (1997): 159–206.

26. José Cabezón argues that "the fully evolved siddhānta schema outlined above [in Cabezón's article] was something that did not develop until Buddhism was already well established in Tibet, this schematization, of course, has its roots in such Indian Buddhist works as the *Mahāprajnāpāramit[opadeśa] śāstra* attributed to Nāgārjuna (second century CE), the *Tarkajvālā* of Bhāvaviveka (sixth century CE), the *Tattvasaṅgraha* of Śāntarakṣita (eighth century CE), the *Tattvaratnāvalī* of Maitrīpa (eleventh century CE), and the *Vimalaprabhā*, a commentary on the Kālacakra Tantra." See José Cabezón, "The Canonization of Philosophy and the Rhetoric of Siddhānta in Tibetan Buddhism," in Paul Griffiths and John Keenan, eds., *Buddha Nature: A Festschrift in Honor of Minoru Kiyota* (Tokyo: Buddhist Books Int'l, 1990), 12–13.

27. Cabezón, "The Canonization of Philosophy and the Rhetoric of Siddhānta in Tibetan Buddhism," 11. However, as Cabezón succinctly points out in his article, as to what exactly it means to follow Madhyamaka, there is generally no consensus.

28. Vose argues, "Virtually every important Tibetan exegete from the thirteenth century to the present ranks Candrakīrti's Prāsaṅgika as the highest interpretation of Buddhist doctrine and delineates the ways in which it is superior to Svātantrika." See Vose, *Resurrecting Candrakīrti*, 138.

29. See Lindtner, "Cittamātra in Indian Mahāyāna until Kamalaśīla," 160. Lindtner suggests that the term might even have its origin in the Pāli Canon. See ibid., 161.

30. See M. D'amato, "Three Natures, Three Stages: An Interpretation of the Yogācāra Trisvabhāva-Theory," *Journal of Indian Philosophy* 33 (2005): 188.

31. Cittamātra or Yogācāra was probably not seen as a distinct Mahāyāna school until the time of Bhāviveka, who clearly criticizes Yogācāra by drawing a doctrinal distinction between Madhyamaka and Yogācāra, putting the latter on the lower rung of the hierarchy. For instance, Dreyfus and McClintock argue: "In the case of Madhyamaka, for example, the main Mādhyamikas, at least after Bhāvaviveka, knew themselves as such, and the term has since been used by a lengthy succession of thinkers, who understood it, for the most part, in relatively similar way." See Dreyfus and McClinctock, *The Svātantrika-Prāsaṅgika Distinction*, 2. Furthermore, both Candrakīrti and Śāntideva criticize Yogācāra in *Madhyamakāvatāra* and *Bodhisattvacaryāvatāra* respectively by embracing Madhyamaka as their ultimate view of the Buddha's teachings.

32. For more on some of the earliest proponents of Cittamātra, see Williams, *Buddhist Thought*, 154–56. Also see, Robert Kritzer, *Vasubandhu and the Yogācārabhūmi: Yogācāra Elements in the Abhidharmakośabhāṣya* (Tokyo: The International Institute for Buddhist Studies, 2005), xii. Hereafter, *Vasubandhu and the Yogācārabhūmi*.

33. Dölpopa argues, "It is mentioned that the Ultimate Cittamātra is the whole appearance of reality as the appearance of gnosis, and the Conventional Cittamātra is the whole appearance of mistaken phenomena as the appearance of consciousness." *chos nyid kyi snang ba thams cad ye shes kyi snang ba don dam pa'i sems tsam dang chos can 'khrul pa'i snang ba thams cad rnam shes*

kyi snang ba kun rdzob kyi sems tsam du bshad. See Dölpopa, *dpal yongs grub dgu'i bshad pa khyad 'phags gyu rnying,* in *The Collected Works of Kun mkhyen dol po pa* ('Dzam thang, 'Bar khams rdzong: 'Dzam thang dgon pa, 199–), vol. 5, 229. Henceforth, *The Excellent Exposition on the Nine Glorious Thoroughly Established Natures.* Moreover, Dölpopa states: *'dir sems tsam la yang bden gnyis rnam dbye shes dgos shing/ dom dam gyi sems ni dbu ma dang gcig ste/ don dam gyi sems las gzhan pa'i chos 'ga' yang gshis la med pa'i phyir dang/ don dam gyi sems ni gang gis kyang gzhom du med par rtag tu de bzhin nyid du mkha' khyab tu bzhugs pa'i phyir ro// kun rdzob yin pa'i sems tsam ni deng sang yongs grags pa'i sems tsam 'di dang gcig ste/ 'di la ni rnam par shes par smra ba zhes gsungs so//* See Dölpopa, *Commentary on the Fourth Council,* 252. For an English translation of the Tibetan passage cited here, see Stearns, *Buddha from Dölpo,* 254.

34. Dölpopa says, "There are two [types] of Cittamātra: the Satyākāra-Cittamātra and the the the Alīkākāra-Cittamātra." *sems tsam la rnam bden rnam brdzun gnyis//* See Dölpopa, *Proclamation of the Great Bliss of the Dharmadhātu,* 359. Since Dölpopa believes these two types as a part of what he calls Conventional Cittamātra, he does not elaborate on the distinction between the two schools in his collected works. On the other hand, he has much to say about the other divisions of Cittamātra, since he intends to show that there is a drastic difference between the Cittamātra that he follows as the ultimate system and the Cittamātra that others wrongly describe as the ultimate intention of figures such as Asaṅga and Vasubandhu. For a brief discussion of the origin of the two categories of Cittamātra, see Brunnhölzl, *In Praise of Dharmadhātu,* 380–82, note 542. On discussion of Nirākāravāda and Sākāravāda of Yogācāra system, see Lindtner, "Cittamātra in Indian Mahāyāna until Kamalaśīla," 175–87.

35. "There are two [types] of Cittamātra also: the Ultimate and the Non-Ultimate." *sems tsam la yang don dam yin min gnyis dang/* See Dölpopa, *rang rig rang gsal gyi rab tu dbye ba,* in *The Collected Works of Kun mkhyen dol po pa* ('Dzam thang, 'Bar khams rdzong: 'Dzam thang dgon pa, 199–), vol. 6, 332. Henceforth, *Distinguishing the Self-Illuminating Self-Awareness.*

36. See Hopkins, *Mountain Doctrine,* 239.

37. *rnam par shes pa tsam don dam du 'dod pas sems tsam pa dang/* See Dölpopa, *Abhisamayālaṃkāra Commentary,* 289.

38. *mthar thug gi chos rnams dngos po dang rnam shes su 'dod pa sems tsam pa dang/ dngos po dang rnam shes las 'das pa ye shes su 'dod pa ni dbu ma pa ste/* See Dölpopa, *The Sun that Illuminates the Two Truths,* 721. On the following page of *The Sun that Illuminates the Two Truths,* Dölpopa suggests that Vijñānavāda does not assert mind and perfected nature as ultimately existent, rather it is consciousness that is accepted as ultimately existent.

39. *kun rdzob yin pa'i sems tsam ni deng sang yongs grags pa'i sems tsam 'di dang gcig ste/ 'di la ni rnam par shes par smra ba zhes gsungs so//* See Dölpopa, *Commentary on the Fourth Council,* 252. Stearns translates the sentence as follows, "The Cittamātra that is relative is identical to this Cittamātra that is

nowadays famous. Adherence to this is taught to be 'Vijñānavāda (Advocates of Consciousness).'" See Stearns, *Buddha from Dölpo*, 254.

40. For more on the three natures, see D'amato, "Three Natures, Three Stages."

41. The eight are eye consciousness, nose consciousness, ear consciousness, tongue consciousness, body consciousness, mental consciousness, afflicted mind, and all-basis-consciousness.

42. *ngo bo nyid gsum 'dod mi 'dod dang/ rnam shes tshogs brgyad 'dod mi 'dod dang/ kun gzhi'i rnam shes 'dod me 'dod dang, rigs chad 'dod me 'dod dang/ don dam du grub pa'i chos 'dod mi 'dod las dbu ma dang sems tsam gyi khyad par 'byed pa ni rgyal ba'i bka' yang dag dang sa bcu pa rnams kyis ma gsungs so//* See Dölpopa, *Abhisamayālaṃkāra Commentary*, 292.

43. *mdor bsdus par bstan na, mthar thug gi chos rnams dngos po dang rnam shes su 'dod pa sems tsam pa dang/ dngos po dang rnam shes las 'das pa ye shes su 'dod pa ni dbu ma pa ste/ dpal dus kyi 'khor lor. . . . shes dang/ 'di'i 'grel pa dri med 'od du. . . . zhes dang/* See Dölpopa, *The Sun that Illuminates the Two Truths*, 721. For an English translation of the quotes that Dölpopa cites from the Kālacakra and Vimalaprabhā, see Vesna A. Wallace, *The Kālacakratantra: The Chapter on the Individual together with the Vimalaprabhā* (New York: American Institure of Buddhist Studies at Columbia University, 2004), 241–246. Hereafter, *The Kālacakratantra*.

44. Wallace, *Kālacakratantra*, 244. Also see Vesna A. Wallace, *The Inner Kālacakratantra: A Buddhist Tantric View of the Individual* (Oxford: Oxford University Press, 2001), 34. Hereafter, *The Inner Kālacakratantra*.

45. Tāranātha interestingly argues that some Vijñānavāda commentarial works existed before the time of Nāgārjuna. Tāranātha states, "Even though it is clear that there existed some miscellaneous Cittamātra śāstras, they did not follow the treatises of Maitreya, Asaṅga and his brother Vasubandhu because they were in circulation before Ārya Nāgārjuna since they were rejected in śāstras such as *Bodhicittavivarana*, and so forth that came before Asaṅga. Therefore, it seems to be the case that [the proponents of the Cittamātra] were the five hundred Yogācāra masters such as Mahābande Avitarka, Jñānatala, and so forth, who are known to have existed. [But], their treatises were not translated in Tibetan." *sems tsam pa'i bstan bcos thor bu 'ga' zhig ni yod par gsal na yang byams chos dang thogs med sku mched kyi gzhung gi rjes su 'brang ba ni ma yin te byang chub sems 'grel sogs thogs med kyi sngon du byung ba'i bstan bcos nas bkag pa sogs kyis 'phags pa na gar ju na'i snga rol du byung ba'i phyir ro// des na btsun pa chen po a vi tar ka dang jna na la sogs pa rnal 'byor spyod pa slob dpon lnga brgya byung bar grags pa ltar yin par mngon no de dag gi bstan bcos ni bod du ma 'gyur ba yin//* See Jetsün Tāranātha, *Ornament of the Other-Emptiness Madhyamaka*, 212.

46. Hopkins translates, "Therefore, although the profound sūtras of the third wheel such as the *Sūtra Unraveling the Thought* and so forth, Maitreya's *Ornament for the Great Vehicle Sūtras*, *Differentiation of the Middle and the*

Extremes, and so forth, and Asaṅga's *Grounds of Yogic Practice, Summary of the Great Vehicle, Summary of Manifest Knowledge*, and so forth temporarily teach mind-only." See Hopkins, *Mountain Doctrine*, 249. Tāranātha, second only to Dölpopa in the Jonang tradition, also offers a similar response in two of his texts. "[We] assert that there is no distinct set of sutra for Madhyamaka and Cittamātra because [the two schools] are only different in terms of interpreting one set of sutra." (*dbu sems gnyis la mdo sde tha dad du med par ni 'dod de mdo sde gcig la dgongs pa 'grel lugs kyi khyad par tsam yin pas*). See Tāranātha, *Entry to the Definitive Meaning*, 245. Furthermore, in his *Ornament of the Other-Emptiness Madhyamaka*, Tāranātha responds to the question of whether there are separate sutras and commentarial works for Cittamātra by stating, "There is no separate sutra [for the Cittamātra] just as there is no separate sutra for the two [Hīnayāna] schools of Vaibhāṣika and Sautrāntika." *mdo sde ni logs su yod pa ma yin te/ dper na bye mdo gnyis la yang mdo sde tha dad med pa bzhin no//* See Tāranātha, *Ornament of the Other-Emptiness Madhyamaka*, 212.

47. He says, "This Dharmarāja [referring to *Kun spangs thugs rje brtson 'grus*] studied and excelled in Cittamātra sutras and *śāstras* such as Ārya Asaṅga's treatises, and particularly, Vasubandhu's eight prakaraṇas, such as *Viṃśatikā, Triṃśikā*, and so forth." *chos rje 'dis sems tsam ston pa'i mdo rnams/ 'phags pa thogs med kyi bstsan bcos rnams dang/ khyad par du slob dpon dbyig gnyen gyi sems tsam nyi shu pa dang/ sum cu pa la sogs te pra ka ra na sde brgyad rnams dang sems tsam ston pa'i bka' bstan bcos ma lus pa rnams gsan nas mkhas par bslabs shing.* See Jangsem Gyelwa Yeshé, *dpal ldan dus kyi 'khor lo'i jo nang pa'i lugs kyi bla ma brgyud pa'i rnam thar*, (mi rigs dpe bskrun khang, 2004), 95. Henceforth, *Lineage of the Jonang Kālacakra Tradition*. Furthermore, Jangsem Gyelwa Yeshé lists Nāgārjuna's *Six Collections of Reasoning*, Āryadeva's *Catuḥśatakaśāstrakārikā*, Candrakīrti's *Prasannapadā, Madhyamakāvatāra*, and Bhāviveka's *Prajñāparadīpa* as Prāsaṅgika's treatises and Śāntarakṣīta's *Madhyamakālaṃkāra*, and Kamalaśīla's *Madhyamakāloka* as Svātantrika's texts. See ibid., 102.

48. However, the Madhyamaka categories such as Yogācāra Madhyamaka (*rnal 'byor spyod pa'i dbu ma*), Sautrāntika Madhyamaka (*mdo sde spyod pa'i dbu ma*), Māyopamādvayavādin (*sgyu ma rigs sgrub pa*) and Sarvadharmāpratiṣṭhānavādin (*rab tu mi gnas par smra ba*) are not mentioned in Dölpopa's extant works, as far as I can tell.

49. "Division of the Madhyamaka into Svātantrika and Prāsaṅgika schools is not feasible to be a division of Madhyamaka." *dbu ma pa ni rang rgyud thal 'gyur zhes 'byed pa dbu ma'i dbye bar mi rung ste.* See Dölpopa, *The Great Calculation of the Fourth Council*, 181. Also in his *Commentary to the Summary of the Fourth Council*, Dölpopa argues that Svātantrika and Prāsaṅgika schools can not be the divisions of Madhyamaka as both of them fall into the extreme of existence. See Dölpopa, *bka' bsdu bzhi pa'i bsdus don 'grel pa*, in *The Collected Works of Kun mkhyen dol po pa* ('Dzam thang, 'Bar khams rdzong:

'Dzam thang dgon pa, 199–), 209. Henceforth, *Commentary to the Summary of the Fourth Council.* Also see Stearns, *Buddha from Dölpo,* 259.

50. Stearns says, "Here the terms *snang bcas* (*having appearance*) and *snang med* (*no appearance*) probably refer to the Madhyamaka of perfect appearance (*yang dag snang ba'i dbu ma*), in which it is taught that perfect reality directly appears and is seen in meditative equipoise and is the authentic Madhyamaka of apprehensible emptiness (*dmigs bcas stong nyid*), and to the Madhyamaka of no appearance (*snang med dbu ma*), in which it is taught that seeing nothing is seeing reality." See Stearns, *Buddha from Dölpo,* 410–11, note 764.

51. "There are two [types] of Madhyamaka: [Madhyamaka] with Appearance and [Madhyamaka] without Appearance" (*dbu ma la snang bcas snang med gnyis*). See Dölpopa, *Proclamation of the Great Bliss of the Dharmadhātu,* 359. As will be shown later, in some of his texts, Dölpopa adds adjectives "ultimate" and "temporary" to "Madhyamaka with Appearance" and "Madhyamaka without Appearance" respectively. Hence, we come across nomenclatures "ultimate Madhyamaka with Appearance" (*snang bcas mthar thug gi dbu ma*) and "temporary Madhyamaka without Appearance" (*snang med gnas skabs kyi dbu ma*). For instance, Dölpopa states that "the meaning of the Madhyamaka, which goes beyond Cittamātra, abides within the temporary Madhyamaka without Appearance; [however] the meaning of the last wheel, which goes beyond [the temporary Madhyamaka without Appearance], must remain within the ultimate Madhyamaka with Appearance." *sems tsam las 'das nas bka' bar pa'i dgongs pa snang med gnas skabs kyi dbu ma la gnas pa dang/ de las 'das nas bka' tha ma'i dgongs pa snang bcas mthar thug gi dbu ma la gnas dgos kyi/* See Dölpopa, *The Sun that Illuminates the Two Truths,* 724. Dratsépa is arguably the first Tibetan thinker to criticize Dölpopa's classification of Madhyamaka in the former's *de bzhin gshegs pa'i snying po mdzes rgyan gyi rgyan mkhas pa'i yid 'phrog,* a commentary on Butön's *bde gshegs snying po gsal ba'i rgyan.* See Dratsépa Rinchen Namgyel, *de bzhin gshegs pa'i snying po mdzes rgyan gyi rgyan mkhas pa'i yid 'phrog,* in *The Collected Works of Bu ston rin chen grub* (Lhasa, Zhol par khang, 2000),part 28, 191 Henceforth, *Ornament to the Ornament.*

52. Dölpopa proclaims, "Two levels of Madhyamaka that are beyond Cittamātra are explained in the *Laṅkāvatārasūtra.*" *lang gshegs su sems tsam las 'das pa'i dbu ma pa rim pa gnyis gsungs te/* See Dölpopa, *The Sun That Illuminates the Two Truths,* 724.

53. Dölpopa quotes the verses from the *Laṅkāvatārasūtra,* the English translation of which is taken from Dölpopa's *Mountain Doctrine* (237), where it appears in a similar context. It is interesting that Jangsem Gyelwa Yeshé, the second patriarch of the Jonang School, identifies Kamalaśīla's *Bhāvanakrāma* and the *Kālacakra* as the treatises for meditation-oriented practice (*sgom pa nyams len gyi gzhung*). See Jangsem Gyelwa Yeshé, *Lineage of the Jonang Kālacakra Tradition,* 102. Kamalaśīla's *Bhāvanakrāma* uses *Laṅkāvatārasūtra* as one of its major sources, and it is in this text where the same exact quote that

Dölpopa cites for his justification of the two Madhyamaka categories is also found. See Lindtner, "Cittamātra in Indian Mahāyāna until Kamalaśīla," 160. See Klaus-Dieter Mathes, "'Gos Lo tsā ba gZhon nu dpal's Commentary on the *Dharmatā* chapter of the *Dharmadharmatāvibhāgakārikās*," in *Studies in Indian Philosophy and Buddhism*, vol. 12 (2005), 33, note 70, where Mathes offers an Enlish translation of the same passage cited above. Notice that this version does not have the negation in the last line of the second stanza.

54. *sems tsam las 'das nas bka' bar pa'i dgongs pa snang med gnas skabs kyi dbu ma la gnas pa dang/ de las 'das nas bka' tha ma'i dgongs pa snang bcas mthar thug gi dbu ma la gnas dgos kyi/* See Dölpopa, *The Sun That Illuminates the Two Truths*, 724.

55. While Kamalaśīla obviously does not employ the terms that Dölpopa uses here, the former's *Bhāvanakrāma* quotes the exact verses from the *Laṅkāvatārasūtra* and explains three different modes of realization in a hierarchical order, the last one being the ultimate realization. See Lindtner, "Cittamātra in Indian Mahayana until Kamalaśīla," 159–60.

56. Wallace, *Inner Kālacakratantra*, 11.

57. Dolpopa lists ten definitive sutras in his *Overcoming Nihilism and Superimposition*. They are *sher phyin lnga brgya pa* (*Pañcaśatikāprajñāpāramitāsū tra*), *byang chub sems dpa'i bslab pa rab tu bsdus dbye ba'i le'u cha bcu gnyis byams zhus su'ang grags pa gnyis gcig tu bsdus pa* (the "Maitreya Chapter"), *rgyan stug po'i mdo* (*Ghanavyūhasūtra*), *rab tu zhi ba rnam par nges pa'i chos 'phrul gyi ting nge 'dzin gyi mdo* (*Praśāntaviniścayaprātihāryanāmasamādhisūtra*), *dkon mchog sprin gyi mdo* (*Ratnameghasūtra*), *gser 'od dum chen* (*Suvarṇaprabhāsottamasūtra*), *dgongs pa nges 'grel* (*Saṃdhinirmocanasūtra*), *lang kar gshegs pa* (*Laṅkāvatārasūtra*), *ye shes snang ba rgyan gyi mdo* (*Sarvabuddhaviṣayāvatārajñānālokālaṃkārasūtra*), and *mdo sde phal chen* (*Buddhāvataṃsakasūtra*). See See Dölpopa, *slob ma la spring ba skur 'debs dang sgro 'dogs spang ba* (*Collected Works of Dölpopa Sherap Gyeltsen*, vol. 6, 277–86, Dzamthang, bar khams rdzong), 285–86. Henceforth, *Overcoming Nihilism and Superimposition*. Sometimes Dölpopa makes reference to the five definitive sutras, in that case the last five sutras from the category are taken out. These scriptures become the foundational texts for his presentation of the Jonang system. The Sanskrit titles are taken from Brunnhölzl, *When the Clouds Part*, 5. See also Stearns, *Buddha from Dölpo*, 316–17, n. 29. It is not clear from Dölpopa's writings what criteria he follows for the inclusion into, or exclusion from, the category of the ten definitive sutras or the group of the ten tathāgata-essence sutras. For instance, Dölpopa claims both the *Tathāgatagarbhasūtra* and the *Laṅkāvatārasūtra* as authoritative sources for his school, but the former is included in the group of the ten tathāgata-essence sutras, and the latter in the category of the ten definitive sutras, irrespective of his assertion that both explain tathāgata-essence explicitly.

58. Dölpopa lists ten tathāgata-essence sutras in his *Overcoming Nihilism and Superimposition*. They are: *de bzhin gshegs pa'i snying po'i*

mdo (*Tathāgatagarbhasūtra*), *rnam par mi rtog pa la 'jug pa'i gzhung* (*Avikalpaprave-śadhāraṇi*), *mdo sde dpal 'phreng* (*Śrīmālādevīsūtra*), *rnga bo che* (*Mahābherisūtra*), *sor mo'i 'phreng ba* (*Aṅgulimālīyasūtra*), *stong nyid chen po'i mdo* (*Śūnyatā-nāmamahāsūtra*), *de bzhin gshegs pa'i thugs rje chen po bstan pa'i mdo* (*Tathāgata mahākaruṇānirdeśasūtra*), *de bzhin gshegs pa'i yon tan dang ye shes bsam gyis mi khyab pa bstan pa'i mdo* (*Tathāgataguṇajñānācintyaviṣayāvatāranirdeśasūtra*), *sprin chen po'i mdo rgyas pa* (*Mahāmeghasūtra*), and *myang 'das chen po'i mdo rgyas bsdus gsum gcig tu byas pa* (*Parinirvāṇasūtra* and *Mahāparinirvāṇasūtra*). See Dölpopa, *Overcoming Nihilism and Superimposition*, 285. See Brunnhölzl, *When the Clouds Part*, 986, notes 17 and 18 for more on *stong nyid chen po'i mdo* and *myang 'das chen po'i mdo rgyas bsdus gsum gcig tu byas pa*. The Sanskrit titles are taken from Brunnhölzl's book. Sometimes Dölpopa makes reference to the five tathāgata-essence sutras, in which case he excludes the last five sutras from the category. Stearns, *Buddha from Dölpo*, 316, note 28.

59. For information on how Dölpopa asserts that the middle-wheel teachings are interpretable, see Hopkins, *Mountain Doctrine*, 24. Dölpopa states: "The Bhagavan in the *Saṃdhinirmocanasūtra* states that the First Wheel and the Second Wheel teachings are interpretable." *bka' 'khor lo dang po daṇg gnyis pa drang don du bcom ldan 'das kyis mdo dgongs pa nges 'grel du gsungs la/* See Dölpopa, *The Sun that Illuminates the Two Truths*, 724.

60. As pointed out in the previous section, Jangsem Gyelwa Yeshé does not assert that the works of Maitreya, Asaṅga, and Vasubandhu are authoritative sources for his Great Madhyamaka. Instead Jangsem Gyelwa Yeshé lists Nāgārjuna's *Six Collections of Reasoning*, Āryadeva's *Catuḥśatakaśāstrakārikā*, Candrakīrti's *Prasannapadā* and *Madhyamakāvatāra*, and Bhāviveka's *Prajñā-paradīpa* as Prāsaṅgika treatises; Jñānagarbha's *Satyadvayavibhaṅgakārikā*, Śāntarakṣita's *Madhyamakālaṃkāra*, and Kamalaśīla's *Madhyamakāloka* as the Svātantrika texts; and the *Kālacakra* and Kamalaśīla's *Bhāvanakrāma* as the treatises for meditation oriented practice (*sgom pa nyams len gyi gzhung*). Jangsem Gyelwa Yeshé does not use the term "Great Madhyamaka" to refer to any of these texts, except for the *Kālacakra*. He argues, "Kamalaśīla's *Bhāvanakrāma* and the transmission of the Great Madhyamaka stemming from the bodhisattva and king, Sucandra, etc. are the treatises of meditation oriented practice." *Ka ma la shi la'i sgom rim gsum dang byang chub sems dpa' zla ba rgyal po nas brgyud pa'i dbu ma chen po'i khrid la sogs pa sgom pa nyam len gyi gzhung rnams daṇg.* See Jangsem Gyelwa Yeshé, *Lineage of the Jonang Kālacakra Tradition*, 102. Here one could certainly read the passage in the way that the phrase "transmission of the Great Madhyamaka" could include Kamalaśīla's *Bhāvanakrāma* as well. In that case, Kamalaśīla's *Bhāvanakrāma* would also be a Great Madhyamaka treatise. However, more research needs to be done to get a better assessment of how these terms are used in the literature of early Jonang scholars and other related texts. It is interesting that Jangsem Gyelwa Yeshé lists *Prajñāpradīpa*, a text that obviously criticizes Buddhapālita, as a

Prāsaṅgika text. This goes against the way we sometimes trace the lineages of Svātantrika-Madhyamaka and Prāsaṅgika-Madhyamaka by associating the former with Bhāviveka and the latter with Buddhapālita.

Chapter 4

1. Sam Van Schaik, *Approaching the Great Perfection: Simultaneous and Gradual Methods of Dzogchen Practice in the Longchen Nyingtig* (Boston: Wisdom, 2004), 9. Hereafter, *Approaching the Great Perfection*. Longchenpa received his initial scholastic education at Samye monastery and later went to Sangpu monastery for his scholastic training. For more on Longchenpa's life, see Greg Hillis, *The Rhetoric of Naturalness: A Critical Study of the gNas lugs mdzod*, (Dissertation, Department of Religions Studies, University of Virginia, January, 2003), 112–130. Hereafter, *The Rhetoric of Naturalness*.

2. *theg mchog zab mo'i dgongs don rnam 'byed pa'i/ tshul 'di bla ma dam pas rjes bzung zhing/ blo ldan slob mas yang yang bskul ba'i mthus/ blo gros rgyal mtshan dpal gyis rnam par sbyar.* See Sazang Mati Penchen, *rgyud bla ma'i bstan bcos kyi rnam par bshad pa nges don rab gsal snang ba*, (Khreng tu'u?, 2000?), 518. Henceforth, *Illuminating the Definitive Meaning*.

3. "[The transmission] has been conferred upon Sazang by Künkhyen Chöjé [that is, Dölpopa.]" *kun mkhyen chos rje la/ brgyud de sa bzang pa la gnang ba'o.* See Sazang, *Illuminating the Definitive Meaning*, 519–20.

4. For the quote, see Sazang, *Illuminating the Definitive Meaning*, 16. He also argues that the *Abhisamayālaṃkāra* explains the view of the middle-wheel sutras, the *Sūtrālaṃkāra* delineates both the ultimate view and the Buddhist path as found in the last-wheel teachings, and the *Madhyāntavibhāga* and *Dharmadharmatāvibhāga* explicate the dharma reality, the view of the last-wheel teachings only.

5. Sazang says:

> The ultimate reality, [which is] the essential meaning of dharma-reality,
> Due to becoming free from adventitious defilements of conventionality,
> Becomes the great enlightenment.
> [The texts] that teach such are definitive, the opposites are interpretable.

For the Tibetan, see Sazang, *Illuminating the Definitive Meaning*, 516. In his *Abhidharmasamuccaya Commentary*, Sazang offers a similar definition substantiated by quotes from *Samādhirājasūtra* and Candrakīrti's (although not the author of the *Madhyamakāvatāra*) *Pradīpoddyotana*, a commentary on *Guhyasamāja Tantra*. See Sazang Mati Penchen, *mngon pa kun btus kyi 'grel pa shes bya rab gsal*, (Gangtok: Gonpo Tseten, 1977), 364. Henceforth, *Abhidharmasamuccaya Commentary*.

6. Sazang argues, "The ultimate natural body, which is naturally luminous and which is beautifully adorned by the excellent qualities, should be understood as similar to the statue of the Buddha made of jewel because it naturally exists and it is not newly made through efforts." *dom dam pa ngo bo nyid kyi sku rang bzhin gyis 'og gsal zhing yon tan gyi dpal gyis mchog tu mdzes pa ni rin chen las grub pa'i sangs rgyas kyi sku dang 'dra bar shes par bya ste/ gdod ma nas rang bzhin gyis ni grub pa yin zhing/ 'bad rtsol gyis gsar du byas pa min pa'i phyir//* See Sazang, *Illuminating the Definitive Meaning*, 248.

7. *de lta bas na shin tu rgyas pa las chos thams cad ngo bo nyid med par gsungs kyang/ don la sgra ji bzhin du nges par mi gzung zhing.* See Sazang, *Illuminating the Definitive Meaning*, 269.

8. *sgra ji bzhin par ni ma yin te/ dgongs pa nges 'grel du . . . gsungs pa ltar ro//* For the quote, see Sazang, *Abhidharmasamuccaya Commentary*, 360. Furthermore, Sazang states, "If the statement made in the *Prajñāpāramitāsūtras* that all phenomena are natureless is not literal, what is the intended point? The basis in intention is . . ." *shin tu rgyas pa theg chen las chos thams cad ngo bo nyid med do zhes gang gsungs pa de la sgra ji bzhin pa ma yin na dgongs pa'i don gang yin zhe na, dgongs gzhi ni . . .* See ibid., 357. Sangpu Lodrö Tsungmé leaves the *Saṃdhinirmocanasūtra* out of his list of the supreme definitive sutras, while Sazang asserts it as a supreme definitive sutra, as shown in both his *Uttaratantra* and *Abhidharmasamuccaya* commentaries. Butön's *History of Buddhism* ('krunggo'i bod kyishes rig dpeskrunkhang, 1998) categorizes the *Uttaratantra* and *Saṃdhinirmocanasūtra* as Cittamātra texts.

9. Sazang, *Illuminating the Definitive Meaning*, 14–15.

10. Ibid., 14.

11. *bka' bar pa las gsungs pa thams cad brdzun pa'o snyam du sems na/ de ltar yang mi bsam ste/ glo bur gyi dri ma la dgongs nas gtso cher ngo bo nyid med par ston yang/ med pa la med par gsungs pa'i phyir brdzun pa ma yin zhing sems kyi rang bzhin 'od gsal ba'o zhes pa la sogs pas chos dbyings kyang yod par ston pa'i phyir mthar thug pa'i don ni tha ma dang yang gcig cing mchog tu zab pa nyid yin pa'i phyir ro// 'ong kyang chos kyi dbyings gtso cher ston pa'i phyir phyi ma mchog tu 'phags par shes par bya ste.* See Sazang, *Illuminating the Definitive Meaning*, 278. Sazang gives a similar account in his *Abhidharmasamuccaya Commentary*, "In consideration that conventional adventitious defilements, afflictions, are without inherent existence (*rang bzhin med pa*) under analysis [it is] taught that all phenomena are empty, but it is to be understood that it is not that the dharma-reality, the naturally pure ultimate, does not exist at all." *kun rdzob glo bur gyi dri ma kun nas nyon mongs pa rnams dpyad na rang bzhin med pa la dgongs nas chos thams cad stong pa nyid du bstan pa yin gyi/ don dam rang bzhin gyis rnam par dag pa'i chos kyi dbyings gtan nas med pa ni ma yin no zhes kyang rig par bya'o//* See Sazang, *Abhidharmasamuccaya Commentary*. He cites Nāgārjuna's *Dharmadhātustotra* to substantiate his point here.

12. Although I did not find the terms "permanent entity" (*rtag pa'i dngos po*) or "unconditioned entity" (*'dus ma byas kyi dngos po*) to explain the ultimate truth in Dölpopa's own works, he would not have disagreed with Sazang on the meaning of the terms.

13. *rtag pa yang yin la 'dus ma byas pa'i dngos po yang yin pa zhes brjod pa la ni 'gal ba med de.* For the quote, see Sazang, *Illuminating the Definitive Meaning*, 123. For Sazang, "thing" refers to something that is suitable to perform a function, whereas "conditioned things" are those that are subject to causes and conditions. The latter is what Sazang calls "secondary conditioned thing" (*nyi tshe ba 'dus byas kyi dngos po*). For the reference, see Sazang, *Illuminating the Definitive Meaning*, 123. Gyeltsap, as will be shown later, puts such a view held by Dölpopa and Sazang to criticism in his commentary. While Gyeltsap uses the term "thing" as a synonym for impermanent phenomena, Sazang does not restrict it merely to impermanent phenomena. Furthermore, Sazang argues, "If someone says that since the buddha-gnosis exists since beginningless, pursuing the path would be pointless, and there also would be no difference between the cause and the effect. [Our response is that] because adventitious afflictions have to be eliminated, there is a great purpose in cultivating paths, and because of that there also is a difference between the cause and the effect in terms of being defiled and not defiled [respectively]." *ci ste sangs rgyas kyi ye shes gdod ma nas yod na lam la 'bad dgos pa med par 'gyur zhing/ rgyu dang 'bras bu khyad par med par yang 'gyur ro zhe na/ glo bur gyi dri ma nyon mongs pa rnams spang dgos pa'i phyir lam sgom pa ni don chen po dang ldan zhing/ de nyid kyi phyir rgyu dang 'bras bu dag dri ma dang bcas pa dang dri ma med pa'i khyad par kyang yod de.* See Sazang, *Illuminating the Definitive Meaning*, 120.

14. *de bzhin nyid de thams cad la khyab par kun tu 'gro ba'i phyir cha shas dang bcas par 'gyur ram snyam na/ ma nges te/ rgyud las cha med kun 'gro khyab pa po.* For the quote, see Sazang, *Illuminating the Definitive Meaning*, 123. Gyeltsap, as will be shown later, repeatedly criticizes the way that Dölpopa and his followers explicate the pervasive nature of the dharma-body in all beings in his *Uttaratantra* commentary.

15. *de bzhin gshegs pa'i chos kyi sku ni rnam par shes pa glo bur gyi dri ma kun tu rtog pa thams cad las yang dag par 'das shing.* See Sazang, *Illuminating the Definitive Meaning*, 51. Closely following Dölpopa, Sazang makes a distinction between ultimate truth that is not subject to conceptual thought and conventional truth that is subject to mind basis of all. Dölpopa argues, "There are two all-bases that are basis for the object of abandonment and the basis for antidote. What are the two? [The two are] all-basis-consciousness and all-basis-gnosis. The first, as is widely known, refers to that which has fruition and seeds, the root consciousness, perpetuating consciousness, and neutral. The all-basis-gnosis is dharma reality itself, and it is referred to by many names such as tathāgata-essence, seed, element, [buddha] lineage." *spang bya dang gnyen po'i chos dag 'jug pa'i rten kun gzhi gnyis yod pa'i phyir ro// gnyis po*

gang zhe na/ kun gzhi'i rnam shes dang kun gzhi'i ye shes so// de la snga ma ni rnam smin dang sa bon thams cad pa dang rtsa ba'i rnam shes dang len pa'i rnam shes dang lung du ma bstan pa yin par deng sang yongs su grags so// kun gzhi ye shes ni chos kyi dbyings nyid yin zhing/ de la de bzhin gshegs pa'i snying po dang/ sa bon dang/ khams dang/ rigs . . . la sogs pa'i ming du mas bstan to. See Döl-popa, *Abhisamayālaṃkāra Commentary*, 385–386. However, these two terms do not appear in Dölpopa's *Mountain Doctrine* and the *Uttaratantra* commentary.

16. "However, [the dharma-body] gradually manifests as different forms of defilements are purified. However the complete [dharma-body] directly appears to those who have completely purified defilements." *'on kyang sgrib pa ci rigs pas dag pa las rim gyis snang bar 'gyur zhing/ sgrib pa ma lus pas dag pa la ni mtha' dag kyang mngon sum du snang ba nyid de . . .* See Sazang, *Illuminating the Definitive Meaning*, 122. What Sazang is arguing here is that although buddha-nature or dharma-body exists inherently in all beings we do not realize it until we begin to eliminate the mental defilements. As we eliminate the defilements, we begin to see the ultimate truth. However, the complete realization of buddha-nature does not occur until we have elimi-nated all defilements.

17. Sazang states, "Because the conventional objects are not truly exis-tent in reality they do not appear to gnosis." *yang dag par na kun rdzob kyi dngos po rnam bden par grub pa med pa'i phyir ye shes la mi snang zhing/* See Sazang, *Illuminating the Definitive Meaning*, 295. Sazang demonstrates the distinction between the two polar opposite truths by arguing that conceptual thought takes conventional truth as its object, whereas gnosis or buddha-nature takes ultimate truth as its object.

18. Sazang claims, "If someone asserts that since [enlightened] qualities such as power, fearlessness, and so forth are generated gradually, they do not exist in the nature of [our] mind since beginningless time, this too is not feasible at all. Since the buddha qualities have an unconditioned nature, they are not newly generated, rather the previously existing [enlightened qualities] get manifested through merely becoming free from defilements." *yang kha cig stobs dang mi 'jigs pa la sogs pa'i yon tan rnams kyang rim gyis bskyed pa las 'grub pa'i phyir gdod ma nas sems kyi rang bzhin du yod pa ma yin no zhes bya bar 'dod na/ de yang shin tu rigs pa ma yin te/ de dag ni 'dus ma byas pa'i rang bzhin yin pas sngar med gsar du bskyed pa ni ma yin zhing, sngar yod pa dri ma dang bral ba tsam gyis mngon sum du 'gyur ba'i phyir ro.* See Sazang, *Illuminat-ing the Definitive Meaning*, 368.

19. After quoting from several texts such as Kamalaśīla's *Madhyamakāloka*, Śāntarakṣita's *Madhyamakālaṃkāra*, and Dignāga's *Prajñāpāramitāpiṇḍārtha*, he conclusively states: These [treatises] clear away the misconception that the *Laṅkāvatārasūtra*, *Saṃdhinirmocanasūtra*, *Sūtrālaṃkāra*, *Madhyāntavibhāga*, *Yogacārabhūmi*, and so forth are treatises of the Cittamātra because they teach the three natures. Even though the three natures that are in conformity with the Cittamātra such as a thoroughly established nature that is the other-

powered mere cognition being empty of the imputed nature, and so forth
are taught temporarily in those texts, they primarily teach the final three
natures asserted by the Madhyamaka School such as the thoroughly established nature that is the dharma-reality being empty of all selves, and so
forth. If they become treatises of the Cittamātra because of explaining the
Cittamātra temporarily, then the *Prajñāpāramitāsūtra*, the *Abhisamayālaṃkāra*,
and so forth also would very absurdly be treatises for Hearers because they
teach the Hearer Vehicle. However, such is not the case. *'di dag gis ni lang*
kar gshegs pa dang dgongs 'grel dang/ mdo sde rgyan dang, dbus mtha' dang/ rnal
'byor spyod pa'i sa la sogs pa rnams ngo bo nyid gsum ston pa'i phyir sems tsam
gyi gzhung yin no zhes smra ba'i 'khrul pa yang bsal ba yin te/ de rnams su gzhan
dbang rnam rig tsam kun brtags kyis stong pa'i yongs grub la sogs pa gnas skabs
sems tsam pa dang mthun pa'i ngo bo nyid gsum yang gsungs mod/ mthar thug
chos kyi dbyings bdag mtha' dag gis stong pa'i yongs grub la sogs pa dbu ma pa
bzhed pa'i ngo bo nyid gsum brjod bya'i gtso bor ston pa'i phyir ro// ci ste gnas
skabs su sems tsam pa bstan pas sems tsam gyi rang gzhung du 'gyur na ni, yum
dang/ mngon rtogs rgyan la sogs par yang nyan thos kyi theg pa bstan pa'i phyir
nyan thos kyi gzhung du ha cang thal bar 'gyur te de ltar yang ma yin no// See
Sazang, *Abhidharmasamuccaya* Commentary, 104–105.

20. He is not mentioned in any of the *Uttaratantra* commentaries and
its related texts that I have consulted for this book.

21. Gendün Özer, *theg pa chen po rgyud bla ma'i rnam bshad don dam rnam*
nges bsdus pa'i snying po'i snying po, Selected Collections of Kadam Tradition,
vol. 20, si khron mi rigs dpe skrun khang, 2006, 457. Henceforth, *Quintes-*
sential Essence.

22. Gendün Özer, *Quintessential Essence*, 457. "Early commentators" usually refers to scholars such as Ngok, Chapa, Naktso, Patsap, and so forth who
flourished between the eleventh and twelfth centuries.

23. He states that "the inappropriate translations [in Ngok's Tibetan
rendering of the *Uttaratantra*] have been made viable in consultation with the
more appropriate translations rendered by Naktso, Patsap, and so forth." *de la*
'gyur mi bde ba rnams nag tsho dang pa tshab la sogs pa'i 'gyur gzhan bde ba rnams
dang don mthun par byas te. For reference, see Gendün Özer, *Quintessential*
Essence, 566. This certainly suggests that Gendün Özer had access to copies of
the Tibetan translations of Naktso, Patsap, and some other Tibetan scholars.

24. See Tsünpa Pelrin and Zhönnu Gyeltsen, *Biographies of Gyelsé Tokmé*
Zangpo.

25. He began his formal study of Buddhist texts such as *Abhidharma-*
samuccaya and the *Five Treatises of Maitreya* at the age of fifteen at Bodong É
(*bo dong e*) monastery, also known as, É Chödra Chenmo (*e chos grwa chen po*)
under Künga Gyeltsen. He then went to Sakya monastery, where he primarily studied texts on Buddhist epistemology. He visited several monasteries
in central Tibet for debates on Buddhist philosophical topics at the age of
twenty-three. In his early thirties, he was requested by his teachers to be the

abbot of the Tara monastery (*rta ra dgon*), where he served for seven years, while maintaining the connection with his main seat of Bodong É. Tsünpa Pelrin and Zhönnu Gyeltsen, *Biographies of Gyelsé Tokmé Zangpo*, 29–31.

26. Gyelsé Tokmé Zangpo, *theg pa chen po rgyud bla ma'i nges don gsal ba'i 'od zer*, in *Collected Works of Kadampa Masters*, vol. 59. Si khron mi rigs dpe skrun khang, 2007. Henceforth, *Illuminating the Definitive Meaning of the Uttaratantra*.

27. Tsünpa Pelrin and Zhönnu Gyeltsen, *Biographies of Gyelsé Tokmé Zangpo*, 35–36. The colophon to the *Uttaratantra* commentary mentions that he wrote the commentary at the Bodong É.

28. *nges don rgyud bla ma zhes pa'i yang dag phul gyi bstan bcos*/ See Gendün Özer, *Quintessential Essence*, 561. A few pages later, Gendün Özer says, "the cream of the excellent treatises known by 'the *Uttaratantra*' in which the definitive meaning of the Mahāyāna is consolidated" *theg pa chen po'i nges don phyogs gcig tu bsdus pa rgyud bla ma zhes pa'i yang dag phul gyi btsan bcos 'di mdzad*// See ibid., 565.

29. *kwa ye, nges don tshogs pa'i bka' 'gyur zer kyang 'di lags te, nges don mdo sde'i dgongs pa mtha' dag 'dir 'tshogs phyir*// *nges don bsdus pa'i bstan 'gyur zer kyang 'di lags te*/ *nges don 'grel pa'i bshad pa mtha' dag 'dir bsdus phyir*// *de phyir nges don don du gnyer ba'i skal ldan rnams 'di la zhugs shig 'dis ni nges don nges par ston*// See Gendün Özer, *Quintessential Essence*, 469.

30. *dri med tshig gi 'dab brgyas rab mdzes shing*/ *nges don mthar thug ge sar snying po cha*/ *mi pham mgon gyi gsung rab pad tshal 'di*/ *gzhan don sbrang rtsi don gnyer don du dbye*// Gyelsé Tokmé Zangpo, *Illuminating the Definitive Meaning of the Uttaratantra*, 334.

31. *gang du gsungs na*/ *bka' bar pa'i mdo de dang der gsungs*// *ji skad gsungs na gzugs sogs shes bya'i 'gres rkang thams cad rnams kun tu rang rang gis stong pa'o zhes gsungs so*// See Gendün Özer, *Quintessential Essence*, 497.

32. *gang du gsungs na de nas yang bka' tha ma'i mdo 'dir gsungs. . . . ji skad gsungs na sems can kun la sangs rgyas kyi khams grub pa snying por gyur pa yod ces gsungs.* See Gendün Özer, *Quintessential Essence*, 497. On the following page of the same text, Gendün Özer says, "It is taught that the [buddha]-element that exists as an essence exists." *khams grub pa snying por gyur pa yod ces bstan to*//

33. *'o na sprin sogs bzhin du mi bden par gsungs pa rnams gang la dgongs zhe na*/ *nyon mongs pa rnams dang des kun nas bslangs pa'i las dang de dag gi rnam smin gyi 'bras bu phung po'i don ni sprin la sogs pa bzhin du brjod do*// See Gyelsé Tokmé Zangpo, *Illuminating the Definitive Meaning of the Uttaratantra*, 394.

34. *de ltar dpe dgus bstan pa'i don 'di ni zab pa bas kyang ches zab pa*/ *nges pa'i don mthar thug pa ste*/ See Gyelsé Tokmé Zangpo, *Illuminating the Definitive Meaning of the Uttaratantra*, 386.

35. Gendün Özer calls it, "the ultimate [buddha]-element endowed with three natures." "*don dam pa'i khams rang bzhin gsum ldan*" See Gendün Özer, *Quintessential Essence*, 496. While the author uses the terms, buddha-element, the buddha-nature, and the sugata-essence, interchangeably in his

commentary, he does not use the word "tathāgata-essence" at all in his commentary.

36. "There is no affliction whatsoever that is the nature of the subject, ultimate element, because [the buddha-element] being free from afflictions is its nature." *don dam pa'i khams 'di chos can/ khyod la bsal bar bya ba'i kun nyon khyod kyi rang bzhin yin pa ni ci yang med de/ khyod de dang ye nas bral ba 'di khyod kyi rang bzhin yin pa'i phyir ro//* See Gendün Özer, *Quintessential Essence*, 496.

37. "There is no single purity that is not the nature of the subject, ultimate element, because [the buddha-element] being endowed with [the purity] since beginning is its nature." *dom dam pa'i khams 'di chos can/ khyod la bzhag par bya ba'i rnam byang khyod kyi rang bzhin min pa ni cung zad kyang med ste/ khyod de dang ye nas ldan pa 'di khyod kyi rang bzhin yin pa'i phyir ro//* See Gendün Özer, *Quintessential Essence*, 496.

38. *sems can ma lus thams cad la/ gdod nas yon tan lhun grub can/ yin la yin bzhin 'chad pa'i phyir/ skur 'debs spangs pa'i sems bskyed do//* See Gendün Özer, *Quintessential Essence*, 457.

39. *nyon mongs pa la sogs pa'i nyes pa rnams ni glo bur du ldan pa yin gyi/ rang bzhin gyis yod pa ma yin la, stobs la sogs pa'i yon tan rnams ni dang po nyid nas rang bzhin gyis ldan pa'i phyir khams de ni ji ltar sngar ma dag pa'i gnas skabs na gnas pa bzhin du phyis shin tu dag pa'i gnas skabs na yang de bzhin du gnas pa'i phyir rang bzhin gyis nam yang 'gyur ba med pa'i chos nyid do//* See Gyelsé Tokmé Zangpo, *Illuminating the Definitive Meaning of the Uttaratantra*, 365.

40. Gyelsé Tokmé Zangpo states: "As for the reason why [the buddha-] element, the tathāgata-essence, pervades all sentient beings, [it is because] the dharma-body of the resultant complete Buddha pervades sentient beings. This is so because when the element is purified from defilements, the dharma-body is born. Or [one could say that since] the naturally purified dharma-body pervades all sentient beings, [the buddha-element pervades all beings.]" *khams de bzhin gshegs pa'i snying pos sems can la khyab pa'i rgyu mtshan ni sems can rnams la 'bras bu rdzogs pa'i sangs rgyas kyi chos kyi sku 'phro ba ste dri mas dag pas na de 'byung ba'i phyir ro/ yang na rang bzhin rnam dag gi chos skus sems can thams cad la khyab pa'o/* See Gyelsé Tokmé Zangpo, *Illuminating the Definitive Meaning of the Uttaratantra*, 356.

41. Tsunpa Pelrin reports Gyelsé Tokmé's view: "The doctrinal presentation of the Omniscient One [that is, Dölpopa] is taught in many sutras and tantras, and it was even an old system in India. Therefore, we do not see any fault with it. The doctrinal presentation of the Abbot Butön is also not merely of his own [new school]; rather it is the intended meaning of most of the sutras and tantra and of most of the Indian and Tibetan scholars and adepts. Therefore, in no way do we see any fault with [Butön's doctrinal presentation]. He [that is, Butön] is right." *kun mkhyen gyi grub mtha' 'di ni mdo rgyud mang po na bshad// rgya gar nas kyis grub mtha' rnying pa yin pas rang res nor bar ma shes// mkhan bu ston pa'i grub mtha' 'di yang ni khong cig pu'i ma yin// mdo rgyud phal mo che thams cad dang rgya bod kyi mkhas grub*

phal che ba thams cad kyi dgongs pa yin pas de bas kyang 'o skol gyis nor bar ma shes khong bden gsung// See Tsünpa Pelrin and Zhönnu Gyeltsen, *Biographies of Gyelsé Tokmé Zangpo*, 85–86.

42. Chapter 3 of the *Treasury of Words and Meaning* deals specifically with the concept of the tathāgata-essence, where buddha-nature is explained as an undefiled essence of all sentient beings. Germano states that "the third chapter [of the *Treasure of Words and Meaning*] describes how this innate purity [the buddha-nature] nevertheless remains unstained at the core of all life." David Germano, *Poetic Thought, the Intelligent Universe, and the Mystery of Self: The Tantric Synthesis of rDzogs Chen in Fourteenth Century Tibet* (Dissertation, University of Wisconsin, Madison, 1992), 77. Hereafter, *Poetic Thought, the Intelligent Universe, and the Mystery of Self*.

43. The *Treasury of Abiding Reality* also explains the tathāgata-essence as found in the last-wheel teachings. Hillis states that "both of these currents [that refer to the emptiness taught in the middle wheel and the positive buddha-nature taught in the last wheel] are strongly evident in the text of *The Treasury of Abiding Reality*." Hillis, *The Rhetoric of Naturalness*, 182.

44. In his *Commentary to the Treasury of the Precious Dharma Reality*, Longchenpa describes the importance of the buddha-nature concept throughout the text. For information on how he discusses the concept of the buddha-nature or dharma-reality, see Longchen Rapjampa, *chos dbyings rin po che'i mdzod kyi 'grel pa lung gi gter mdzod*, vol. 3 (Gangtok, Sikkim: Sherab Gyaltsen and Khyentse Labrang, 1983), 89–92, 95, 113–14, 149, 160, 204. Hereafter, *Commentary to the Treasury of the Precious Dharma Reality*. For quotes from the *Uttaratantra*, see ibid., 95, 113.

45. Mathes, *A Direct Path to the Buddha Within*, 98. For the quotes from the *Uttaratantra*, see Longchen Rapjampa, *theg pa mtha' dag gi don gsal bar byed pa grub pa'i mtha' rin po che'i mdzod*, vol. 2 (Gangtok, Sikkim: Sherab Gyaltsen and Khyentse Labrang, 1983), 625, 633, 672, 676, 678, 747, 824, 860–61, 874, 899–901, 948, 967. Hereafter, *Treasury of Tenets*. For a detailed analysis and an English translation of the *Treasury of Tenets*, see Albion Butters, *The Doxographical Genius of Kun mkhyen kLong chen rab 'byams pa*, (Dissertation, Columbia University, 2006).

46. *sprin dang rmi lam sgyu bzhin de dang der/ shes bya thams cad rnam kun stong pa zhes/ gsungs nas yang 'dir rgyal rnams sems can la/ sangs rgyas snying po yod ces ci ste gsungs//* For reference, see *The Sūtrālaṃkāra and the Uttaratantra*, 93.

47. *bka' bar pa chos thams cad mi rtag pa sprin lta bu dang/ mi bden pa rmi lam lta bu dang, rgyu rkyen tshogs kyang rang bzhin med pa sgu ma lta bu la sogs pa gsungs la 'dir ye nas 'gyur med du yod pas rtag pa dang, rang bzhin du gnas pas dben pa dang, rgyu rkyen gyis ma bskyed pas 'dus ma byas su bstan pa dag 'gal ba'i phyir ji ltar lags zhes . . . pa'i lan du snying po 'di'ang skyon dang 'dus byas pa la sogs pas stong pa'i phyir stong pa yin gyis/ rang gi yon tan gyi chos 'dor ba'i stong pa ma yin te/* See Longchenpa, *Treasury of Tenets*, 899–900.

48. *khams byang chub kyi snying po sems can la lhun grub tu yod pa de yang rang bzhin gyis dag cing yon tan rdzogs pa'i cha nas chos kyi sku'i rang bzhin zhes bya ste* / See Longchenpa, *Treasury of Tenets*, 894. For a similar quote, see Longchenpa, *Commentary to the Treasury of the Precious Dharma Reality*, 113–14. Longchenpa cites the *Uttaratantra* to show that such is the case.

49. Mathes, *A Direct Path to the Buddha Within*, 103. While Longchenpa maintains that these qualities have existed in sentient beings since beginningless time, he does not claim that they are free from adventitious defilements. As he states, "We also do not assert that these qualities exist as free of adventitious defilements now." *"da lta glo bur rnam dag tu yon tan de dag yod ces pa ni kho bo cag kyang mi 'dod"* // See Longchenpa, *Commentary to the Treasury of the Precious Dharma Reality*, 114.

50. *dbyings snying po 'di'i ngo bo la dor bya' dri ma ye nas med de rang bzhin gyis 'od gsal zhing dri ma med pa'i phyir ro* // *sngar med kyi yon tan phyi nas gsar du bsgrub pa med de yon tan lhun grub yin pa'i phyir ro* // See Longchenpa, *Treasury of Tenets*, 860–61.

51. *rigs kyi don 'di ni drang don du mi lta bar nges pa'i don 'ba' zhig tu bzung ste shes par bya'o* // *gnas 'di theg pa chen po'i tshul rab tu gces shing rtogs par dka' ba'i phyir 'dir rgyas par bshad pa'ang de yin no* // See Longchenpa, *Treasury of Tenets*, 905. Mathes also explains how the *Uttaratantra* is definitive: "The superiority of Prāsaṅgika is accepted within the lower analytical approach of the sūtras, but the *Ratnagotravibhāga*, a text whose doctrine is so closely associated with dzogchen, has definitive meaning, counteracting the defects of the analytical approach in a way similar to dzogchen." For the quote, see Mathes, *A Direct Path to the Buddha Within*, 112.

52. See Germano, *Poetic Thought, the Intelligent Universe, and the Mystery of Self*, 78, 567. However, Germano says that "some contemporary Nyingma scholars verbally suggested classifying both the second and the third doctrinal wheels as definitive, with the former emphasizing the "emptiness" and the latter emphasizing the "radiant light" of the mind's abiding reality." See ibid.

53. Germano suggests that the three wheels differ in terms of the subtlety of meanings, ranging from the least subtle to the most subtle meaing: "[T]he point here seems to be that if the second cycle's teaching of absolute emptiness alone is of supreme significance (i.e., the "ultimate" teaching), then the subsequent teaching of yet another distinct teaching cycle makes no sense, as the absolute teaching has already been delivered. However if the third cycle is of supreme significance and a further refinement of the second, then the three cycles would reflect an ordered, rational progression to the ultimate teaching based on soteriological considerations." See Germano, *Poetic Thought, the Intelligent Universe, and the Mystery of Self*, 567. Also see Longchenpa, *Treasury of Tenets*, 654, for a similar description of the three wheels.

54. Longchenpa, *Treasury of Tenets*, 628.

55. Ibid., 630.

56. Ibid., 631.

57. See Northrop Frye, *The Double Vision: Language and Meaning in Religion* (Toronto: University of Toronto Press, 1991; reprint 1995), 3. Hereafter, *The Double Vision*.

Chapter 5

1. Dratsépa says: *dus phyis gzhan gyis bskul nas byas pa'i lan yi ge ma legs po zhig btsun chung zhig gis bris pa nged rang gi thel tshes mnan pa zhig yod// 'di da gzod ce na dgos pa zhig yod pas ma stor ba gyis byas yod// 'di la lung rigs kyi sgrub byed mang po yod cing/ 'di nged rang gis dge bshes byams pa la zhun thar byas yod pas the tshom mi dgos so//* Dratsépa, *Ornament to the Ornament*, 284.

2. Dratsépa employs the short title *"nges rgyam"* to refer to the text, almost as if it is an anathema to call it by the full title, but he does not criticize Dölpopa by name. Dratsépa, *Ornament to the Ornament*, 167–70, 182, 184, 191–92, 220, 233.

3. See Stearns, *Buddha from Dolpo*, 22 for the possible completion date of the *Mountain Doctrine*.

4. *des na rgyud bla ma zhes bya ba yang/ bla ma dang phyi ma skad dod gcig ste, phyi ma'i don/ yang na gong ma ste theg pa chen po'i rgyud gong ma yin pas de skad du brjod do//* See Butön Rinchen Drup, *bde gshegs snying po gsal ba'i rgyan*, Collected Works of Bu-Ston, part 20 (VA) (New Delhi: International Academy of Indian Culture, 1971), 3. Henceforth, *The Ornament*. Butön gives a smilar explantion in his *History of Buddhism*: "Because the *Uttaratantra* is the supreme of the continuum or the continuous flow of the Mahāyāna teachings, that is, [because it] is the higher of [the Mahāyāna] teachings it is called as such. Or "'uttara' can mean 'later' [in which case it means that] because the *Uttaratantra* comments on the later continuum of the Mahāyāna teachings it is called as such." *rgyud bla ma ni theg pa chen po'i rgyud dam rgyun chags pa'i chos rnams kyi bla ma ste/ chos rnams kyi gong mar gyur pas de skad ces bya'o// yang na ut ta ra ni phyi ma ste theg pa chen po'i rgyud phyi ma'i dgongs pa 'grel bas de skad ces bya zhing.* See Butön, *History of Buddhism*, 30. In his *Precious Garland of Rebuttals*, Butön argues that the meaning of the *Uttaratantra* conforms to that of the Madhyamaka, although the *Uttaratantra* presents it provisionally. *de yang dgongs te gsungs pa'i tshul cung zad mi 'dra ba ma gtogs pa dbu ma dang 'dra bar gtogs so//* See Butön, *Precious Garland of Rebuttals*, 204.

5. Butön does not address the issue of the tathāgata-essence in any detail in his commentary to the *Abhisamayālaṃkāra* and *History of Buddhism*. In his *Abhisamayālaṃkāra Commentary*, Butön certainly cites the *Uttaratantra* several times when he discusses the concept of the buddha-body and the buddha-nature idea, but he does not develop his explication of the buddha-nature concept into any elaborate form. For reference, see Butön Rinchen Drup, *phar phyin lung gi snye ma*, Collected Works of Butön, vol. 18 (Lhasa: Zhol, 2000). Henceforth, *Abhisamayālaṃkāra Commentary*. In his *History of Buddhism*,

Butön makes reference to the *Uttaratantra* here and there, but because of the nature of the work he does not elaborate on it.

    6. *shin tu zab pa bde gshegs snying po'i don/ bde gshegs dgongs pas gsungs pa ngo mtshar chos// ma rtogs dri mas gos pa'i mi mdzes pa/ bsal nas mdzes par byed pa'i rgyan brjod bya//* See Butön, *The Ornament*, 2.

    7. Ibid., 22–41.

    8. Ibid., 48–63.

    9. Ibid., 59–65.

    10. *yang dag par rdzogs pa'i sangs rgyas la dad pa 'ba' zhig gis rtogs par bya ba 'di'i don shin tu rtogs dka' zhing dpyad par dka' ba yin pa'i phyir de bzhin gshegs pa'i lung gi rjes su 'brangs la rtogs par bya dgos la/ lung yang shin tu rgyas pa min pa gzhan gyis 'di'i don mi khrol te/ de dag tu ma bstan pa'i phyir// shin tu rgyas pa'ang rgyud phyi ma ma rtogs pa gzhan gyis gsal bar gtan la mi phebs te/ de dag tu don gyis bstan yang gsal bar ma bstan pa'i phyir// des na de bzhin gshegs pa'i snying po'i don gtan la 'bebs pa'i mdo rgyud bla rtsa 'grel du khungs su smros pa rnams dang/ der dngos su khungs su ma smros su zin kyang rnga bo che chen po'i mdo la sogs pa de dang rigs su mthun pa'i mdo sde rnams kyi don bcom ldan 'das byams pa dang/ 'phags pa thogs med kyis gtan la phab pa bzhin du dgongs gzhi dgongs pa'i dgos pa dngos la gnod byed dang bcas pa'i sgo nas dgongs te gsungs pa'i don zab mo bcom ldan 'das nyid kyis mdo las gtan la phab pa bzhin du gsal bar shes byed kyi lung dang bcas pa mdo gzhan gyi lung yang med/ lung rdzun ma yang med/ mdo'i don rang bzos bcos pa yang med de/ bcom ldan 'das nyid tshad ma yin pa'i phyir//* Ibid., 73–74.

    11. See chapter 1, note 18 for the verse.

    12. See Butön, *The Ornament*, 29, and Dratsépa, *Ornament to the Ornament*, 216–17.

    13. See Butön, *The Ornament*, 29, 37–39, and Dratsépa, *Ornament to the Ormanent*, 216.

    14. Butön states that since sentient beings do not have gnosis (*ye shes*), as it has to be achieved through immeasurable accumulations, there is no tathāgata-essence in sentient beings. For reference, see Butön, *The Ornament*, 37. Dratsépa says, "If someone asks, 'Is there a reason refuting the explicit remarks?' Indeed, there is. The actual sugata-essence is the dharma-body of a complete buddha, and it never exists in corporal sentient beings." *dngos la gnod byed kyi rigs pa yod dam zhe na/ shin tu'ang yod de/ bde gshegs snying po mtshan nyid pa de rdzogs pa'i sangs rgyas kyi chos sku yin la/ de sems can gyi phung po chen po rnams la nam yang med do//* See Dratsépa, *Ornament to the Ornament*, 206. Furthermore, Dratsépa shows how the dharma-body, the sugata-essence, the tathāgata-essence, and the emptiness-gnosis are the same and how they exist only in buddhas, not in sentient beings. See Dratsépa, *Ornament to the Ornament*, 206–9. Hopkins mentions that some of the later Geluk scholars criticize Butön for confusing the causal tathāgata-essence with resultant dharma-body. For reference, see Jeffrey Hopkins, *Emptiness in the Mind-Only School of Buddhism: Dynamic Responses to Dzong-ka ba's The*

Essence of Eloquence: I (Berkeley and Los Angeles: University of California Press, 1999); 130–31 footnotes a, b, a. Hereafter, *Emptiness in the Mind-Only School of Buddhism*.

15. Much of this material has appeared in my article "In Defense of His Guru: Dratsepa's Rebuttal to the Challenges Articulated by the Proponents of the Other-Emptiness Doctrine," *Journal of Indian Philosophy* 39, no. 2, (2011): 147–65.

16. See Dratsépa, *Ornament to the Ornament*, 163–64. Rendawa would later call Dölpopa "an evil teacher" (*bshes gnyen ngan pa*) because of the latter's interpretation of other-emptiness. Rendawa also uses a similar language to refer to Dölpopa and the latter's view in Rendawa's *The Lamp That Illuminates Suchnesss*, 170.

17. *sangs rgyas kyi bstan pa la log par rtog pa dgag/* See Dratsépa, *Ornament to the Ornament*, 166.

18. *bcom ldan 'das kyi mdo'i dgongs pa zab mo bstan//* See Dratsépa, *Ornament to the Ornament*, 166.

19. *phyin ci log gi rtog pas kun nas bslangs nas bstan pa dkrugs pa'i phyi rgol gyi rtsod spang/* See Dratsépa, *Ornament to the Ornament*, 166.

20. *des na de bzhin gshegs pa'i snying po sems can thams cad la thog ma med pa nas yod par ston pa'i mdo 'grel thams cad drang don dgongs pa can yin gyi/ nges don min no//* See Dratsépa, *Ornament to the Ornament*, 237.

21. See Dratsépa, *Ornament to the Ornament*, 206. See also ibid, 206–9 where he shows how dharma-body, sugata-essence, tathāgata-essence, and the emptiness-gnosis are the same, and they exist only in buddhas.

22. See chapter 1, note 18 for the verse.

23. Dratsépa claims that Asaṅga in his *Uttaratantra* commentary cites sutras to show that sentient beings do not have tathāgata-essence. See Dratsépa, *Ornament to the Ornament*, 207.

24. Dratsépa cites Kamalaśīla to argue that sentient beings do not have tathāgata-essence; rather they only have a potential to achieve enlightenment. See Dratsépa, *Ornament to the Ornament*, 247–48, 262.

25. Dratsépa cites a verse from Candrakīrti's *Madhyamakāvatāra* to argue that the tathāgata-essence teachings are provisional. See Dratsépa, *Ornament to the Ornament*, 254.

26. Dratsépa cites a passage from Ngok's *Uttaratantra* commentary to show that the tathāgata-essence teachings are provisional. See Dratsépa, *Ornament to the Ornament*, 201.

27. Dratsépa cites verses from Sapen's *Distinguishing the Three Vows* to show that sentient beings do not have tathāgata-essence. See Dratsépa, *Ornament to the Ornament*, 253–54.

28. See Dratsépa, *Ornament to the Ornament*, 200. Dratsépa asserts that tathāgata-element is not the same as tathāgata-essence (*de bzhin gshegs pa'i snying po*), as the former exists in all sentient beings, whereas the latter exists only in enlightened beings. The five metaphors that he refers to are

1) precious jewels, 2) kernels, 3) a precious image of the Buddha, 4) a universal king, and 5) a golden form. For Dratsépa, these five metaphors show that all sentient beings have a precious causal factor, notably buddha-nature, that will eventually mature into a fully enlightened entity through Mahāyāna path. See also note 13 in the introduction on the metaphors.

29. See Dratsépa, *Ornament to the Ornament*, 210–11.

30. *phyi mas bar pa las lhag par ston te drang nges 'dres ma ston cing, gdul bya drang ba'i don du drang dgos pa can dbang po rnon po ma gtogs pas rtogs par dka' ba rnams ston gyi, bar pa las nges don 'ba' zhig gtso bor ston no// bar pas bstan pa las lhag pa'i nges don mi ston te de bas lhag pa'i nges don mi srid pa'i phyir ro//* See Dratsépa, *Ornament to the Ornament*, 211.

31. "Moreover, having primarily explained the object of negation, the conventional self-emptiness that is not beyond dependent arising, in the middle wheel, the ultimate other-emptiness—the basis for purification and beyond dependent arising—is primarily taught in the last wheel. However, it is not the case that the basis for purification [that is ultimate truth] is not explained in the middle wheel." *de yang 'khor lo bar pa yang dgag bya'i chos kun rdzob rang stong dang/ rten 'brel las ma 'das pa gtso cher bstan nas dgag pa'i gzhi don dam gzhan stong rten 'brel las 'das pa ni 'khor lo tha mar gtso cher bstan te/ 'khor lo bar par yang dgag bya'i gzhi ma bstan pa yang ma yin no//* See Dölpopa, *A Brief Distinction*, 390. See Hopkins, *Mountain Doctrine*, 196–97, for a similar statement. Also see Kapstein, *Reason's Traces*, 301.

32. For the passage from the *Saṃdhinirmocanasūtra* cited in the *Ornament to the Ornament*, see Dratsépa, 183–84.

33. *'di ni rtsod pa'i gzhi dngos yin pas drang nges 'byed pa'i gzhung du mi rigs te/* See Dratsépa, *Ornament to the Ornament*, 184.

34. *'khor lo bar pas yang dag pa'i don spros bral ston pas dbu ma yin zhing/ tha mas yang dag pa'i don gzung 'dzin gnyis med kyi shes pa rang rig rang gsal sogs su ston pas sems tsam yin no//* See Dratsépa, *Ornament to the Ornament*, 184.

35. *'di na mi mkhas gang dag lta ba nyams pas dngos la zhen pa'i gdon chen gyis/ zin pa'i dbang gis blo gros nyams pas che ba'i che ba zla grags la sogs pa/ smod par byed kyang bdag nyid phung pa 'ba' zhig byed du bzad pa de dag gi/* See Dratsépa, *Ornament to the Ornament*, 163–64.

36. See Khedrup, *rgyud sde spyi'i rnam par gzhag pa rgyas par bshad pa* (The Collected Works of the Lord mkhas grub rje dge legs dpal bzang, vol. 8 (New Delhi: Mongolian Lama Gurudev, 1980; 461–63). Henceforth, *Presentation of the General Tantric Systems*. Khedrup argues that the *Prajñāpāramitāsūtras* are the "actual middle wheel sutras" (*bka' bar pa'i mdo dngos*), while the tathāgata-essence teachings, such as the *Dhāraṇīṣvararājasūtra*, *Vajracchedikasūtra*, *Laṅkāvatārasūtra*, and so forth are sutras "that are included within the middle wheel" (*'khor lo bar pa'i mdor gtogs*) because the meaning of these sutras is similar to the actual middle wheel, the *Prajñāpāramitāsūtras*. On the other hand, he lists the *Saṃdhinirmocanasūtra* as an "actual last wheel sutra" (*'khor lo tha ma'i mdo dngos*), but he does not list any sutras that could be asserted as scriptures "included within the last wheel" (*'khor lo tha ma'i mdor gtogs*).

37. See Hopkins, *Mountain Doctrine*, 116.

38. *kun rdzob tu gzhan stong dang don dam du rang stong khas shin tu yang blangs kyang/ khyed 'dod pa bzhin don dam gzhan stong dang kun rdzob rang stong gzhi ma grub de 'dra mi 'dod cing/ gzhan stong stong nyid tha shal yin pas don dam stong pa'i go mi chod do//* See Dratsépa, *Ornament to the Ornament*, 266.

39. Dratsépa quotes from the *Laṅkāvatārasūtra* in his *Ornament to the Ornament*: "The Great Wise One, the one-being-empty-of-other is the lowest of all [emptinesses], you must completely abandon this [view]." *blo gros chen po gcig gis gcig stong pa 'di ni kun gyi tha shal te/ de ni khod kyis yongs su spang bar bya'o//* See Dratsépa, *Ornament to the Ornament*, 264.

40. For information on how Dölpopa explains the emptiness that is the-one-being-empty-of-the-other (*gcig gis gcig stong pa'i stong nyid*) delineated in the *Laṅkāvatārasūtra*, see Hopkins *Mountain Doctrine*, 228). Also see Mathes, "The *gzhan tong* model of reality," 195–98 for more on the emptiness that is the-one-being-empty-of-the-other. Also, see Dratsépa, *Ornament to the Ornament*, 188–89 for a response from a Jonang proponent to such a critique.

41. *dad pa ye shes kyi kun gzhi zhes bya ba bde gshegs snying po rtag pa brtan pa ther zug pa gyung drung gzhan spang bya 'khor ba'i chos kyis stong pa'i gzhan stong/ don dam pa gdod ma nas spangs rtogs kyi yon tan thams cad rang chas su ldan pa kun rdzob rang stong dang bral ba bsgom par bya'o zer ba'i lung gtsang ma zhig khyer la shog//* See Dratsépa, *Ornament to the Ornament*, 267.

42. Dölpopa would completely disagree with Dratsépa. He would say that his position is justified based on the Buddha's and highly realized bodhisattvas' teachings.

43. *des na kho bo cag dbu ma pa'i lugs la rang stong gi ngos 'dzin tha snyad tsam du snang ba'i chos de nyid dang stong pa nyid don gzhan du brjod du med la/ don dam par spros pa'i mtha' bral la byed kyi/ rang stong zhes bya ba ri bong ra dang mo gsham gyi bu lta bu la zer ba min//* See Dratsépa, *Ornament to the Ornament*, 191.

44. *des na 'dir yod med rtag chad 'khor 'das rang gzhan dgag sgrub stong mi stong gzung 'dzin la sogs gnyis thams cad spangs shing, chos thams cad rang rang gi ngo bos stong pa don dam par gnyis chos kyi spros pa'i mtha' thams cad dang bral ba dbu ma'i lta ba yin cing/ de ston pa dbu ma'i gzhung yin te/* See Dratsépa, *Ornament to the Ornament*, 186.

45. *'di na kha cig mkhas par rlom yang thub pa'i gsung rab gzhan du 'chad// phyogs zhen dug chus blo ngan ngoms pas yang dag lta ba'i bdud rtsi 'dor// dus ngan 'di 'drar drang por smras kyang bden par 'dzin pa shin tu dka'// de phyir rang gi yid la goms phyir ma nor lta ba cung zad smras//* See Dratsépa, *Ornament to the Ornament*, 282–83. This quote appears at the end of Dratsépa's text.

Chapter 6

1. *slob dpon de dag gis klu sgrub kyi dgongs pa ji lta ba bzhin ma rtogs par dpal ldan zla ba grags pa'i gzhung las bshad pas 'phags pa'i dgongs pa ma yin no//*

For the quote, see Rendawa Zhönnu Lodrö, *theg pa gsum gyi 'phags pa'i rtogs pa rnam par 'byed pa* (*Collected Works of Rendawa*, vol. 2, Kathmandu: sa-skya rgyal yons gsun rab slob gner khan, 1999), 134. Henceforth, *Distinguishing the Realizations*. This position will later be included by Tsongkhapa in his *Illuminating the Thoughts of the Madhyamaka* as one of the eight uncommon views of the Prāsaṅgika-Madhyamaka. For reference, see Tsongkhapa, *dbu ma dgongs pa rab gsal*, Drepung Loseling Library Society, 1992. Hereafter, *Illuminating the Thoughts of the Madhyamaka*.

2. See Rendawa, *Distinguishing the Realizations*, 135–36, 146 for the quotes.

3. *sngon gyi bstan bcos mdzad pa po thogs med dang dbyig gnyen la sogs pa'i skye bos klu sgrub lugs bzang gang dag rgyang ring du spangs pas/* See Rendawa, *The Lamp That Illuminates Suchness*, 296.

4. "Because this Ārya [that is, Nāgārjuna] refutes all conventional phenomena as ultimately existent and shows that they are not ultimately existent in his *Collection of Reasoning*, the position that conventional phenomena ultimately exist is damaged. On the other hand, because the middle way of suchness, the dharma reality, the unchanging thoroughly established nature is negated as not existing ultimately and shown as ultimately existent [in his] *Collection of Praises*, the position that nothing ultimately exists is refuted." *'phags pa 'dis dbu ma rigs pa'i tshogs kyis tha snyad pa'i dngos po thams cad don dam par yod pa bkag cing med par bstan pas kun rdzob kyi chos don dam du yod par 'dod pa'i phyogs bshig la/ dbu ma bstod pa'i tshogs kyis 'gyur ba med pa'i yongs grub chos dbyings de bzhin nyid kyi dbu ma don dam du med pa bkag cing yod par bstan pas don dam par ci yang med par 'dod pa'i phyogs bshig go//* See Dölpopa, *Abhisamayālaṃkāra Commentary*, 285. From this one can deduce that Dölpopa does not assert that Nāgārjuna's *Mūlamadhyamakakārikā*, which is one of the *Collection of Reasonings*, primarily explains the ultimate truth of dharma-reality, rather he takes it as teaching conventional phenomena as empty of ultimate existence, which is not the ultimate other-emptiness for Dölpopa.

5. *'dir mdor bsdus pa'i don ni 'di yin te bcom ldan 'das kyis de bzhin gshegs pa'i snying po gsungs pa de sgra ji bzhin pa lags na/ mu stegs can gyi bdag tu smra ba dang khyad par med par 'gyur la/ dgongs te gsungs pa yin na/ dgongs gzhi dang dgos pa gang lags zhes pa ni 'dri ba po'i bsam pa'o// 'di ni sgra ji bzhin pa ma yin gyi/ dgongs pa can yin la dgongs gzhi stong pa nyid dang mtshan ma med pa la sogs pa la brtsams nas dgos pa gdul bya mu stegs can gyi lta ba la goms pa zab mo'i snod du mi rung ba rnams rim gyis bdag med pa la drang ba'i phyir bstan to zhes pa ni lan gyi don to//* See Rendawa, *The Lamp That Illuminates Suchness*, 169–70.

6. "The element that exists since beginningless time is the basis for phenomena. Due to this all sentient beings [exist], and nirvāṇa is also achieved."

7. *'on kyang bshes gnyen ngan pas nye bar bstan pa'i dug chus myos pa'i blo gros kyi mig ldongs pa dag bcom ldan 'das kyis dgongs te gsungs pa'i mdo sde zab mo rnams la sgra ji bzhin du bzung nas bde bar gshegs pa'i snying po'i zol gyis rtag pa dang khyab pa'i bdag tu smra bar byed cing rang nyid kyang log pa'i lam*

la gnas nas gzhan dag kyang log pa'i lam la 'jug par byed// de ltar zhugs pa dag la bsngags pa brjod cing mthun pas dg'a bar byed do// gang dag bde bar gshegs pa'i bstan pa'i snying po bdag med pa dang stong pa nyid kyi don phyin ci ma log par smra ba dag la dngos su tshig dor dang ltag chod la sogs pa'i sgo nas gya tshoms su rgol zhing/ lkog tu chad pa zhes ngan smras su byed pa dag gis deng sang gangs can gyi bstan pa bud shing zad du nye ba'i me lce 'di'ang lta ba ngan pa'i dri mas shin tu ma rungs par byas so// For reference, see Rendawa, *The Lamp That Illuminates Suchness*, 170–71.

8. Stearns, *Buddha from Dölpo*, 56.

9. *gang dag rnam par shes pa las gzhan pa'i bde bar gshegs pa'i snying po rtag pa khas blangs nas de nyid bka' tha ma'i dgongs pa yin par bsams nas lung 'di nyid kyis bka' tha ma nges don du sgrub par byed pa ni sna bcad ma gyar po'i rgyan gyis mdzes par rlom pa dang 'dra ste/ lugs de ni bka' tha ma nges don du bzhed pa'i shing rta chen po dag gi lugs las kyang phyi rol tu gyur pa'i phyir ro//* For reference, see Rendawa, *The Lamp That Illuminates Suchness*, 11.

10. *gzhan du na nyam nga'i lam du long ba gya tshoms su gom pa 'dor ba ltar gdon mi za bar gyang sa chen por lhung bar 'gyur ro//* For reference, see Rendawa, *The Lamp That Illuminates Suchness*, 25.

11. *'o na grub mtha' bzhi las gang zhig bde bar gshegs pa'i dgongs pa yin zhe na/ 'phags pa klu sgrub kyi lugs 'ba' zhig de bzhin gshegs pa'i bka'i dgongs pa 'khrul pa med pa yin te/* See Rendawa, *The Lamp That Illuminates Suchness*, 28.

12. *'di ltar 'phags pa klu sgrub kyi rjes su 'brang pa dag ni mdo sde gang stong pa nyid mkhyud cing kun rdzob kyi bden pa gtso bor ston pa de dag ni drang ba'i don yin la/ mdo sde gang stong pa nyid don dam pa'i bden pa gtso bor ston pa de dag ni nges pa'i don gyi mdo sde yin no// . . . tha mar yang yang dag pa ma yin pa'i kun tu rtog pa yod par bstan pa'i phyir drang ba'i don yin la/ bar par ni stong pa nyid kyi rnam pa gsal por stan pa'i phyir nges pa'i don yin par bzhed do//* See Rendawa, *The Lamp That Illuminates Suchness*, 7. Moreover, Rendawa offers this definition: "Because the meaning of those sutras that clearly teach emptiness, productionlessness, and so forth explicitly cannot be interpreted into something else, it should be understood as definitive meaning." *mdo gang zhig dngos su stong pa nyid dang skye ba med pa la sogs pa gsal bar byed pa de dag gi don de ni rnam pa gzhan du drang bar mi nus pa'i phyir nges pa'i don yin par shes par bya'o//* See Rendawa, *The Lamp That Illuminates Suchness*, 172.

13. For the quotes from the two sutras, which are the basis for his formulation of definitive and provisional meanings, see also Rendawa, *The Lamp That Illuminates Suchness*, 172.

14. *de la mdo gang zhig rten cing 'brel bar 'byung ba skye ba med pas khyad par du byas pa'i de kho na nyid don dam pa'i bden pa dngos su gsal byed ma yin/ dngos su kun rdzob kyi don can bshad na stong pa nyid kyi don can du drang du rung ba de dag ni rang bzhin med pa la 'jug pa'i thabs su gsungs pa tsam yin pas drang don yin la/* See Rendawa, *The Lamp That Illuminates Suchness*, 171–72.

15. Dölpopa states, "Moreover, having primarily explained the self-emptiness of conventional phenomena—the object to be negated and that

which is not beyond dependent arising—in the middle wheel, [the Buddha] taught the ultimate other-emptiness—the basis of negation and that which is beyond dependent arising—in the last wheel." *de yang 'khor lo bar pa yang dgag bya'i chos kun rdzob rang stong dang/ rten 'brel las ma 'das pa gtso cher bstan nas dgag pa'i gzhi don dam gzhan stong rten 'brel las 'das pa ni 'khor lo tha mar gtso cher bstan te/* See Dölpopa, *A Brief Distinction,* 390.

16. *bla ma rjes bka' tha ma'i dgongs 'grel lta ba sems tsam ston par bzhed//* For the quote, see Khedrup, *Presentation of the General Tantric Systems,* 495–96. Similarly, Khedrup juxtaposes the two lamas, when commenting on whether the *Abhisamayālaṃkāra* is a Cittamātra or a Madhyamaka text, by utilizing the same respectful apellations "Lama Jé" (*bla ma rje*) to refer to Rendawa and "Jé Rinpoché" (*rje rin po che*) for Tsongkhapa, the latter being preceded by "in our system" (*rang lugs la*). See ibid., 498. In their English translation of Khedrup's *Presentation of the General Tantric Systems,* Ferdinand D. Lessing and Alex Wayman mention that Lama Jé is presumably Rendawa, who excludes the *Ratnāvalī* as one of Nāgārjuna's discourses of reason. For reference, see Ferdinand D. Lessing and Alex Wayman, *Fundamentals of the Buddhist Tantras* (Paris: Mouton, 1968), 86, note 24. In order to show that Rendawa asserts Nāgārjuna's five reason discourses, Wayman and Lessing point out in the same footnote that Könchok Jikmé Wangpo (*dkon mchog 'jigs med dbang po*) says in his *rten 'grel rtsom 'phro sogs ljags rtsom 'phro can gyi skor,* "The reverend Red mdah pa held that the *Ratnāvalī* should not be included among the sets of reasons because it is a set of reports [to a king], and so held that there are five 'sets of reasons.' " Furthermore, Rendawa lists *Mūlamadhyamakakārikā* (*dbu ma rtsa ba'i shes rab*), *Yuktiṣaṣṭīkā* (*rigs pa drug cu pa*), *Vigrahavyāvartanī* (*rtsod zlog*), *Śūnyatāsaptati* (*stong nyid bdun cu pa*), and *Vaidalyasūtra* (*zhib mo rnam 'thag*) as the collection of reasons, excluding *Ratnāvalī.* See Rendawa, *The Lamp That Illuminates Suchness,* 22–23.

17. Roerich, *Blue Annals,* 349.

18. "In the later part of his life Rendawa lived in semiseclusion at a hermitage in the region of Kangbuley, where he composed his most substantial work on the Kālacakra, entitled *A Jewel Lamp Illuminating the Definitive Meaning of the Glorious Kālacakra* (*Dpal dus kyi 'khor lo'i nges don gsal bar byed pa rin po che'i sgron me*). Unlike his two earlier polemic works, the first of which was certainly written while Rendawa was not yet thirty years of age, this fascinating treatise is a thorough and positive analysis of the meditation practices of the Kālacakra." For reference, see Stearns, *Buddha from Dölpo,* 58.

19. Shakya Pel, *rin chen rnam rgyal gyi rnam par thar pa snyim pa'i me tog las 'khrungs pa ngo mthar ze 'bru'i nor bu* (No publication date), 46. Hereafter, *Biography of Dratsépa Rinchen Namgyel.*

20. *chos dbang grags pa'i dpal.*

21. Zhamar Chödrak Yeshé (*zhva dmar chos grags ye shes,* 1453–1524) reports that Tsongkhapa taught an alternative way of distinguishing provi-

sional from definitive based on the *Uttaratantra*, but Mathes points out that he does not tell his readers how exactly Tsongkhapa might have done it. For this, see Mathes, *A Direct Path to the Buddha Within*, 136.

22. *rang lugs la rje rin po che'i bzhed pas bka' bar pa'i phyogs mthun gyi mdo bde gshegs snying po'i mdo dang/ gzungs kyi dbang phyug rgyal pos zhus pa'i mdo dang/ ye shes snang ba rgyan gyi mdo dang/ sor mo phreng ba la phan pa'i mdo dang/ 'phags pa dpal 'phreng gi mdo la sogs pa'i dgongs pa gtso bor 'grel la/ dgongs pa thal 'gyur du gnas shing/* See Khedrup, *Presentation of the General Tantric Systems*, 497.

23. *mngon rtogs rgyan dang rgyud bla ma'i lta ba mthar thug pa thal 'gyur du gnas so zhes rje btsun thams cad mkhyen pas mkhas pa'i tshogs kyi dbus su yang dang yang du seng ge'i nga ro sgrog par mdzad la/* For reference, see Chöwang Drakpa, *shes rab kyi pha rol tu phyin pa'i man ngag gi bstan bcos mgnon par rtogs pa'i rgyan gyi mthar thug pa'i lta ba thal 'gyur du 'grel tshul gnad don gsal ba'i zla zer*, in Khedrup Je's *Collected Works*, vol. 1 (New Delhi, 1980), 704.

24. Jeffrey Hopkins, *Reflections on Reality: The Three Natures and Non-Natures in the Mind-Only School* (Berkeley, University of California Press, 2002), 536. Henceforth, *Reflections on Reality*.

25. Robert Thurman, *Tsong Khapa's Speech of Gold in the Essence of Eloquence: Reason and Enlightenment in the Central Philosophy of Tibet* (New Jersey, Princeton University Press, 1984), 30. Henceforth, *Speech of Gold*.

26. Ruegg, *Three Studies*, 74–76.

27. *des na dbu ma pa ni sems kyi rang bzhin gshis la cir yang ma grub pa'i stong nyid de rtogs pa na tha snyad du sgyu ma lta bu'i 'dzin pa mtha' dag zhi bar 'gyur zhing sgyu ma lta bu'i gnyen po mtha' dag skye bar 'gyur bas sems kyi rang bzhin de nyid la kun rdzob kyi ngos nas sgro btags te 'di ni rang bzhin du gnas pa'i rigs so zhes 'jog go// sems tsam pa ni sems kyi rang bzhin 'od gsal ba de gshis la rang gi ngo bos dus thams cad du grub cing dri ma de dag de la gnyen pos 'bral du rung la ci tsam bral ba de tsam du yon tan mtha' dag skyed par 'gyur bas de gnyis kyi gzhi byed pas chos nyid rigs su 'dod de snga ma ni rgyan 'di dang phyi ma ni rgyud bla ma'i bshad tshod du mthong ngo// de lta na chos nyid rigs su 'dod par mtshungs kyang dri ma'i sbyang gzhi bden par 'dod mi 'dod mi 'dra bas rigs su 'jog pa'i rgyu mtshan mi mtshungs so//* See Tsongkhapa Lozang Drakpa, *legs bshad gser phreng* (Taipei: The Corporate Body of the Buddha Educational Foundation, 2000); 339–340. Hereafter, *Golden Rosary of Excellent Exposition*.

28. Tsongkhapa, *Golden Rosary of Excellent Exposition*, 333–34.

29. Ibid., 334–37.

30. See Matthew Kapstein, *The Tibetans* (Malden, MA: Blackwell, 2006), 119–23.

31. *slob dpon chen po thogs med kyis kyang rgyud bla ma'i dgongs pa rnam par rig tsam gyi lugs su ma bshad par dbu ma'i lugs su bshad la/* See Tsongkhapa, *Illuminating the Thoughts of the Madhyamaka*, 243.

32. *theg pa chen po rgyud bla ma'i bstan bcos kyi rnam par bshad pa* in *The Sūtrālaṃkāra and the Uttaratantra*, 197.

33. *theg bsdus su kun gzhi rnam shes kyi sgrub byed du drangs pa'i chos mngon pa'i lung rgyud bla ma'i 'grel pa las sems can la de bzhin gshegs pa'i khams grub pa snying por gyur pa yod mod kyi/ sems can de dag gis shes pa ma yin no zhes gsungs so// de skad du/ thog ma med pa'i dus kyi khams/ chos rnams kun gyi gnas yin te/ de yod pas na 'gro kun dang/ mya ngan 'das pa'ang thob pa yin zhes sems can la chos nyid kyi rigs yod pa'i sgrub byed du drangs pas/* See Tsong-khapa, *Illuminating the Thoughts of the Madhyamaka,* 243. The quote from the *Uttaratantra* commentary that is cited here is slightly different from the one that appears in *The Sūtrālaṃkāra and the Uttaratantra,* 197.

34. *gang zhig gang na med pa de ni/* For the passage, see *The Sūtrālaṃkāra and the Uttaratantra,* 201.

35. *rgyud bla ma'i 'grel par gang zhig gang na med pa de ni zhes sogs kyi don bkral ba ni snga ma gnyis dang gtan mi 'dra bar dbu ma'i 'grel tshul du yod de mangs pas 'jigs nas ma bris so//* See Tsongkhapa, *Illuminating the Thoughts of the Madhyamaka,* 253.

36. *dbus mtha' dang mdo sde rgyan dang chos nyid rnam 'byed du kun gzhi rnam par bzhag pa dang phyi rol med pa'i phyogs bshad la/ mngon rtogs rgyan dang rgyud bla ma las kun gzhi rnam shes rnam par ma bzhag pa dang phyi rol ma bkag pa'i phyogs bshad do//* See ibid., 243.

37. Ibid., 323–24.

38. *re zhig gtso bo rnams brjod na/ tshogs drug las ngo bo tha dad pa'i kun gzhi rnam shes dang/ rang rig 'gog lugs thun mong ma yin pa dang rang rgyud kyi sbyor bas phyir rgol gyi rgyud la de kho na nyid kyi lta ba skyed pa khas mi len pa gsum dang/ shes pa khas len pa bzhin du phyi rol gyi don yang khas blang dgos pa dang/ nyan rang la dngos po rang bzhin med par rtogs pa yod pa dang/ chos kyi bdag 'dzin nyon mongs su 'jog pa dang/ zhig pa dngos po yin pa dang/ de'i rgyu mtshan gyis dus gsum gyi 'jog tshul thun mong ma yin pa sogs yin no//* See Tsongkhapa, *Illuminating the Thoughts of the Madhyamaka,* 226.

Chapter 7

1. Gyeltsap says that those who intend to know more about the com-plementary nature of the emptiness of inherent existence and the conventional nature of causal connection should read Tsongkhapa's great exposition on the *Mūlamadhyamikakārikā (rtsa shes ṭik chen), Illuminating the Thoughts of the Madhyamaka, Essence of Excellent Exposition,* the *Great Exposition of the Stages of Path,* etc. For reference, see Gyeltsap Darma Rinchen, *theg pa chen po rgyud bla ma'i ti ka, Collected Works of Gyeltsap,* vol. 3 (Kubum Monastery: sku 'bum byams pa gling par khang), 96. Henceforth, *Uttaratantra Commentary.* This also points out that Gyeltsap's commentary is certainly composed after the *Essence of Excellent Exposition.* It is important to note that he does not mention the *Golden Rosary of Excellent Exposition* by its name here.

2. *rje btsun bla ma'i gsung gi man ngag las/* See Gyeltsap, *Uttaratantra Commentary,* 341.

3. *rgyud bla ma'i btsan bcos 'grel ba dang bcas pa'i rnam par bshad pa . . . dus phyis . . . rje rin po che thams cad mkhyen pa blo bzang grags pa'i dpal bzang po'i zhal snga nas las bka' drin rdzogs par mnos shing/* See Gyeltsap, *Uttaratantra Commentary*, 457. Gyeltsap also states, "[Initially] I heard the exposition of the *Uttaratantra* along with [Asaṅga's] commentary from the Supreme Jetsün Rendawa Zhönnu Lodrö, and later . . ." *rgyud bla ma'i btsan bcos 'grel ba dang bcas pa'i rnam par bshad pa rgyal ba ring lugs pa chen po rje tsun dam pa red mda' pa ku ma ra ma ti zhal snga las kyang thos shing, dus phyis . . .* See Gyeltsap, *Uttaratantra Commentary*, 457.

4. Khedrup clearly states, "Followers of the older school [such as Ngok and Chapa] assert that the *Uttaratantra* presents the view of the Svātantrika-Madhyamaka; the followers of the Jonang School say that the *Uttaratantra* is a commentarial work on the last wheel and presents his [that is, Dölpopa's] own doctrinal view [of other-emptiness]. Lama Jé [that is, Rendawa] asserts that it is a commentarial work on the last wheel and presents the Cittamātra view." *lnga pa rang rgyud ston par snga rabs pa rnams bzhed la/ jo nang pas bka' tha ma'i dgongs 'grel lta ba khong gi lta ba ston par bzhed do// bla ma rjes bka' tha ma'i dgongs 'grel lta ba sems tsam ston par bzhed//* See Khedrup, *Presentation of the General Tantric Systems*, 495–96.

5. *de bzhin gshegs pa'i snying po ni 'bras bu de bzhin gshegs pa'i 'bras bu nyid kyi sgo nas bshad pa dang/ de bzhin gshegs pa'i rang bzhin gyi sgo nas bshad pa dang/ de bzhin gshegs pa'i rgyu'i ngos nas bshad pa'o// 'chad byed gsum gyi sgo nas de ltar bshad pa yin gyi/ de bzhin nyid tsam dang yang dag par rdzogs pa'i sangs rgyas kyi chos sku de bhzin gshegs pa'i snyign po'i mtshan gzhir byed pa ni ma yin te/ bstan bcos 'di rtsa 'grel du sems can gyi gnas skabs dang rgyu'i gnas skbas 'ba' zhig la bshad pa'i phyir ro// mtshan gzhi bzung na khams rnam par sbyong byed kyi lam bsgoms pas thob pa'i 'bras bu yang dag par rdzogs pa'i sangs rgyas kyi chos kyi sku'i 'phrin las sems can thams cad la 'phro zhing khyab pa ste/ sems can gyi shes rgyud 'ba' zhig gi khyad par gyi chos su ldan pa'i chos sku'i 'phrin las 'jug rung de nyid yod pas sems can thams cad de bzhin gshegs pa'i snying po can du bshad de . . . de bzhin nyid dri mas rang bzhin gyis dben pa ni sems can dang sangs rgyas gnyi ga'i rang bzhin yin mod kyi/ sangs rgyas kyi rang bzhin yin pa rgyu mtshan du byas nas de nyid sems can gyi rgyud kyi dri ma dang bcas pa'i tshe de bzhin gshegs pa'i snying po yin la/ dri ma dang bcas pa'i de bzhin nyid du gyur pa'i sems can gyi rgyud kyi dri ma rang bzhin gyis dben pa sems can thams cad la yod pa la dgongs nas sems can thams cad de bzhin gshegs pa'i snying po can du gsungs pa dang sku gsum thob par byed pa'i rgyu'i gnas skabs sangs rgyas kyi rigs sems can thams cad la yod pa la dgongs nas sems can thams cad de bzhin gshegs pa'i snying po can du gsungs so//* See Gyeltsap, *Uttaratantra Commentary*, 148–49.

6. *bstan bcos 'di rtsa 'grel du mthar thug theg pa gcig dang nyan rang 'phags pa la yang chos kyi bdag med rtogs pa yod par bsgrub par shes par bya'o//* See Gyeltsap, *Uttaratantra Commentary*, 22.

7. It says: Śāripūtra, if Hearers and Solitary Realizers do not even realize, observe, and analyze this point correctly for the time being with their own wisdom, there is no mention that the childish ordinary beings

cannot. However, this does not include the realization of this point [generated through] faith in the Buddha. *shā ri'i bu don 'di ni re zhig nyan thos dang rang sangs rgyas thams cad kyis kyang rang gi shes rab kyis yang dag par shes pa'am lta ba'am brtag par mi nus na/ byis pa so so'i skye bo'i dag gis lta ci smos te/ de de bzhin gshegs pa la dad pas rtogs pa ni ma gtogs so//* See *The Sūtrālaṃkāra and the Uttaratantra*, 120.

8. *des na nyan thos dang rang sangs rgyas 'phags pa rnams kyis kyang don dam pa'i bden pa mngon sum du gzigs mod kyi/ dbu ma rtsa ba shes rab nas bstan pa ltar don dam pa'i bden pa la spros pa gcod pa'i rigs pa'i tshogs mtha' yas pa'i sgo nas khong du chud par mi byed cing/ theg pa chen po'i gang zag dbang po rnon po ltar don dam pa'i bden pa la rang stobs kyi shes rab gong nas gong du rgyas par 'gyur pa'i tshul gyis rtogs mi nus pas.//* See Gyeltsap, *Uttaratantra Commentary*, 21–22.

9. *slob dpon rang nyid rnam rig par ston par mi bsam ste/ bstan bcos 'di'i 'grel par mthar thug theg pa gcig tu bsgrubs shing/ stong nyid phra mo rgyas par gtan la phab pa dang shin tu 'gal ba'i phyir ro//* See Gyeltsap, *Uttaratantra Commentary*, 9. A similar remark is seen in Gyeltsap's *Abhisamayālaṃkāra Commentary*: "It is not acceptable to assert that the Ācārya Asaṅga interpreted the *Uttaratantra* according to the Vijñāptimātra system because it would contradict the establishment of one-vehicle theory and the establishment of the subtle emptiness in an elaborate form in the commentary." See Gyeltsap Darma Rinchen, *rnam bshad snying rgyan, Collected Works of Gyeltsap*, vol. 2 (sku 'bum monastery: sku 'bum byams pa gling par khang), 8. Henceforth, *Abhisamayālaṃkāra Commentary*.

10. *chos thams cad bden pas stong pa don dam pa'i bden pa spros pa thams cad dang bral ba mdo rgyas 'bring bsdus gsum dang de bzhin gshegs pa'i snying po'i mdos khyad par med par gsal bar ston la/ de nyid bstan bcos 'dir brjod bya'i gtso bor ston pa slob dpon gyis dgongs pa ji lta ba bzhin du gsal bar mdzad pa yin no//* See Gyeltsap, *Uttaratantra Commentary*, 8.

11. *yang kha cig slob dpon 'phags pa thogs med kyis theg bsdus su rgyas par gtan la phab pa'i tshogs drug las ngo bo tha dad pa'i kun gzhi'i rnam par shes pa de bzhin gshegs pa'i snying por byas nas de snying po'i mdo dang bstan bcos 'di rtsa 'grel gyi don du byed pa ni ma brtags pa chen po yin te de 'dra'i kun gzhi bstan bcos 'di rtsa 'grel du bshad pa zur tsam yang med pa'i phyir dang bstan bcos 'di rang lugs la kun gzhi khas mi len cing phyi rol gyi don khas len pa'i lugs yin te 'chad par 'gyur ro//* See Gyeltsap, *Uttaratantra Commentary*, 152–53.

12. *'khor lo tha mar bstan pa'i khams rang bzhin rnam dag de nyid 'khor lo bar par bshad pa'i stong pa dang don gcig par rtogs nas snga phyi mi 'gal bar khong du chud par 'gyur ro//* See Gyeltsap, *Uttaratantra Commentary*, 336.

13. *de bzhin gshegs pa'i snying po'i mdo dgongs 'grel du gsungs pa'i 'khor lo gsum pa'i mtshan gzhir 'dod pa ni phyogs tsam yang ma rtogs pa'i mu cor du smra ba yin te/* See Gyeltsap, *Uttaratantra Commentary*, 48.

14. *kun brtags bden pas stong pa//* See Gyeltsap, *Uttaratantra Commentary*, 49.

15. *gzhan dbang dang yongs grub bden grub//* Ibid.

16. *mthar thug theg pa gsum//* Ibid.

17. *chos thams cad bden pas stong pa//* Ibid.

18. *mthar thug theg pa gcig//* Ibid.

19. See footnote chapter 5, note 36. See Khedrup, *Presentation of the General Tantric Systems,* 461–63.

20. Khedrup, however, argues that the *Uttaratantra* comments on middle-wheel teachings, not on last-wheel teachings because he does not categorize sutras such as *Tathāgatagarbhasūtra* and others as a part of the last-wheel scriptures. He says that "the *Uttaratantra* is a commentarial work of the middle wheel." *rgyud bla ma bka' bar pa'i dgongs 'grel/* See Khedrup, *Presentation of the General Tantric Systems,* 497.

21. *de la spyir bcom ldan 'das kyi gsung rab las drang don dang nges don 'byed pa'i tshul gnyis gsungs te/ 'phags pa blo gros mi zad pa'i mdo dang ting nge 'dzin rgyal po'i mdo las gsungs pa sogs dang don zab dgongs pa nges par 'grel pa'i mdo las gsungs pa'o//* See Gyeltsap, *Abhisamayālaṃkāra Commentary,* 5. The same exact quote appears in Gyeltsap's *Uttaratantra Commentary,* 5–6.

22. *mdo snga ma'i rjes su 'brangs nas mgon po klu sgrub kyis drang don dang nges don 'byed pa'i shing rta'i srol legs par phye bas mdo gnyis pa drang ba'i don du 'bad pa med par grub par mdzad do//* See Gyeltsap, *Uttaratantra Commentary,* 6.

23. *dang po ni chos thams cad rang gi mtshan nyid kyis grub pas stong par ston pa nges pa'i don dang gang zag dang phung po la sogs pa tshig dang yi ge sna tshogs kyis ston pa drang ba'i don du bstan la mdo sde phyi mas ni kun btags rang gi mtshan nyid kyis ma grub pa dang gzhan dbang dang yongs grub rang gi mtshan nyid kyis grub par bstan nas thams cad rang gi mtshan nyid kyis ma grub par phyogs gcig tu ston pa dang/ phyogs gcig tu rang gi mtshan nyid kyis grub par ston pa drang don dang/ rang gi mtshan nyid kyis grub pa dang ma grub pa'i sa tshigs gsal bar phye nas ston pa nges pa'i don du gsungs so//* See Gyeltsap, *Uttaratantra Commentary,* 6.

24. See note 23 of this chapter for the definitions.

25. *sems can gyi rgyud la gdod ma nas yang dag par rdzogs pa'i sangs rgyas yod par 'dod pa ni mu stegs dbang phyug pa rtag pa rang byung gi thams cad mkhyen pa khas len pa dang ming mi mthun pa tsam du zad do//* See Gyeltsap, *Uttaratantra Commentary,* 24.

26. *yang kha cig don dam pa'i bden pa rtag dngos su khas blangs nas de kun rdzob mtha' dag gis stong pa gzhan stong zab mo'o zhes smra ba ni mun sprul gyi tshig 'ba' zhig ste/ gzhan stong gi don de don dam pa'i bden pa kun rdzob kyi bden pa yin pas stong pa'i don yin nam/ 'on te kun rdzob yod pas stong pa'i don yin// phyi ma ltar na don dam pa'i bden pa brtan gyo mtha' dag la khyab par yod par khas blangs pa dang 'gal te don dam bden pa shes bya mtha' dag la khyab byed du yod pa dang don dam bden pa kun rdzob yod pas stong pa ji ltar mi 'gal ba soms shig// dang po ltar na khyod kyis gzhan stong zab mo bstan rung gi gdul bya de dbang po yang rab mthar thug pa yin pa nyams te don dam pa'i bden pa rtag dngos*

de kun rdzob kyi bden pa yin snyam du dogs nas de'i dogs pa bcad dgos kyi gdul bya yin pa'i phyir// See Gyeltsap, *Uttaratantra Commentary,* 40.

27. *dag pa gnyis ldan gyi chos sku sems can gyi rgyud la yod pa'i don 'di dpyad par bya ste sems can gyi sems de nyid rang bzhin gyis rnam par dag pa la glo bur gyi dri ma mtha' dag gis dben pa'i don nam/ 'on te dag pa gnyis ldan gyi chos sku sems can gyi rgyud la rang gi sems dang ngo bo gcig tu yod pa'am/ don gzhan gyi tshul du yod pa'am/ 'brel pa med pa'i tshul du yod pa yin//* . . . *dang po ltar na/ sems can de nyid sangs rgyas su thal ba ldog tu med do.* . . . . *gnyis pa ltar na sems can gyi rgyud la yod pa'i dag pa gnyis ldan gyi chos sku de khyad par gyi gzhir gzung nas de sems can gyi rgyud kyi glo bur gyi dri ma des bsgribs sam ma bsgribs/ dang po ltar na dag pa gnyis ldan gyi chos skur 'gal la/ gnyis pa ltar na sems can gyi sems rgyud dag pa gnyis ldan dang ngo bo gcig tu yod la/ sems can gyi sems rgyud dri mas legs par bslad pa yang yin pa nyams so//* . . . *gsum pa ltar na don gzhan dus mnyam pa rgyu 'bras su mi rung ba'i phyir/ sems can dang sangs rgyas tshogs pa gcig tu khas len dgos na de yang mi rigs pa kho na'o// bzhi pa ltar na/ dag pa ngyis ldan gyi chos sku sems can dang 'brel ba med bzhin du thog ma med pa nas de'i rgyud la rang chas su gnas pa'o zhes smra ba ni rigs pa mtha' dag dang 'gal ba'o//* See Gyeltsap, *Uttaratantra Commentary,* 138–39.

28. *thub pa'i gsung rab 'chad pa'i zol gyis mu stegs byed kyi bdag tu smra ba rgyas par byed pa kha cig na re/ shes rab kyi pha rol tu phyin pa'i mdo rgyas 'bring bsdus gsum las ni kun rdzob rang stong tsam zhig bstan gyi/ don dam pa'i bden pa mthar thug pa ma bstan la/ don dam pa'i bden pa mthar thug pa ni 'khor lo tha mas bstan cing/ de'i dgongs pa phyin ci ma log pa theg pa chen po rgyud bla rtsa 'grel gyis 'grel par byed pa yin no zhes zer ba ni 'grel pa 'di dag blta ba'i skal ba tsam yang med par shes par bya'o//* See Gyeltsap, *Uttaratantra Commentary,* 89–90.

29. See Gyeltsap, *Uttaratantra Commentary,* 8.

30. See Roerich, *Blue Annals,* 777.

Conclusion

1. Donald Lopez, *Elaborations on Emptiness: Uses of the Heart Sutra,* Princeton University Press, Princeton, NJ, 1996, 18. In this work I do not study the "effects" of the *Uttaratantra* in the way that Lopez examines the "effects" of the *Heart Sūtra* in his book.

2. Many of the *Uttaratantra* commentaries (e.g., Gelong Chöshé's and Kyotön Monlam Tsültrim's commentary) found in the recent publications of the collected works of Kadam masters are yet to be systematically examined. Although future research on them will shed more light on how the early Kadam scholars engaged with the Indian treatise, my cursory reading suggests that they follow either Ngok's tradition of the *Uttaratantra* or Tsen Khawoché's tradition of the *Uttaratantra.* It is clear that several of early Kadam masters followed Tsen Khawoché's tradition as opposed to that of Ngok.

3. Georges Dreyfus, *The Sound of Two Hands Clapping: The Education of a Tibetan Buddhist Monk* (Berkeley: University of California, 2003), 17–31.

4. I am following Anne Blackburn's rendering of the phrase. She says, "the term 'textual community' remains a useful tool with which to think about the lives of texts in relation to the lives of men and women. I use the term to describe a group of individuals who think of themselves to at least some degree as a collective, who understand the world and their appropriate place within it in terms significantly influenced by their encounter with a shared set of written texts or oral teachings based on written texts, and who grant special social status to literate interpreters of authoritative written texts. Although members of a given textual community are oriented by and toward shared texts, their interpretations of these texts are not homogeneous." See Anne Blackburn, *Buddhist Learning and Textual Practice in Eighteenth-Century Lankan Monastic Culture* (Princeton University Press, 2001), 12.

5. See Stanley Fish, *Is There a Text in This Class?: The Authority of Interpretive Communities* (Cambridge: Harvard University Press, 1980), particularly chapter 6. Fish says, "Interpretive communities are made up of those who share interpretive strategies not for reading (in the conventional sense) but for writing texts, for constituting their properties and assigning their intentions. In other words, these strategies exist prior the act of reading and therefore determine the shape of what is read rather than, as is usually assumed, the other way around." See ibid., 171.

6. Ibid., 169.

7. Kadam interpretive method is not a homogeneous category. For instance, early Kadam scholars such as Gelong Choshé and Kyotön Monlam Tsültrim comment on the *Uttaratantra* using what I would call "Kadam contemplative method" as opposed to "Kadam scholastic method" employed by Rinchen Yeshé and others.

8. For more on these thinkers and their views on buddha-nature as presented in the *Uttaratantra*, see Christian Bernert, *Rong-ston on Buddha-Nature: A Commentary on the Fourth Chapter of the Ratnagotravibhāga* (MA Thesis, University of Vienna, 2009); Ngawang Jorden, *Buddha-Nature through the Eyes of Go ram pa Bsod nams seng ge in Fifteenth-Century Tibet* (Dissertation, Cambridge, Harvard University, 2003); Klaus-Dieter Mathes, *A Direct Path to the Buddha Within* on Gö Lotsawa's interpretation of the *Uttaratantra*; Yaroslav Komarovski, *Visions of Unity: The Golden Pandita Shakya Chokden's New Interpretation of Yogācāra and Madhyamaka* (Albany: State University of New York Press, 2011) on Shakchok's interpretation of the Mahāyāna path structure in general; and Yaroslav Komarovski, "Reburying the Treatise—Maintaining the Continuity: Two Texts by Sakya Mchog Ldan on the Buddha-Essence," in *Journal of Indian Philosophy* 34 (2006): 521–70; "Shakya Chokden's Interpretation of the *Ratnagotravibhāga*: 'Contemplative' or 'Dialectical?'" *Journal of Indian Philosophy*, 38, no. 4 (2010): 441–52 on Shakchok's *Uttaratantra* com-

mentary; Khenpo Tsultrim Gyamtso and Rosemarie Fuchs, *Buddha Nature: The Mahayana Uttaratantra Shastra with Commentary* (Ithaca: Snow Lion, 2000) on Kongtül's *Uttaratantra* commentary; and Douglas Duckworth, *Mipam on Buddha-Nature: Ground of the Nyingma Tradition* (Albany: State University of New York Press, 2008).

9. This is a short list of scholars who wrote texts related to buddha-nature in that time period. See Kano, *rNgog Blo-ldan-shes-rab's Summary*, 597–600 for a comprehensive list of the *Uttaratantra* commentaries written between the fifteenth and twentieth centuries in Tibet.

10. Bernert, *Rong-ston on Buddha Nature*.

11. Ibid., 25–42.

12. Rongtön, *Explanation of the Uttaratantra*, 53. However, in my conversation with Sakya Khenpo Ven. Drakpa Singgé on the issues explicated in Rongtön's commentary, he said that Rongtön interprets the *Uttaratantra* to be a commentary on the middle-wheel teachings, not the last-wheel teachings.

13. José Cabezón and Geshe Lobsang Dargya, *Freedom from Extremes: Gorampa's "Distinguishing the Views" and the Polemics of Emptiness* (Boston: Wisdom, 2007), 43. Henceforth, *Freedom from Extremes*.

14. See Jorden, *Buddha-Nature through the Eyes of Go ram pa Bsod nams seng ge in Fifteenth-Century Tibet*, 69. For Gorampa's criticism of Tsongkhapa's and Dölpopa's views of ultimate truth, see Cabezón, *Freedom from Extremes*, 41–56 and chapters 2 and 3.

15. See Jorden, *Buddha-Nature through the Eyes of Go ram pa Bsod nams seng ge in Fifteenth-Century Tibet*, 69–72.

16. Ibid., 71–72.

17. See Cabezón, *Freedom from Extremes*, 52, in relation to Gorampa's critique of Tsongkhapa's view.

18. Ibid., 51.

19. Ibid.

20. Ibid.

21. See Jorden, *Buddha-Nature through the Eyes of Go ram pa Bsod nams seng ge in Fifteenth-Century Tibet*, 76–77.

22. Taktsang Lotsawa Sherap Rinchen (b. 1405), a Sakya master who was very critical of Tsongkhapa's view, also wrote a commentary on the *Uttaratantra*, but it is not available as far as I can tell.

23. *"gangs can mdzes pa'i rgyan drug"* in Tibetan. The other three luminaries are Yakton Sangyé Pel (1348–1414), Ngorchen Kunga Zangpo (1382–1456), and Dzongpa Kunga Namgyel (1432–1496).

24. Komarovski, *Visions of Unity*, 20–21.

25. Ibid., 28–29, 122–36.

26. Ibid., 5–6, 122–36.

27. Ibid., 130.

28. Komarovski, *Shakya Chokden's Interpretation of Ratnagotravibhāga*, in particular, 6.

29. For a detailed analysis of Shakchok's classification of different Mahāyāna schools, see Komarovski, *Visions of Unity*.

30. Komarovski, *Reburying the Treatise*, 538.

31. Komarovski, *Shakya Chokden's Interpretation of Ratnagotravibhāga*, 10–11.

32. Ibid., 5.

33. Ibid.

34. See Mathes, *A Direct Path to the Buddha Within*, 368.

35. Ibid., 351.

36. Ibid., 368–73.

37. Ibid., 354.

38. See Kano, *rNgog Blo-ldan-shes-rab's Summary*, 598.

39. See Penchen Sonam Drakpa, *The Moonlight That Illuminates the Difficult Points* (*dka' 'grel gnad kyi zla 'od*), vol. 5, (Mundgod: Drepung Loseling Library Society, 1982–1990), 371–468. Penchen Sonam Drakpa's commentary follows Gyeltsap's reading of the *Uttaratantra* and is reflective of Geluk polemical works where he argues against thinkers such as Dölpopa, Rongtön, Gorampa, and Shakchok. The three Sakya scholars, as we know, wrote in response to the growing demographic of the followers of Tsongkhapa and his direct disciples such as Gyeltsap and Khedrup. For references to Dölpopa and his Jonang School, see Penchen Sonam Drakpa, *The Moonlight That Illuminates the Difficult Points*, 398, 434; for references to Rongtön, see ibid., 389. It is interesting that Penchen Sonam Drakpa claims that Rongtön asserted the *Uttaratantra* to be a treatise from the Cittamātra perspective. For references to Gorampa and Shakchok, see Penchen Sonam Drakpa, ibid., 400. Penchen Sonam Drakpa says, "Ta [lung pa] and Dzi [lung pa] are the two well-known later followers of [Sakya]" *rjes 'brangs phyis su grags che ba la rta zi gnyis las*. Although he never mentions Gorampa and Shakchok by name, it is clear that Ta lung pa refers to Gorampa, who founded a monastery in Tanak, and Zi lung pa refers to Shakchok, who headed the monastery in Dzi. For more on Gorampa's and Shakchok's criticized positions, see Penchen Sonam Drakpa, ibid., 400–404, 404–406.

40. See Coné Drakpa Shedrup, *theg pa chen po rgyud bla ma'i don gyi snying po gsal byed kyi snang ba chen po* (*A Great Light That Illuminates the Essential Meaning of the Uttaratantra*), *The Collected Works of Coné Drakpa Shedrup*, vol. 3, 83–102. True to his words, "[I] have explained the essential meaning of [the *Uttaratantra*] in a concise manner in accordance with the presentation of the Master [Tsongkhapa] and his Disciple [Gyaltsab]" / *bstan bcos 'di'i don gyi snying po bsdus te rje yab sras kyi bzhed pa bzhin du bshad pa yin la*. Coné Drakpa Shedrup's commentary is short and does not elaborate much on any essential topics. For the quote, see ibid., 100. However, an interesting aspect of his commentary in the history of the *Uttaratantra* commentaries within the Geluk tradition is that he makes reference to tantra a few times. For tantric references, see ibid., 91, 93.

41. Although the text is believed to have been published, I have not been able to obtain a copy of it. Judging from the title of the text, *A Short Elucidation on the Concise Meaning of the Uttaratantra* (*theg pa chen po'i rgyud bla ma'i bsdus don nyung ngu rnam gsal*), it is most likely a short summary.

42. See E. Gene Smith, Introduction to *Kongtrul's Encyclopedia of Indo-Tibetan Culture* (New Delhi, Ngawang Gelek Demo, 1970), especially 24–36.

43. Two other eminent figures, Paltrül Rinpoché (*rdza dpal sprul rin po che che*, 1808–1887) (who taught Mipam) and Khenpo Zhenphen (*mkhan po gzhan phan chos kyi snang ba*, 1871–1927) each wrote a commentary. I have not been able to find Paltrül Rinpoché's text, *An Outline of the Uttaratantra* (*theg pa chen po'i bstan bcos rgyud bla ma'i sa bcad*); however, judging from the title and the length (12 fols.) of the text, it appears to be an outline of the *Uttaratantra*, not an exposition. Khenpo Zhenphen's commentary, *An Interlinear Commentary on the Uttaratantra* (*rgyud bla ma'i bstan bcos zhes bya ba'i mchan 'grel*), provides literal glosses to the *Uttaratantra*. It, therefore, does not give any detailed exposition providing his own view in response to, or critique of, other Tibetan thinkers. As Duckworth, following Nyoshul Khenpo (1931–1999), argues, "His [Zhenphen's] commentaries can be seen as a means to circumvent sectarian disputes by appealing to Indian originals rather than some specific strand of nearly one thousand years of Tibetan commentary. His work contrasts not only with Kongtrül, who embraced an explicit other-emptiness interpretation, but also with Mipam. Mipam's works have a stronger Nyingma sectarian identity." See Duckworth, *Mipam on Buddha-Nature*, xxii. For Khenpo Zhenphen's role in instituting a commentarial school, see Georges Dreyfus, "Where Do Commentarial Schools Come From? Reflections on the History of Tibetan Scholasticism," in *Journal of the International Association of Buddhist Studies* 28, no. 2 (2005): 273–97.

44. See Kongtrül, *Lion's Roar of the* Uttaratantra, 4.

45. He completed the commentary either in 1869 or in 1870. See Richard Barron, trans., *The Autobiography of Jamgon Kongtrul: A Gem of Many Colors* (Ithaca, NY: Snow Lion, 2003), 153–154. Not only did Kongtrül write a commentary on it, but he also gave teachings on it. See Barron, *The Autobiography of Jamgon Konttrul*, 154, 239.

46. See Kongtrül, *Lion's Roar of the* Uttaratantra, 13, and Mathes, *A Direct Path to the Buddha Within*, 32–34.

47. See Kongtrül, *Lion's Roar of the* Uttaratantra, 12.

48. For more on Kongtrül's description of other-emptiness or experiential approach, see Kongtrül, *Lion's Roar of the Uttaratantra*, 20–25, 139–41. In one of my interviews with Thrangu Rinpoche, he says, "The commentary by Jamgon Kongtrül Rinpoche and the commentary by Dölpopa Sherap Gyeltsen boil down to the same meaning apart from the differences in words." *'jam mgon kong sprul rin po che'i 'grel pa dang dol po pa shes rab rgyal mtshan gnyis kyi 'grel pa de phal cher tshig mi 'dra ba red ma gtogs don gcig la 'dra po babs kyi yod red//*

49. See Kongtrül, *Lion's Roar of the* Uttaratantra, 143–45.

50. Ibid., 13–16.

51. Ibid., 20–21.

52. Ibid., 24–25.

53. Ibid., 139–40.

54. Ibid., 140.

55. Ibid., 20–25.

56. Despite Mipam's work on the other-emptiness concept, both Duckworth and Wangchuk argue that Mipam does not adhere to the view of other-emptiness. See Dorji Wangchuk, "The rNying-ma Interpretation of the Tathāgatagarbha Theory," *Vienna Journal of South Asia Studies* 48 (2004: 171–213), 177, 189–90, and Duckworth, *Mipam on Buddha-Nature*, chapter 3.

57. Dreyfus tells an anecdote about how Khenpo Zhenphen (also known as Khenpo Zhenga) spoke of the other-emptiness view as "the worst wrong view whose adoption is worse than killing all the Buddhas and Bodhisattvas." See Dreyfus, "Where Do Commentarial Schools Come From?" 290–91 for the whole anecdote.

58. Duckworth, *Mipam on Buddha-Nature*, xxvi. In a private conversation with Khenpo Yeshe, a Nyingma Khenpo who is a doctoral student in the Buddhist Studies Program at UC Berkeley, the Khenpo tells me that Khenpo Zhenphen's *Uttaratantra* commentary is studied and preferred over Mipam's *Uttaratantra* commentary at Nyingma commentarial institutes, if the *Uttaratantra* is studied.

59. Since Mipam's *Uttaratantra* commentary mentions his *Lion's Roar* (*stong thun seng ge'i nga ro*), which was completed in 1891, one could perhaps see his *Uttaratantra* commentary as one of his later works. For a complete English translation of *Lion's Roar*, see Duckworth, *Mipam on Buddha-Nature*, 147–80. For Mipam's commentary, see Mipam, *theg pa chen po rgyud bla ma'i bstan bcos kyi mchan 'grel mi pham zhal lung* (*Instruction from Mipam: Interlinear Glosses to the Uttaratantra*), *Collected Works of Mipam*, vol. 17, Chengdu: 'jam dpal dhi yig ser po'i dpe skrun tshogs pa, 2008. Henceforth, *Instruction from Mipam*.

60. See Mipam, *Instruction from Mipam*, 16. However, as Duckworth states, "Since he depicts Buddha-nature with the qualities of the Buddha present at the time of a sentient being, his presentation shares an important feature with the Jonang tradition. His presentation also shares a quality with the Geluk tradition, given that he equates Buddha-nature with emptiness." See Duckworth, *Mipam on Buddha-Nature*, 115.

61. John Pettit, *Mipham's Beacon of Certainty: Illuminating the View of Dzogchen, the Great Perfection* (Boston: Wisdom 1999), 134.

62. Mipam, *Instruction from Mipam*, 21–22.

63. See ibid., 16, and Duckworth, *Mipam on Buddha-Nature*, 19, 102.

64. Irrespective of the value in using the terms "self-emptiness" and "other-emptiness" in a decontextualized manner, as Dorji Wangchuk notes,

followers of Nyingma "prefer to designate themselves as exponents of *raṅ stoṅ* [self-emptiness]." See Wangchuk, "The rÑiṅ-ma Interpretations of the Tathāgatagarbha Theory," 202. Many contemporary Nyingma scholars also share this sentiment. However, Mipam wrote a text from the other-emptiness perspective. Furthermore, Duckworth shows that Mipam's overall view is more in line with other-emptiness.

65. See Georges Dreyfus, "The Shuk-den Affair: History and Nature of a Quarrel," *Journal of the International Association of Buddhist Studies* 21 no. 2 (1998): 227–70.

66. Dzemé Rinpoché, *theg pa chen po rgyud bla mai'i bstan bcos kyi mchan 'grel. (Interlinear Glossary to the Uttaratantra)*, Collected Works, vol. 3 (Delhi: Dze smad blab rang, 1996).

Bibliography

Tibetan Language Works Cited

Asaṅga. *theg pa chen po rgyud bla ma'i bstan bcos kyi rnam par bshad pa* (*The Sūtrālaṃkāra and the Uttaratantra*). In the *gangs can rig brgya'i sgo 'byed lde mig*, 27, mi rigs dpe skrun khang, 1998.

Butön Rinchen Drup. *'phrin yig gi lan rin po che'i phreng ba* (*Precious Garland of Rebuttals*). The Collected Works of Bu-Ston, part 26 (LA) ed. Lokesh Chandra. New Delhi: International Academy of Indian Culture, 1971.

———. *bde gshegs snying po gsal ba'i rgyan* (*The Ornament That Illuminates Sugata-Essence*). The Collected Works of Bu-Ston, part 20 (VA). New Delhi: International Academy of Indian Culture, 1971.

———. *bstan 'gyur gyi dkar chag yid bzhin nor bu'i dbang gi rgyal po'i phreng ba* (*Catalogue for the Translated Treatises*). The Collected Works of Bu-Ston, vol. 26. Lhasa: Zhol Publications, 2000.

———. *chos 'byung* (*History of Buddhism*). krung go'i bod kyi shes rig dpe skrun khang, 1998.

———. *phar phyin lung gi snye ma* (*Abhisamayālaṃkāra Commentary*). The Collected Works of Butön, vol. 18. Lhasa: Zhol, 2000.

Candrakīrti. *Commentary on the Madhyamakāvatāra* (*dbu ma la 'jug pa'i bshad pa*). Cazadero, CA: ye shes sde'i chos 'khor 'khrul dpar khang, 2003.

Chapa Chökyi Senggé. *theg pa chen po rgyud bla ma'i bstan bcos kyi tshig dang don gyi cha rgya cher bsnyad pa phra ba'i don gsal ba* (*Illumination of the Meaning of the Uttaratantra*). The Collected Works of Kadam Masters, vol. 7. Chengdu: si khron mi rigs dpe skrun khang, 2006.

Chomden Rikpé Reldri. *rgyud bla ma'i ti ka rgyan gyi me tog* (*Flowers of Ornament*). The Collected Works of Kadam Masters, vol. 62. Chengdu: si khron mi rigs dpe skrun khang, 2009.

Chöwang Drakpé Pel. *shes rab kyi pha rol tu phyin pa'i man ngag gi bstan bcos mgnon par rtogs pa'i rgyan gyi mthar thug pa'i lta ba thal 'gyur du 'grel tshul gnad don gsal ba'i zla zer* (*Prāsaṅgika-Madhyamaka's Interpretation of the Abhisamayālaṃkāra*). Khedrup Je's Collected Works, vol. 1. New Delhi, 1980.

Coné Drakpa Shedrup. *theg pa chen po rgyud bla ma'i don gyi snying po gsal byed kyi snang ba chen po (A Great Light that Illuminates the Essential Meaning of the Uttaratantra)*. Collected Works of Coné Drakpa Shedrup, vol. 3. Taipei: Corporate Body of the Buddha Educational Foundation, 2010.

Dölpopa Sherap Gyeltsen. *bka' bsdu bzhi pa'i bsdus don 'grel ba (Commentary to the Summary of the Fourth Council)*. The Collected Works of Dol po pa shes rab rgyal mtshan, vol. 6. Dzamthang: bar khams rdzong.

———. *bka' bsdu bzhi pa'i don bstan rtsis chen po (The Great Calculation of the Fourth Council)*. The Collected Works of Dol po pa shes rab rgyal mtshan, vol. 6. Dzamthang: bar khams rdzong.

———. *bka' bsdu bzhi pa'i don bstan rtsis chen po phyogs med ris med ces bya ba'i 'grel ba (Commentary on the Fourth Council)*. The Collected Works of Dol po pa shes rab rgyal mtshan, vol. 6. Dzamthang: bar khams rdzong.

———. *bden gnyis gsal ba'i nyi ma (The Sun that Illuminates the Two Truths)*. The Collected Works of Dol po pa shes rab rgyal mtshan, vol. 6. Dzamthang, bar khams rdzong.

———. *chos dbyings bde ba chen po'i 'ja' sa (Proclamation of the Great Bliss of Dharma Reality)*. The Collected Works of Dol po pa shes rab rgyal mtshan, vol. 6. Dzamthang, bar khams rdzong.

———. *dpal yongs grub dgu'i bshad pa khyad 'phags gyu rnying (The Excellent Exposition on the Nine Glorious Thoroughly Established Natures)*. The Collected Works of Dol po pa shes rab rgyal mtshan, vol 5. Dzamthang, bar khams rdzong.

———. *dpon byang ba'i phyag tu phul ba'i chos kyi shan 'byed (A Letter to Pönjangwa)*. The Collected Works of Dol po pa shes rab rgyal mtshan, vol. 6. Dzamthang, bar khams rdzong.

———. *gshags 'byed bsdus pa (A Brief Distinction)*. The Collected Works of Dol po pa shes rab rgyal mtshan, vol. 6. Dzamthang, bar khams rdzong.

———. *lta ba shan 'byed yid kyi mun sel (Distinguishing Views)*. The Collected Works of Dol po pa shes rab rgyal mtshan, vol. 6. Dzamthang, bar khams rdzong.

———. *rang rig rang gsal gyi rab tu dbye ba (Distinguishing the Self-Illuminating Self-Awareness)*. The Collected Works of Dol po pa shes rab rgyal mtshan, vol. 6. Dzamthang, bar khams rdzong.

———. *shes rab kyi pha rol tu phyin pa man ngag gi bstan bcos mngon par rtogs pa'i rgyan gyi rnam bshad mdo'i don bde blag tu rtogs pa (Abhisamayālaṃkāra Commentary)*. The Collected Works of Dol po pa shes rab rgyal mtshan, vol. 5. Dzamthang, bar khams rdzong.

———. *slob ma la spring ba skur 'debs dang sgro 'dogs spang ba (Overcoming Nihilism and Superimposition)*. The Collected Works of Dol po pa shes rab rgyal mtshan, vol. 6. Dzamthang, bar khams rdzong.

———. *so so skye bo'i pan di ta la sogs pa'i 'khrul pa lung bstan pa (Criticism against Ordinary Scholars)*. The Collected Works of Dol po pa shes rab rgyal mtshan, vol. 6. Dzamthang, bar khams rdzong.

————. *theg pa chen po rgyud bla ma'i bstan bcos legs bshad nyi ma'i 'od zer* (*The Sunlight Exposition*). The Collected Works of Dol po pa shes rab rgyal mtshan, vol. 2. Dzamthang: bar khams rdzong.

Drakpa Gyeltsen. *rgyud kyi mngon par rtogs pa rin po che'i ljon shing* (*Precious Tree of the Tantric Path*). Collected Works, vol. 3. Sarnath: C.I.H.T.S., 1987.

Dratsépa Rinchen Namgyel. *de bzhin gshegs pa'i snying po mdzes rgyan gyi rgyan mkhas pa'i yid 'phrog* (*Ornament to the Ornament*). Collected Works of Bu-Ston, part 28 (SA), Lhasa, Zhol par khang, 2000.

Dzemé Rinpoché. *theg pa chen po rgyud bla mai'i bstan bcos kyi mchan 'grel.* (*Interlinear Glossary to the Uttaratantra*). Collected Works, vol. 3: 441–532. Delhi: Dze smad blab rang, 1996.

Gampopa Sonam Rinchen. *phyag rgya chen po gsal byed kyi man ngag* (*Instruction on the Mahāmudra*). Gampopa's Collected Works, vol. 2, (ZHA). Darjeeling: Kargyud Sungrab Nyamso Khang, 1982.

————. *phyag rgya chen po'i rtsa ba la ngo sprod pa zhes kyang bya, snang ba lam khyer gyi rtog pa cig mchog ces kyang bya, phyag rgya chen po gnyug ma mi gyur ba zhes kyang bya* (*Introduction to the Mahāmudra*). Gampopa's Collected Works, vol. 2, (YA). Darjeeling: Kargyud Sungrab Nyamso Khang, 1982.

————. *rje dvags po lha rje'i gsung zhal gyi bdud rtsi thun mong ma yin pa* (*The Uncommon Nectar*). Gampopa's Collected Works, vol. 2, DZA. Darjeeling: Kargyud Sungrab Nyamso Khang, 1982.

————. *rje dvags po'i zhal gdams dang rje sgom tshul gyi zhus lan, phag gru'i zhus lan* and *rje sgom tshul gyi zhus lan* (*Responses to Questions*). Gampopa's Collected Works, vol. KHA. Kathmandu: Shri Gautam Buddha Vihara, 2000.

————. *snying po don gyi gdams pa phyag rgya chen po'i 'bum tig* (*Instruction on the Essence*). Gampopa's Collected Works, vol. 2, A. Darjeeling: Kargyud Sungrab Nyamso Khang, 1982.

————. *thar pa rin po che'i rgyan* (*Ornament of the Precious Liberation*). The Dalai Lama Tibeto-Indological Series 26, ed. Khenpo Sonam Gyalpo, Sarnath: CIHTS, 1999.

Gelong Chöshé. *bstan bcos rgyud bla ma'ai gdams ngag bsam mi khyab kyi yi ge* (*The Words of Inconceivable Instruction on the Uttaratantra Treatise*). *The Collected Works of Kadam Masters*, vol. 76, dpal brtsegs bod yig dpe rnying zhib 'jug khang, 2009.

Gendün Özer. *theg pa chen po rgyud bla ma'i rnam bshad don dam rnam nges bsdus pa'i snying po'i snying po* (*Quintessential Essence*). The Collected Works of Kadam Masters, vol. 20, si khron mi rigs dpe skrun khang, 2006.

Gö Lotsawa Zhönnu Pel. *theg pa chen po rgyud bla ma'i bstan bcos kyi 'grel bshad de kho na nyid rab tu gsal ba'i me long* (*The Mirror That Illuminates Suchness*). Kathmandu: Franz Steiner Verlag Stuttgart, 2003.

Gyelsé Tokmé Zangpo. *Theg pa chen po rgyud bla ma'i nges don gsal ba'i 'od zer* (*Illuminating the Definitive Meaning of the Uttaratantra*). The Collected

Works of Kadam Masters, vol. 59. Si khron mi rigs dpe skrun khang, 2007.

Gyeltsap Darma Rinchen. *rnam bshad snying rgyan* (*Abhisamayālaṃkāra Commentary*). The Collected Works of Gyeltsap, vol. 2. Kubum Monastery: sku 'bum byams pa gling par khang.

————. *theg pa chen po rgyud bla ma'i tik ka*, (*Uttaratantra Commentary*). The Collected Works of Gyeltsap, vol. 3. Kubum Monastery: sku 'bum byams pa gling par khang.

Jangsem Gyelwa Yeshé. *dpal ldan dus kyi 'khor lo'i jo nang pa'i lugs kyi bla ma brgyud pa'i rnam thar* (*Lineage of the Jonang Kālacakra Tradition*). Beijing: mi rigs dpe bskrun khang, 2004.

Jayānanda. *dbu ma la 'jug pa'i 'grel bshad* (*Explanation of the Madhyamakāvatāra*). snga 'gyur rnying ma'i glegs bam rin po che'i dbu phyogs (no publication date).

Jetsün Tāranātha. *gzhan stong dbu ma'i rgyan* (*Ornament of the Other-Emptiness Madhyamaka*). rdzogs ldan chos mchog dbu ma gzhan stong gi chos skor, vol. 7. shang kang then ma dpe skrun khang, 2005.

————. *tshul gnyis rnam 'byed nges don 'jug ngogs* (*Entry to the Definitive Meaning*). rdzogs ldan chos mchog dbu ma gzhan stong gi chos skor, vol. 7, shang kang then ma dpe skrun khang, 2005.

Jonang Zangpo. *chos rje kun mkhyen chen po yab sras bco lnga'i rnam thar nye bar bsdus pa ngo mtsar rab gsal* (*Biographies of the Great Omniscient One, the Father, and His Fourteen Lineage Sons*). The Collected Works of Dol po pa shes rab rgyal mtshan, vol. 1. 'Dzam thang, 'Bar khams rdzong: 'Dzam thang dgon pa, 199–.

Kamalaśīla. *Madhyamakāloka*, bstan 'gyur, vol. dbu ma (SA), krung go'i bod kyi shes rig dpe skrun khang, 2000.

Khedrup Gelek Pelzang. *rgyud sde spyi'i rnam par gzhag pa rgyas par bshad pa* (*Presentation of the General Tantric Systems*). The Collected Works of the Lord mkhas grub rje dge legs dpal bzang, vol. 8 (nya). New Delhi: Mongolian Lama Gurudev, 1980.

Khenpo Zhenpen Chökyi Nangwa. *rgyud bla ma'i mchan 'grel.* (*Interlinear Glosses to the Uttaratantra*). Bylakuppe: Ngagyur Nyingma Institute, 2002.

Kongtrül Lodrö Tayé. *theg pa chen po rgyud bla ma'i bstan bcos snying po'i don mngon sum lam gyi bshad srol dang sbyar ba'i rnam par 'grel pa phyir mi ldog pa seng ge'i nga ro* (*Lion's Roar of the* Uttaratantra). Varanasi: Kagyu Relief and Protection Committee, 1999.

Longchen Rabjampa. *chos dbyings rin po che'i mdzod kyi 'grel ba lung gi gter mdzod* (*Commentary to the Treasury of the Precious Dharma Reality*), vol. 3. Gangtok, Sikkim: Sherab Gyaltsen and Khyentse Labrang, 1983.

————. *theg pa mtha' dag gi don gsal bar byed pa grub pa'i mtha' rin po che'i mdzod* (*Treasury of Tenets*). vol. 2, Gangtok, Sikkim: Sherab Gyaltsen and Khyentse Labrang, 1983.

Mabja Jangchup Tsöndü. *dbu ma rtsa ba shes rab kyi 'grel ba 'thad pa'i rgyan* (*Commentary* to *the Madhyamakakārikā*). Sikkim: dpal rgyal ba kar ma pa'i Collections, 1975.

Maitreya. *theg pa chen po rgyud bla ma'i bstan bcos* (*The Uttaratantra*). *gangs can rig brgya'i sgo 'byed lde mig*, vol. 27. mi rigs dpe skrun khang, 1998.

Mipam Namgyel. *theg pa chen po rgyud bla ma'i bstan bcos kyi mchan 'grel mi pham zhal lung* (*Instruction from Mipam: Interlinear Glosses to the Uttaratantra*). Collected Works of Mipam, vol. 17. Chengdu: 'jam dpal dhi yig ser po'i dpe skrun tshogs pa, 2008.

Ngok Loden Sherap. *theg chen rgyud bla ma'i bsdus don* (*Condensed Meaning of the Uttaratantra*). Dharamsala: Library of Tibetan Works and Archives, 1993.

Pawo Tsuklak Trengwa. *chos 'byung mkhas pa'i dga' ston* (*A Joyous Feast for Scholars*). Sarnath: Vajra Vidya Institure, 2003.

Penchen Sonam Drakpa. *dka' 'grel gnad kyi zla 'od* (*The Moonlight that Illuminates the Difficult Points*). Collected Works of Penchen Sonam Drakpa, vol. 5, 371–468. Mundgod: Drepung Loseling Library Society, 1982–1990.

Rendawa Zhönnu Lodrö. *dbu ma la 'jug pa'i rnam bshad de kho na nyid gsal ba'i sgron ma* (*The Lamp That Illuminates Suchness*). dpal ldan sa skya pa'i gsung rab, vol. 13. Beijing: mi rigs dpe skrun khang, 2003.

———. *theg pa gsum gyi 'phags pa'i rtogs pa rnam par 'byed pa* (*Distinguishing the Realizations*). Collected Works of Rendawa, vol. 2. Kathmandu: sa-skya rgyal yons gsun rab slob gner khan, 1999.

Rinchen Yeshé. *rgyud bla ma'i 'grel ba mdo dang sbyar ba nges don gyi snang ba* (*Rays of the Definitive Meaning*). The Collected Works of Kadam Masters, vol. 20. Sichuan, *dpal brtsegs bod yig dpe rnying zhib 'jug khang*, 2006.

Rongtön Sheja Künrik. *theg pa chen po rgyud bla ma'i bstan bcos legs par bshad pa* (*Explanation of the Uttaratantra*). New Delhi: Yashodhara, 1998.

Sakya Paṇḍita Kūnga Gyeltsen. *sdom gsum rab dbye* (*Distinguishing the Three Vows*). The Collected Works of the Founding Masters of Sa-skya, vol. 12. NA, Dehradun: Sakya Center, 1993.

———. *thub pa'i dgongs pa rab tu gsal ba* (*Illuminating the Thoughts of the Buddha*). The Collected Works of the Founding Masters of Sa-skya, vol. 10 (tha). Dehradun: Sakya Center, 1993.

Sangpu Lodrö Tsungmé. *theg pa chen po rgyud bla ma'i bstan bcos kyi nges don gsal bar byed pa'i rin po che'i sgron me* (*The Precious Lamp That Illuminates Definitive Meaning*). Tibetan Nyingma Monastery, Arunachal Pradesh, 1974.

Sazang Mati Penchen. *mngon pa kun btus kyi 'grel pa shes bya rab gsal* (*Abhidharmasamuccaya Commentary*). Gangtok: Gonpo Tseten, 1977.

———. *rgyud bla ma'i bstan bcos kyi rnam par bshad pa nges don rab gsal snang ba* (*Illuminating the Definitive Meaning*). Khreng tu'u?, 2000?.

Shakya Pel. *rin chen rnam rgyal gyi rnam par thar pa snyim pa'i me tog las 'khrungs pa ngo mtshar ze 'bru'i nor bu* (*Biography of Dratsépa Rinchen Namgyel*). (n.d.,n.p.)

Sonam Tsemo. *rgyud sde spyi rnam (General Tantric Presentation).* The Collected Works of Sakya, vol. GA (n.d.,n.p.).

———. *spyod 'jug gi 'grel ba (Bodhicāryavatāra Commentary).* The Collected Works of Sakya, vol. CA (n.d.,n.p.).

Tsongkhapa Lozang Drakpa. *dbu ma dgongs pa rab gsal (Illuminating the Thoughts of Madhyamaka).* Drepung Loseling Library Society, 1992.

———. *drang nges legs bshad snying po (Essence of Excellent Exposition).* Sarnath: *dge ldan spyi las khang,* 1973.

———. *legs bshad gser phreng (Golden Rosary of Excellent Exposition).* Taipei: The Corporate Body of the Buddha Educational Foundation, 2000.

Tsünpa Pelrin and Zhönnu Gyeltsen. *rgyal sras dngul chu thogs med kyi rnam thar (Biographies of Gyelsé Tokmé Zangpo).* Paltseg Boyig Penying Zhibjug Khan, (n.d.,n.p.).

English Language Works Cited

Barron, Richard. trans. *The Autobiography of Jamgon Kongtrul: A Gem of Many Colors.* Ithaca, NY: Snow Lion, 2003.

Bernert, Christian. *Rong-ston on Buddha-Nature: A Commentary on the Fourth Chapter of the Ratnagotravibhaga.* MA Thesis, University of Vienna, 2009.

Blackburn, Anne M. *Buddhist Learning and Textual Practice in Eighteenth-Century Lankan Monastic Culture.* Princeton: Princeton University Press, 2001.

Brunnhölzl, Karl. *In Praise of Dharmadhātu: Nāgārjuna and the Third Karmapa, Rangjung Dorje.* Ithaca, NY: Snow Lion, 2007.

———. *When the Clouds Part: The Uttaratantra and Its Meditative Tradition as a Bridge between Sūtra and Tantra.* Boston: Snow Lion, 2014.

Butters, Albion Moonlight. *The Doxographical Genius of Kun mkhyen kLong chen rab 'byams pa.* (Dissertation). Columbia University, 2006.

Cabezón, José. *Buddhism and Language: A Study of Indo-Tibetan Scholasticism.* Albany: State University of New York Press, 1994.

———. "The Canonization of Philosophy and the Rhetoric of Siddhānta in Tibetan Buddhism." In Paul Griffiths and John Keenan, eds., *Buddha Nature: A Festschrift in Honor of Minoru Kiyota,* Tokyo: Buddhist Books Int'l, 1990.

Cabezón, José, and Geshe Lobsang Dargya. *Freedom from Extremes: Gorampa's "Distinguishing the Views" and the Polemics of Emptiness.* Boston: Wisdom, 2007.

D'amato, M. "Three Natures, Three Stages: An Interpretation of the Yogācāra Trisvabhāva-Theory." *Journal of Indian Philosophy* 33 (2005): 185–207.

Dreyfus, Georges. *Recognizing Reality: Dharamakīrti's Philosophy and Its Tibetan Interpretations.* Albany: State University of New York Press, 1997.

———. "The Shuk-den Affair: History and Nature of a Quarrel." *Journal of the International Association of Buddhist Studies* 21, no. 2 (1998): 227–70.

————. *The Sound of Two Hands Clapping: The Education of a Tibetan Buddhist Monk*. Berkeley: University of California, 2003.

————. "Where Do Commentarial Schools Come From? Reflections on the History of Tibetan Scholasticism." *Journal of the International Association of Buddhist Studies* 28, no. 2 (2005): 273–97.

Dreyfus, Georges, and Sara McClintock (ed.). *The Svātantrika-Prāsaṅgika Distinction: What Difference Does a Difference Make?* Boston: Wisdom, 2003.

Duckworth, Douglas. *Mipam on Buddha-Nature: Ground of the Nyingma Tradition*. Albany: State University of New York Press, 2008.

Fish, Stanley. *Is There a Text in This Class?: The Authority of Interpretive Communities*. Cambridge, MA: Harvard University Press, 1980.

Frye, Northrop. *The Double Vision: Language and Meaning in Religion*. Toronto: University of Toronto Press, 1991 (Reprint 1995).

Germano, David. *Poetic Thought, the Intelligent Universe, and the Mystery of Self: The Tantric Synthesis of rDzogs Chen in Fourteenth Century Tibet*. (Dissertation) University of Wisconsin, Madison, 1992.

Gold, Jonathan. *Paving the Great Way: Vasubandhu's Unifying Buddhist Philosophy*. New York: Columbia University Press, 2015.

Griffiths, Paul J. *Religious Reading: The Place of Reading in the Practice of Religion*. New York: Oxford University Press, 1999.

Grosnick, William H., "The Tathāgatagarbha Sūtra." In Donald S. Lopez, Jr., ed. *Buddhism in Practice*. New Jersey: Princeton University Press, 1995.

Gyamtso, Khenpo Tsultrim, and Rosemarie Fuchs. *Buddha Nature: The Mahayana Uttaratantra Shastra with Commentary*. Ithaca, NY: Snow Lion, 2000.

Hillis, Greg. *The Rhetoric of Naturalness: A Critical Study of the gNas lugs mdzod*. (Dissertation) University of Virginia, January, 2008.

Hoffman, Helmut. "Early and Medieval Tibet." In Alex McKay, ed. *The History of Tibet*. London and New York: RoutledgeCurzon, 2003.

Hookham, S. K. *The Buddha Within: Tathagatagarbha Doctrine according to the Shentong Interpretation of the Ratnagotravibhaga*. Delhi: Sri Satguru, 1992.

Hopkins, Jeffrey. *Emptiness in the Mind-Only School of Buddhism: Dynamic Responses to Dzong-ka ba's The Essence of Eloquence: I*. Berkeley and Los Angeles: University of California Press, 1999.

————. *Mountain Doctrine: Tibet's Fundamental Treatise on Other-Emptiness and the Buddha-Matrix*. Ithaca: Snow Lion, 2006.

————. *Reflections on Reality: The Three Natures and Non-Natures in the Mind-Only School*. Berkeley: University of California Press, 2002.

————. *The Essence of Other Emptiness*.Ithaca, NY: Snow Lion, 2007.

Jackson, David. "An Early Biography of rNgok Lo-tsa-ba bLo ldan shes rab." In Per Kvaerne, ed. *Tibetan Studies: Proceedings of the 6ᵗʰ Seminar of the International Association for Tibetan Studies*. Oslo: The Institute for Comparative Research in Human Culture, 1994.

————. *The Entrance Gate for the Wise: Sa-skya Pandita on Indian and Tibetan Traditions of Pramana and Philosophical Debate*. Vienna: Arbeitskreis fur Tibetishe und Buddhistische Studien Universitat Wien, 1987.

Johnston, E. H. *Ratnagotravibhāga Mahayanottaratantraśāstra*. Patna: Bihar Research Society, 1950.

Jorden, Ngawang. *Buddha-Nature through the Eyes of Go ram pa Bsod nams seng ge in Fifteenth-Century Tibet*. (Dissertation) Cambridge: Harvard University, 2003.

Kano, Kazuo. *rNgog Blo-ldan-shes-rab's Summary of the Ratnagotravibha: The First Tibetan Commentary on a Crucial Source for the Buddha-nature Doctrine*. (Dissertation) Hamburg, 2006.

Kapstein, Matthew. *Reason's Traces: Identity and Interpretation in Indian and Tibetan Buddhist Thought*. Boston: Wisdom, 2001.

———. *The Tibetans*. Malden, MA: Blackwell, 2006.

Komarovski, Yaroslav. "*Reburying the Treatise—Maintaining the Continuity: Two Texts by Sakya Mchog Ldan on the Buddha-Essence.*" *Journal of Indian Philosophy* 34 (2006): 521–70.

———. "Shakya Chokden's Interpretation of the Ratnagotravibhaga: 'Contemplative' or 'Dialectical'?" *Journal of Indian Philosophy* 38, no. 4 (2010): 441–52.

———. *Visions of Unity: The Golden Pandita Shakya Chokden's New Interpretation of Yogacara and Madhyamak*. Albany: State University of New York Press, 2011.

Kramer, Ralf. *The Great Translator: Life and Wroks of rNgog Blo ldan shes rab*. München: Indus Verlag, 2007.

Kritzer, Robert. *Vasubandhu and the Yogācārabhūmi: Yogācāra Elements in the Abhidharmakośabhāṣya*. Tokyo: The International Institute for Buddhist Studies, 2005.

Lessing, Ferdinand D., and Alex Wayman. *Fundamentals of the Buddhist Tantras*. Paris: Mouton, 1968.

Lindtner, Christian. "Cittamātra in Indian Mahāyāna until Kamalaśīla." *Wiener Zeitschrift für die Kunde südasiens und Archiv für indische Philosophie* 41 (1997): 159–206.

Lopez, Donald S. *Elaborations on Emptiness: Uses of the Heart Sutra*. Princeton: Princeton University Press, 1996.

Lusthaus, Dan. "What Is and Isn't Yogācāra." Yogācāra Buddhism Research Association. http://www.acmuller.net/yogacara/articles/intro.html.

Mathes, Klaus-Dieter. *A Direct Path to the Buddha Within: Gö Lotsawa's Mahāmudra Interpretation of the Ratnagotravibhāga*. Boston: Wisdom, 2008.

———. "'Gos Lo tsā ba gZhon nu dpal's Commentary on the *Dharmatā* Chapter of the *Dharmadharmatāvibhāgakārikās*." *Studies in Indian Philosophy and Buddhism* 12 (2005): 3–39.

———. "The gzhan stong model of reality: Some more material on its origin, transmission, and interpretation." *Journal of International Association of Buddhist Studies* 34 (2012): 187–223.

Obermiller, Eugene. *The Sublime Science of the Great Vehicle to Salvation, Being a Manual of Buddhist Monism, the Work of Ārya Maitreya with a Commentary By Āryāsaṅga.* Acta Orientalia, vol. 9, parts 1, 3, and 4, 1931.

Onodo, Shunzu. "Abbatial Successions of the Colleges of gSang phu sne'u thog Monastery." *Bulletin of the National Museum of Ethnology* 15, no. 4 (1990): 1049–71.

Petech, Luciano. "The Disintegration of the Tibetan Kingdom." In Alex McKay, ed., *The History of Tibet.* London and New York: RoutledgeCurzon, 2003.

Pettit, John Whitney. *Mipham's Beacon of Certainty: Illuminating the View of Dzogchen, the Great Perfection.* Boston: Wisdom, 1999.

Powers, John. *Hermeneutics and Tradition in the Saṃdhinirmocana-Sūtra.* Leiden: Brill, 1993.

Rhoton, Jared Douglas. trans. *A Clear Differentiation of the Three Codes: Essential Distinctions among the Individual Liberation, Great Vehicle, and Tantric Systems.* Albany: State University of New York Press, 2002

Roerich, George. trans. *The Blue Annals.* Delhi: Motilal Banarsidaas, 1976.

Ruegg, David Seyfort. "Purport, implicature and presupposition: Sanskrit abhipraya and Tibetan *dgoṅs pa/dgoṅs gži* as hermeneutical concepts." *Journal of Indian Philosophy* 13 (1985): 309–25.

———. *The Buddhist Philosophy of the Middle: Essays on Indian and Tibetan Madhyamaka.* Boston: Wisdom Publications, 2010.

———. *The Life of Bu-Ston Rin Po Che*, Roma, Istituto Italiano per il Medio Estremo Oriente, 1966.

———. *The Literature of the Madhyamaka School of Philosophy in India*, vol. vii, Fasc. 1, Wiesbaden: Harrassovitz, 1981.

———. *The Meanings of the Term Gotra and the Textual History of the Ratnagotravibhāga.* Bulletin of the School of Oriental and African Studies, vol. 39, part 2 (1976): 341–63.

———. *Three Studies in the History of Indian and Tibetan Madhyamaka Philosophy, Studies in Indian and Tibetan Madhyamaka Thought Part 1.* Vienna: Arbeitskreis fur Tibetishe und Buddhistische Studien Universitat Wien, 2000.

Schaeffer, Kurtis. *The Enlightened Heart of Buddhahood: A Study and Translation of the Third Karma pa Rang byung rdo rje's Work on Tathāgatagarbha.* MA Thesis, University of Washington, 1995.

Schaeffer, Kurtis, and Leornard van der Kuijp. *An Early Tibetan Survey of Buddhist Literature: The Bstan pa rgyas pa rgyan gyi nyi 'od of Bcom ldan ral gri.* Cambridge: Harvard University Press, 2009.

Schaik, Sam Van. *Approaching the Great Perfection: Simultaneous and Gradual Methods of Dzogchen Practice in the Longchen Nyingtig.* Boston: Wisdom, 2004.

Siderits, Mark, and Shōryū Katsura, *Nāgārjuna's Middle Way.* Boston: Wisdom, 2013.

Smith, Gene. Introduction to *Kongtrul's Encyclopedia of Indo-Tibetan Culture*. New Delhi: Ngawang Gelek Demo, 1970.

Smith, Wilfred. *What Is Scripture?: A Comparative Approach*. Minneapolis: Fortress, 2005.

Stearns, Cyrus. *The Buddha from Dölpo: A Study of the Life and Thought of the Tibetan Master Sherab Gyaltsen*. Albany: State University of New York Press, 1999.

Takasaki, Jikido. *A Study on the Ratnagotravibhāga: Being a Treatise on the Tathāgatagarbha Theory of Mahāyāna Buddhism*. Roma: Istituto Italiano per Il Medio Ed Estremo Oriente, 1966.

Thrangu, Khenchen. *On Buddha Essence: A Commentary on Rangjung Dorje's Treatise*. Boston: Shambala, 2006.

Thurman, Robert. *Tsong Khapa's Speech of Gold in the Essence of Eloquence: Reason and Enlightenment in the Central Philosophy of Tibet*. New Jersey: Princeton University Press, 1984.

van der Kuijp, Leonard W. J. *Contributions to the Development of Tibetan Epistemology: From the Eleventh to the Thirteenth Century*. Wiesbaden: Franz Steiner, 1983.

———. "The Monastery of Gsang-phu ne'u-thog and Its Abbatial Succession from ca. 1073 to 1250." *Berliner Indologische Studien* 3 (1987): 103–27.

Vose, Kevin A. *Resurrecting Candrakīrti: Disputes in the Tibetan Creation of Prāsaṅgika*. Boston: Wisdom, 2009.

Wallace, Vesna A. *The Inner Kālacakratantra: A Buddhist Tantric View of the Individual*. Oxford: Oxford University Press, 2001.

———. *The Kālacakratantra: The Chapter on the Individual together with the Vimalaprabhā*. New York: American Institure of Buddhist Studies at Columbia University, 2004.

Wangchuk, Dorji. "The rÑiṅ-ma Interpretation of the Tathāgatagarbha Theory." *Vienna Journal of South Asian Studies* 48 (2004): 171–213

Wangchuk, Tsering. "Can We Speak of Kadam Gzhan Stong?: Tracing the Sources for Other-Emptiness in Early-Fourteenth-Century." *Journal of Buddhist Philosophy* 2 (2016): 9–22.

———. "Dol po pa shes rab rgyal mtshan on Mahāyāna doxography: Rethinking the distinction between Cittamātra and Madhyamaka in fourteenth-century Tibet." *Journal of the International Association of Buddhist Studies* 34, nos. 1–2 (2012): 321–48.

———. "In Defense of His Guru: Dratsepa's Rebuttal to the Challenges Articulated by the Proponents of the Other-Emptiness Doctrine." *Journal of Indian Philosophy* 39, no. 2 (2011): 147–65

Williams, Paul (with Anthony Tribe). *Buddhist Thought: A Complete Introduction to the Indian Tradition*. London and New York: Routledge, 2000.

Zimmerman, Michael. *A Buddha Within: The Tathāgatagarbhasūtra, the Earliest Exposition of the Buddha-Nature in India*. Bibleotheca Philologica et Philosophica Buddhica IV. Tokyo: Soka University, 2002.

Index